EDUCATIONAL ETHICS

Practical and Professional Ethics Series

Vol. 1: The Primer of Applied Ethics
Vol. 2: Environmental Ethics
Vol. 3: Bio-Medical Ethics
Vol. 4: Educational Ethics
Vol. 5: Economic and Business Ethics
Vol. 6: Socio-Political Ethics

About the Author

Dr. Debashis Guha, teaches Ethics, and Phenomenology and Existentialism in the Post Graduate Department of Philosophy, Ranchi University, Ranchi. After doing masters course in Philosophy from Delhi University in 1980, he was conferred the Ph.D. degree of Jadavpur University in 1988. Dr. Guha takes interest in Philosophy of Religion, Social and Political Philosophy, Philosophy of Science and Analytic Philosophy. He taught at the undergraduate level in a constituent college of Ranchi University from 1981 to 1989 and was then asked to serve the Post Graduate Department. Dr. Guha is teaching Ethics for twenty-four years. He was awarded the Visiting Associateship of the U.G.C. (1994-96) in Jadavpur University, Calcutta, where he worked out *An Inquiry into the cases of Pain and Suffering,* which awaits publication. He was further awarded U.G.C.'s Major Research Project (1997-2000) on *Applied Ethics in Indian Context,* which has been now shaped in Six volumes, of which the present work is the fourth one under the series: **Practical and Professional Ethics**. Dr. Guha has fifteen papers to his credit. He has presented philosophical papers in different Seminars, Symposia and Congress, two of them were presented in International Congress; one in the Platinum Jubilee Celebrations of the Indian Philosophical Congress, 2000-01, and the other in the XVth International Congress of Aesthetics in Tokyo, Japan in 2001. During his Major Research Project work, Dr. Guha has talked to many people from different walks of life, interviewed them and also arranged ethical dialogues leading to resolution of value-laden practical problems of urgency. Dr. Guha envisions people's participation in Practical and Professional Ethics.

Practical and Professional Ethics

Volume - Four

Educational Ethics

DEBASHIS GUHA

CONCEPT PUBLISHING COMPANY, NEW DELHI-110059

Cataloging in Publication Data—DK
Courtesy: D.K. Agencies (P) Ltd. <docinfo@dkagencies.com>

Guha, Debashis.
Practical and professional ethics / Debashis Guha.
v. 4. cm.
Includes bibliographical references.
Includes indexes.
Contents: v. 4. Educational ethics.
ISBN 13: 9788180693144 (set)
ISBN 10: 8180693147 (set)
ISBN 13: 9788180694769 (v. 4)
ISBN 10: 81806934763 (v. 4)
ISBN 13: 9788180694776 (pbk.) (v. 4)
ISBN 10: 81806934771 (pbk.)(v. 4)

1. Applied ethics. 2. Professional ethics. 3. Environmental ethics. 4. Bioethics. 5. Medical ethics. I. Title.

DDC 170 22

ISBN -13: 978-81-8069-314-4 (Series) ISBN -10: 81-8069-314-7 (Series)
ISBN -13: 978-81-8069-476-9 (H.B.) ISBN -10: 81-8069-476-3 (H.B.)
ISBN -13: 978-81-8069-477-6 (P.B.) ISBN -10: 81-8069-477-1 (P.B.)

First Published 2007

Published and Printed by
Ashok Kumar Mittal
Concept Publishing Company
A/15-16, Commercial Block, Mohan Garden
New Delhi-110059 (INDIA)
Phones : 25351460, 25351794
Fax : 091-11-25357103
Email : publishing@conceptpub.com

Sri Bhupendra Chandra Guha Mustafi,
Smt. Binapani Bose, Sri Bhanurashmi Guha
Mustafi, Sri Gopal Chandra Guha Mustafi,
Smt. Ava Roy and Smt. Beauty Guha

—The sources of my inspiration

Foreword

Dr. Debashis Guha has given us a very valuable book on the unusual topic of Educational Ethics. Dr. Guha treats this branch of Ethics with great skill and competence. In the long introduction, he analyse the concept of Education, not based on etymology or on some theories, but through what he calls "nature analysis", which consists in finding out what education is by considering the different tasks and requirements of education, viz. the doable aspects of education.

Education is realising an end through a cluster of tasks performed by oneself or others. It involves the initiative of the self to adopt processes leading to a standard of life, where one knows and masters many things. He rightly lays great stress on the self-initiative of the one who wants to be educated. Thus education enables human beings to initiate themselves by their free will towards a desirable standard of life, towards desirable actions and thought processes. The important tasks to be performed through education are, e.g. skill formation, training especially in moral values, by seeking to participate in a moral way of life and knowing the "Why" of ought and ought not, instruction, experiential learning etc. He strongly argues against an education which produces fixity in beliefs and knowledge and against indoctrination. He stresses the need of developing a critical attitude and develop a person's character in a more holistic fashion. The "whole man" is to be educated and the physical, psychological, intellectual and moral dimensions have to be integrated.

Education has a moral aim, irrespective of debates about relativism and scepticism. But the moral task of education does not amount to teaching and learning academic ethics viz.various theories of ethics or various ethical systems.

In the first chapter he explains the nature of Educational Ethics. It is a field of study within ethics. It is an ethics which intercepts a number of ethically relevant problems in the field of education. Its task is not "moralizing" or theory churning". The value of education cannot, e.g. be based on a material basis, such as economics, material well-being because the quality of life is not synonymous with material well-being.

The main justification of the moral task of education is that it is necessary for "moral goodness". This is a matter of judgment on other than theoretical grounds, but mainly on practical grounds, when our moral knowledge is put to some real life test in the face of questions of value. Moral education is a practical enterprise to learn to do what should be done in life.

What then is Educational Ethics? The answer to this question is best obtained by an analysis of the tasks of Educational Ethics. These tasks are meta-ethical, normative-ethical and practical ethical discussions relevant to educational matters. In simpler words: Educational Ethics is an ethical reflection on educational matters that have close relations with the fields of education and ethics.

In the following chapters, Dr. Guha elaborates the First and Second order Tasks of Educational Ethics (ch. 2), the Value and the Virtue related tasks of Educational Ethics (ch. 3) and the Practical tasks of Educational Ethics (ch. 4).

Dr. Debashis Guha is to be congratulated for giving us a very good understanding of what are Education and Educational Ethics.

Fr. Jonckheere S.J.
Emeritus Professor of Ethics
St. Albert's College
Ranchi

Preface

Educational Ethics is the Fourth Volume of the Series: Practical and Professional Ethics. It is natural that a teacher of some experience takes up ethical issues in education because these are issues closer to his or her heart. Teaching is not merely a profession; it is bathing in the light of wisdom and smearing the hue of eternal love. To me, education is a mysterious realm of unfolding of both wisdom and love, not abruptly but gradually. A teacher is a party to it on the one hand as a professional encouraging the said unfolding, whereas students are another party to the same as unfolding mystery. But this is a figurative way of explaining education and teaching, something more has to be said concretely to find out what education, educating and teaching consists in. For a teacher, who is still striving for the mysterious realm to unfold more vigorously, education, educating and teaching are also soaked in challenges—practical and moral. This work is not about the several theoretical and practical intricacies of education, educating, teaching and training rather, considers more elaborately the value-laden practical problems in education, teaching and training because that is another way to unfold the mysterious realm of education to become wiser and loving. There is no positive bearing of living in value crises in education because such crises bereft the teacher of both wisdom and love, and the student of being a lover of wisdom. Civil states having civil teachers and students do not and need not thrive in value crises — crises are to be resolved but not relished. Let us enter into this field of challenge in this work. However, some theoretical groundwork of educational ethics is also needed. I hope to be simple while I perform these tasks in this book because I know that jargons do not please common readers, including the students. The work is, therefore, not only for professional teachers, educational mangers and philosophers, it strives to involve other readers.

For the completion of a work, we are obliged to a number of people. I must thank a number of students, teachers and common men for their support in holding intersubjective dialogues. I thank Sr. Mary Paul and the librarian of St. Albert's College, Ranchi, for their support in lending me a number of useful books. I owe much to Mr. G. Kumarappa of the National Library, Calcutta. I thank Mr. Sanjay Singh for carefully typing the manuscript and the family of Concept Publishers to publish the book.

Contents

Introduction

To crack a joke first: 'the difference between the Indian schools of 1950s to 1980s and those of Gen X, Y and Z is that the students of the schools of Gen X, Y and Z either wants to become engineers or doctors, whereas those of 1950s to 1980s wanted to become *khalasis* (conductors) or drivers'. May be some Indian students before 1950s wanted to become birds or rivers or some after 2006 would like to become mushroom clouds over atomic fields. However, initially I wanted to become a teacher bubbling with energy, smart, fantastic speaker in the class who mesmerized the students with zeal, smartness and oratory. However, as days passed to make me older and weaker, I now want to fall in an eternal *karmic cycle* to be born again and again with a guarantee of becoming nothing but a teacher. Yes, this is a blunt, most unreligious desire on the part of a teacher because he feels that the field of education and educating is still so challenging and one is surely still so unsocial and unloving, he should have rebirth. But what is this field of education and educating? This is the first issue I want to take up before elaborating on the structure of the work later on. So let us consider nature analysis of the concepts of "education", "teaching" and "educating".

Philosophers are enthusiastic about a job of clarification, namely, "nature analysis" because without having basic wisdom of what consists in "education", that is, what this term signifies, we are really not in any position to talk about value-crises in education and their resolution. However, getting involved in nature analysis of "education" does not mean necessarily to find out a satisfactory definition of the term. I have said in the Preface that a figurative way of defining the term need not be taken too seriously because it leaves so many gaps for us to fill up for a proper understanding of the concept. It may well be that we discuss at length about the need of providing any satisfactory definition of "education" at all which is good enough for our understanding of the subject. Further, there might be some confusion about clarification of the nature of the concept "education" and analysing its literal meaning according to the *origin* of the term, the historical linguistic *usages* and how differently people having different language take up a *conventional meaning*. In fact, an interesting linguistic analysis of the English term "education" in the context of the dynamics of English language-use is not my concern here because I do not think that it will do any justice to reveal properly the "nature" of the concept. Similarly, how conventionally the term has been used or is used amounting to fixity of conventional meaning will not be good enough for my aim. Another important point to remember is that confusing the nature analysis of the concept "education" (which is an English expression) is different from linguistic analysis of the concepts "*vidyā*" or "*śikṣā*" or many other non-English parallels. Analysing "education" and "*vidyā*" or "*śikṣā*" and so on are different propositions altogether.

From this, we come to know that the best way to analyse the "nature" of the concept "education" (or any of its parallel in different languages) is to consider the different *tasks* and *requirements* of education or to be precise, to consider the *doable* aspects of education. Doing this as philosophers we will be a satisfied lot telling others what is implicit in the notion which otherwise raises a lot of confusion. This would tragically annoy many of our readers who waited for me to give another definition or definitions or to tell them how the term originated, used, meant and so on. Extremely annoying for some other readers will be that I have little or no regard for very deep analysis of "education" understood as "*vidyā*" or "*śikṣā*" having spiritual significance. Equally annoyed will be those who have the habit of analysing the term as essentially an economic phenomenon involving notions of stakeholders, stockholders and material good for men. Not least perturbed will be those people who waited for me to explain in all details what different philosophers, great educators and other great people thought were the aims of education because these numerous explanations of great people taken in isolation do not bring out clearly the realms of the "doable" in education. It is not always good to go along with some or all great thinkers when it comes to 'nature analysis', therefor. However, most of us nurture a poor idea that "quotable-quotes" are good means for 'nature analysis' of a concept which is otherwise not explicitly clear to us. In fact, these "quotes" blur the nature of the concept more than not. Hence, let us now expect that knowing about "education" is to know clearly about its important tasks or to unfold its "doable" aspects.

In an interesting essay "What is an educational process?" Mr. R.S. Peters[1] says that he, like Gilbert Ryle, thinks that the "logical geography" of the concept "education" and concepts in education are yet to be mapped properly. He felt that there is a need "at the start of what amounts to a bird's eye view of the contours of this territory"[2] And to do so Peters starts with the "task-achievement analysis" of education, exactly what is unfolding the "doable contours of education". It is important to notice here that the so-called "aim" or "aims" of education as enlisted through the ages by the thinkers of education are the same as the doable contours of education. Hence, it is natural to imagine that the "aims" and "tasks" of education are the same. And, therefore, there is no point in overlooking what "great thinkers" have said. There is no hidden neglect in my analytic project. Rather, it transcends and in some sense remains neutral within the barrage of particular opinions about aims or tasks of education. It wants to find out the broadly underlined tasks after much has been said by numerous thinkers (and hopefully many more of them would say further about "tasks"). Bringing out what is characteristic to education despite opinions and disagreements about its tasks is the task of an analyst. However, it will be over expecting on my part to put at one place *all* those characteristic tasks of education because we have the habit of skimping in analysis. Perhaps not many of us have at hand the several opinions and disagreements about aims of education as well as the sweeping ability to discover whatever is essential for education to take up. But that is not a great disadvantage or even a mistake on our part because "nature analysis" does not boast about a finalistic analysis of the concept in consideration. In fact, the intellectual capacity of analysis is so varied that it leaves many gaps for many others to fill up.

Another important point is *relativism* in the analysis of the aims or tasks owing to the changing social, political, economic and spiritual settings influencing the thinkers of education. It is undeniable that there have been changes in the perceptions of thinkers of education regarding its tasks because the above mentioned factors were responsible in influencing and shaping their perceptions. The history of the changing perception of what education ought to undertake, as a meaningful social enterprise in any country will be interesting to find out. This might give us an idea of the way people throughout the world have thought differently at different times about the tasks of education. The project of the analysis of nature of education in terms of unfolding the tasks of education is not apathetic to see these changes but the analyst is not expected to act like a historian of education. There is a difference in an analyst's approach about the matter. He or she would try to find out some of the *characteristic tasks of education* despite the tensions of social, economic, political and spiritual changes throughout history of education. However, from the two points discussed just now we get an idea that nature analysis amounts to put at one place in a more or less sweeping fashion the *universal* aims or tasks of education. Where "universal" bears a sense of "transcending the several controversies in opinions of thinkers in the changing perspectives of social life". This may be a *partial* truth nevertheless because apart from the difficulties in finding out and putting common points together about which there was or is or will be no disagreement, relativism itself rules out any such thing to be successful because there was, is and will be disagreements about such and such task or tasks being universaliy acceptable. Is there any flaw in relativistic stance? If everything changes, none can be really universally or objectively true as task in education. Hence, education has tasks but no well-defined universal or objectively valid tasks. To carry the spirit further amounts to the acceptance of *scepticism* about planning in education for planning is based on goals or tasks well accepted, and the acceptance of *agnosticism* about what *ought* or *should* be the tasks of education despite the tensions of several so-called changes or relative perspectives *external* to education, which results into a callous *trans-valuation attitude* among people engaged in the process of educating people. Here, 'trans-valuation attitude' is not a big jargon; it is simply an attitude of disregard and neutrality towards the "value" or "desirability" or "good" of the aim of education. This is crucial for an understanding of what went wrong with the relativistic approach that there can be no universal task or tasks of education in the tension-maze of social changes.

What I want to assert finally as an analyst is that though it is extremely difficult to find out and put at one place *all* the "universally" acceptable aims or tasks of education thereby unfolding its nature, we are able to find out at least those "universal" or "objectively" valid tasks which *should* be undertaken by us, irrespective of what people opine when they are under many external influences. In one of his seminal essays, James Rachels has appreciated relativists' conception (or misconception) that nothing universally valid could be found out particularly when we speak about "values". Rachels reminds relativists like J.L. Mackie that even if Greeks thought that burning dead bodies were better than the Callatians eating dead bodies, on simple biological and hygienic grounds, it will be well accepted that dead bodies "should" not be eaten whatever the controversy or dogma there may be in history. Certainly, at one epoch in history, in India people believed that women need not be given education in free or mixed schools, and at another epoch others thought that such education is needed. We do not say that both were good given the then social conditions shaping perspectives of thinkers of education. We find that free or mixed schooling in particular is good for the overall growth of a girl child, though we did not out rightly reject women's schools and colleges either because we *discovered* that having both judiciously in our society is practical as well as *desirable*, or that is objectively or universally good in education to champion the cause of universal education in our societies. It may well be that at any later "talibanization" of Indian education, most of the then living thinkers would prefer women education at 'their homes up to a secondary level under the shadows of male-chauvinism' but it would be still *good or desirable* to have free universal women's education up to any level with some place for women—only institutions. Or, will it not be the case? Hence, as analyst when I am trying to find out the universal aims or tasks of education to thus analyse the nature of "education", I am not sweeping the granary that suits for any donkey, I am finding what is suitable for a suitable person.

Much has been said about our analytic project. Let us turn to concrete findings in this regard. Our first finding is that "education" is a concept and not precept like book or blackboard. It is also not a concept like "yellow" which is a simple and non-natural property; or, like "good" which is a non-natural property; or like "The Idea of the Good" which an abstract, metaphysical entity; or, like "teaching" or "instructing" which are demonstrable natural phenomena. The later distinction is of further use to notice that when we speak of teaching philosophy, we do speak of instructing in philosophy but we do not necessarily speak of educating in philosophy because educating and teaching are not two alternative processes. Hence, we may say that we educate someone by teaching or instructing philosophy. Clearly, "educating" bears a different sense than the teaching and instructing, both are not synonymous. Therefore, "education" and "educating" conveys different meaning to us than what is conveyed in "teaching" and "instructing". In one sense, when we find that "teaching" is one process (observable) through which we "educate" or impart "education", teaching comes out as means towards an end, the end being "education" (or "educating"). In this sense, "education" is through which, we achieve an end. Hence, there is no one-to-one correspondence of "a process" and "and end" when we speak of "education" and "educating". Clearly, it is not an observable instance by which someone has something. However, it cannot be ruled out that "education" signifies a broad notion consisting of several processes or a family of processes each contributing separately and conjointly to achieve several good or valuable ends for man, like growth of sense of freedom, love, justice and so on. There is thus no one end of education, it fulfils life in many ways and education is fulfilled by a set of process like teaching, instructing, training, indoctrinating, reforming, studying, researching, counselling and so on. We may say that "education" is not 'a process' but an epitome of standard understandable and realizable in terms of several contributing processes, and the standard itself may be valued for "worth" when some good for man is in view. It will be too simplistic, therefore, to hold as do the absolutists that "education" is that which "frees us of corporeal bondages" or that which "liberates us of sufferings" or that which "makes us dutiful" and so on. Education as a good itself might be good in many ways, not in one way. It is realizable in many good ways, not in one good way. Hence, to say that when one reads books, attends classes, where teachers teach subjects, pupils write pages, appears in examinations, passes out and gets a passing certificate, put together conveys the sense of "education" or "educating" and "educated", is completely out of way to understand what "education" is because teaching, instructing, reading, examining etc. are few processes to understand the standard called "education". To understand the standard fully one has to broaden the perspectives of fulfilling "processes". Some good processes are like exploring the environment, caring life, protecting the inanimate substances, telling a truth when needed, to travel, converse, debate, play, sing, dance, draw, listen to music and so on. Another interesting process may be to de-class oneself to learn from all possible contributors. We shall come to this later on. Education may be really unfulfilled without remaining faithful and eager student. The last assertion speaks of "education" in terms of "self-education", that is, in one way "education" is an interaction of the self (non-spiritual self, to be clear).

Much talk in education is, therefore, about the methods or processes in which one is able to come closer to the standard called "education" and "educated" for that matter. Coming closer is nevertheless an extremely difficult but probable proposition. However, we come to know that education is an *incessant activity* of the self, to be clearer, it consists in continuous act of performing certain "tasks" given to oneself and other selves as well but whatever is "given" is not great, what is great is to *freely* accept the "given" as "my task" and then perform it most gleefully. No one can neglect the truth, therefore, that education and educating refers to standard in which certain task performance activities of both the teacher and the taught may be involved. In this sense, we can say that "education" means realizing an end through a family of tasks performed by one self or other selves or both. It is due to this Schiller noticed that "education" ("teaching" as well) acts as an "achievement verb", which Gilbert Ryle would not contest. However, Peters argues in his essay that "education" need not be taken merely as 'performing certain tasks given to us and achieving something that was intended by us' because when both teachers and students are involved in such performances and achievements, they both put to perform or achieve or both. As a teacher often I fail to perform the task of teaching practical ethics in classroom without any practical work done there, and therefore, fail to achieve the desired goal to teach and thus educate pupils in applied ethics. Similarly, students often fail to perform the task of preparing a project on application of ethics and thus fail to achieve the ground knowledge of applied ethics. Yet, most interesting is that our failures do not least rob us of being educated, involved in educating and in education. Hence, "education" need not be necessarily and sufficiently understood as standard fulfilled by the performance of certain tasks and achieving some goals. Peters prefers to say (and rightly to a great extent) that "education" mainly involves an *initiation* of the self to adopt processes leading to a standard in life wherein one knows and masters many things. He comes to this simple point through another distinction between "being educated" in terms of a teacher and a learner. As I have just said that both teachers and students may be involved in education and thus involved in educating and being educated, the student, being the learner does not necessarily and sufficiently depend on a teacher or teachers, though teaching involves a learner and not otherwise. Hence, education may be possible without task allotment and task performance but it can never be without allotting task and performing them by *me*. It is perhaps due to this that for the evaluation of a teacher, we need to evaluate the performance of the students but for evaluation of the students, evaluating teachers are not necessary and sufficient. To this, I may add that more often than not in task allotment and performance, the learners become teachers by contributing as inquirers, critics, evaluators, appreciators and discoverers. Hence, much success of teachers depends on learners but this may not be always the case when we speak of success of learners. Interestingly, going by our former description of teachers spread all around us, the whole nature so to say, a teacher may be non-task allotters and achievement initiators and yet "teach" us in especial sense, that is, allows us to unravel the "implicit" to know it to some extent. In this sense, we get education through a teaching of nobility of a dog, tranquillity of the deep woods, the music of passing wind and so on. In any case, education is a standard fulfilled in the main by several processes involving teaching and learning but in any case, it is not possible without the *self-initiative* of the one who proceeds for the standard or one who is getting education or is educated. To be careful here, education does not rule out teaching, task allotment and initiation to achieve goals, education is "self-initiation" when we view it from the perspective of the teacher as well because it is the teacher who by virtue of his or her freedom fixes tasks and initiates us to perform for a goal to be realized. If teachers are not free in this regard, that they do not initiate themselves in the process of teaching or educating, there is no teaching at all. "Self-initiation" is one important aspect of "education", therefore, Peters says, "This presumably is the logical truth dormant in saying that all education is self-education. This is what makes the notion of "initiation" an appropriate one to characterize an educational situation; for a learner is "initiated" by another into something, which he has to master, know or remember. Education picks out processes by means of which people get started on the road to such achievements."[3] What I want to stress is that "self-initiation" is true of both teachers and students because in one sense both participate in a 'knowing' process as well as educating process. Broadly, people in education have an ideal in mind, which they realizes by participating in processes needing self-initiation to move on the path of goal realization.

Thus far we were engaged in the understanding of the nature of the concept "education" in terms of its basic performing or doable aspect, which as we have said, is to enable human beings to initiate themselves at their free will towards an ideal or a standard in life which they realize is worth pursuing through several means or processes like learning, teaching, training and so on. Let us continue further with these processes because they highlight the basic 'doable' aspect more clearly. The element of "initiation" in "education" brings out the need to go on with certain *desirable activities* and *forms of thought and conduct* which people master gradually to come closer to what is the standard, namely, 'educated'. An 'educated man' is, therefore, involved in intentional desirable actions and thought processes all by him. It is here that the aspect of what education *should* be like comes to the fore but we will leave it now. It is important to notice that the intentional desirable actions and thought processes are distinguishable from the perspective of the teachers and the learners because the former gets involved in actions and thought processes that targets the learner's good, that is, to initiate them closer to the ideal of "education", and in doing so the teacher comes closer to the said ideal to initiate himself to adopt a process of learning. One cannot overlook the *primacy* of the good of the learners from the perspective of the teachers. From the perspective of the learner, the desirable intentional action and thought processes must be for his or her good or well-being and for the well-being around him or her. The learner must be aware of what exactly he is trying to learn or master and why. Bereft of what someone is trying to do and why, there is no education. Education is an ideal achievable in the conscious efforts of man, which are desirable by public standards as well. It is important to notice here that though the perspectives of doing is different when we consider teachers and learners, both are in need of some aids in the "process of doing". As such, these "aids" to education are different from the "processes" of education. Clearly, teaching may be a "process" in educating people, teaching aids are not similar in nature. In fact, "processes" of education are "intrinsic" to education, "aids" in education are extrinsic to education. These "aids" are, therefore, catalysts or facilitators that contribute towards the effectiveness of the processes in education. Hence, panel discussions on euthanasia in a class may be an aid for a teacher to participate well in the process of educating in applied ethics. However, using aids in education is only relative to the need and interest of the learners for they are used for learners' good. More often than not learners may not need them at all or these things are adverse to their basic urge to learn. Hence, a judicious use of aids is another mastery to be learnt on the part of the teachers in the teaching process. In education, when we speak of the process of teaching aids, they might be evaluated as useful and interesting, but these are surely *extrinsic* means to raise interest. Nothing is as good as *intrinsic* interest of a pupil, which does not rely on aids. The ability of a teacher in the process of teaching and thus educating should be to stimulate intrinsic interests in pupils to become free and "do" themselves, and thus help in initiating one's own self to education. But any intrinsic interest may not be desirable. Hence, *desirable interests* of learners to "do" something to be educated at some freedom, is the crux of the issue. Similarly, in the process of teaching the learners there are certain elements surrounding the learners, which they go on 'picking up' or are 'conversant with' quite naturally. For instance, students pick up some good manners and gestures, mixing with a group of students and bad tongue. Clearly, they pick up something desirable and something undesirable. These things (even if we stress on extremely good or desirable things that are picked up like speaking clearly without any hesitation or oratory skills) are neither intrinsic interests nor extrinsic "aids", rather *additional skills* commendable for the development of the learner as a person. Sometimes, we call them "skills of all-round character formation". Naturally, not everything in way of a teaching-learning atmosphere is a teaching process though in some sense, something has positive effect on the learner or that they flourish one's personality and character. To conclude, a number of "doings" amounts to get education.

With an idea of what does *not* amount to the process within the field of education, we have to know what the processes in education are. This gives us an idea about what are some of the important "tasks" to be performed in education. Keeping in mind the importance of "initiation" and certain achievements such as learning skills, having proper knowledge an understanding of basic theories and principles, we may find irrespective of several thesis about "tasks" that education consists in "training", "instructing", "learning by experience", "teaching and knowing about basic theories and principles", "growth of critical acumen", "development of conversational abilities" and the "evolution of the whole man". Let us touch on these aspects briefly. Education properly understood, undertakes the learning of different skills. "Skill formation" is thus one aim of education, though it is always difficult to master. Yet, one should strive to master with some effort and to do so, we need expert standing as guides having exemplary skills to encourage or initiate any learner because without the learner getting proper initiation, he or she will not exert constantly for a skill formation. Practice is basic to educational and other skill formation. These and initiation of experts go hand in hand in the educational process called "training". Most basic to training from the perspective of an expert or teacher are encouraging to read, write, calculate and compute. From the perspective of the learner, these basic things ought to be taken for their intrinsic value to achieve an ideal in education and thus the need of constant practice of reading, writing and computing are needed. Hence, the aim or task of education is to train through different practices at the initiative of the teacher and the self-motivation of the student without much question for rationale of process. It is important to notice that in "training" in education we always do not need verbal or gesture instructions of the skilled masters. Some specific training like discipline, punctuality and so on cannot be instructed by a skilled person. It is also not possible to pick them up just as we do while playing cricket, throw the ball straight in the line of the wicket without even a word has been uttered to us. Honesty, punctuality, discipline are not picked up by habit or even by expert initiation and training. These need specific *habit formation* as a way of life that is, constantly shaping certain habits, which were alien to us but most needed for at some epoch in life. Hence, "training" need not be taken merely as "skill formation" by experts, and initiation and practice, it is something more. Training is also not instructing the way some habit ought to be formed, it is something more. Equally true is that training is not always an uncanny way to do certain things by watching others do the same. Training, when it comes to specific training like moral or value training, seeks participation in a *moral way of life* and knowing the *rationale* of ought and ought-not, that is, why something should be done or should not be done. In any case, training as an educational process or a task of education does not necessarily involve "rationale" of "doing" certain things.

The task of education is to allow the process of "instruction" and "experiential learning" so that one assimilates what is understood to be desirable for a person's growth. Both instructions and experiential learning are related to the development of the cognitive or the conceptual status of the person, which helps in the qualitative growth of a learner. Instruction primarily needs to be on the basis of language-use so that learners are able to grasp what has been said. Thus, instruction is the initial or the basic experience a learner gets in order to have knowledge of something. Yet, any instruction has to fail if the learner is not self-motivated and if they are unfit as per their mental growth to understand what has been said. Hence, any instruction to any group of learner is not a process in education. The instructor has to carefully gauge the cognitive development of the learners at different epochs of life to find out what things are best to instruct and to what level or degree so that the age-wise inquisitiveness is satisfied and instigated to a great extent. A part of such instruction is to back-up language with "what is", that is, to take the learners to matters of fact to have real experience of what they have listened in so many words or in figures. Education, therefore, involves experimental learning by "seeing" what the case is. This contributes tremendously to the conceptual growth of the learner. This is also a good way to instigate the inquisitive mind of the learners because when they "see" for themselves, they ask more to find out more. This is one way in which self-motivation reaches its climax in education and knowing becomes interesting and ever moving, it becomes the root of all discoveries. However, this does not mean that "going out" is enough for educating, there must be intelligent ways to ask questions, give answers and demonstrate certain things in concrete situations than making a merry picnic.

Another important task of education is to teach and learn basic theories and principles needed for the growth of knowledge because experiential learning might be more useful at the lower level of education, whereas at higher levels of education we need basic principles to be taught so that what really goes on in nature or around us could be understood properly. A thousand apples dropped, our teachers and precursors "saw" them dropping but it further required reflection about the inherent principle behind the dropping of apple. Similarly, in education we have to learn the principles or discover them at some pain. Yet, it is always not the case that principles are taught with ease because grasping them need some mental calibre and the calibre of the teacher to express them so well as to leave no ambiguity in understanding. Naturally, therefore, in education we should know how to strike the right balance between primary or basic experiential knowledge and the knowledge of what is basic to the basic experiential knowledge. It is never possible to teach Newton's laws of gravitation before we have some basic understanding and experiences regarding natural phenomena at some stage. Hence, both the above processes are needed in education. However, we have to remember that not all principles are absolutely true, educating in principles should not be thus absolutist in nature. A difficult proposition is to rationalize and teach principles, which has perhaps nothing to do with experiential knowledge. We have to know how to deal with the knowledge of such bizarre principles given the cognitive status and motivation of the learner.

The aim of education is also to prevent fixity in belief and knowledge. More often than not, we have fixed beliefs, dogmas and blind faiths rather than dynamic knowledge, which faces challenges with courage and sustains all ways to change them rapidly and yet if they need a change, the same is done without a fuss. This way in education, we avoid indoctrination and encourage teaching in a manner that encourages the development of critical acumen in learners so that knowledge does not remain shallow and obstinate. Hence, the task of education is to develop critical attitude while having knowledge about something. It is important to notice that being critical is not the way we should be taught because overactive critical mind does more harm than good to the learner. It is also important to notice that it is difficult to train or teach to become critically appreciative about a subject; what we can do at best is that while teaching a subject we need to raise further questions or queries in term of clarification that might end up in a revision or addition or rejection. The ability to ask for more than what has been stated is a good sign in education but with a care that we ought to know where to stop or what not to ask for the sake of asking. In fact, history of any subject is a history of belligerence of conflicting beliefs and attitudes, one being the *assertive attitude* that "this must be true finally, nothing better than this" and the other being the *negative attitude* that "this must be revised, something is better than this truth". Tragically, best minds have been assertive in nature; best teachers need not be so. The role of education is to enable to read the best minds in best way possible and to communicate in a way that the learners are initiated to know whether best minds did the best things. I will come to the "negative" attitudes in education at a proper place to throw more light on this. Undoubtedly, one task of education is to find out the methods in which becoming "negative" to "assertive" in attitude is possible. One good method is, "dialogue" wherein we attend to the assertive, have a chance to negate them to find out finally the truth. This is the way in which more often than not isolated private mind has access to the public mind to have a broader look at any issue. In this way we become catholic to any assertion and negation — there is no hidden agenda. It is in this way that we shape, reshape, completely change or revise our opinions, our thesis and those of others. Education aims at this "openness". I will come to this at a proper place in a different way.

The aim of education is, therefore, to "liberalize", making us "catholic" in spirit through discourses, debates in formal and informal situations and to shape the person's character in a more holistic fashion — the "whole man" is most desirable. Let us come briefly to this conception of "whole man" and "holistic development of man". In fact, the making of the "whole man" is a touted goal of education believes many but the conception may be wholly confused particularly when it becomes handy with the spiritualists. Let us not fall into too many ambiguities and read this passage by Charles C. Miltner in his book *The Elements of Ethics* (1959): "It (education) means a progressive and well-ordered development of man's threefold powers, physical, intellectual and moral the proper formation of the whole man — body, mind and will"[4]. Consequently, he enlists three important tasks of education, namely, imparting training necessary for the perfection of the physical abilities and powers, for preserving health and basic hygiene, which we often call *physical education*. There is further training necessary to sharpen the mental powers, powers of thinking, imagining, problem solving, reflecting, analysing, critically appreciating and to cope up with the socio-cultural changes, which is *intellectual education*. Finally, training is needed to grow strong will power in us so that people choose, decide and act according to the principles of right, good and just — they act rationally, judiciously and freely, which we call *moral education*. In this way thinks many that the tasks of education should be better rolled in one, that is, "man-making" or "holistic" education. Yet, the unknown gap exists in this holistic scheme as people like Miltner and others think that: learners may become not merely intellectual Hercules or graceful Apollo, but gentlemen of solid Christian character. And that "the genuine educators will keep in mind not only man's end as a citizen of this world, but also his destiny as a Child of God". Hopefully, the "gap" is filled by "religious education or indoctrination". We shall come to this later on, but for now, we must mention that "man-making" need not universally, necessarily and sufficiently include Christian or any other religious man-making. The controversy over "whole man-making" is stiff, which perhaps we do not realize before we have not critically examined it. In any case, there is least controversy over the physical, intellectual and the moral goals or aims of education, but we have still not touched about the moral goal. Let us proceed with "man-making" a little farther. We have neglected psychological education to same extent, that is, the goal of education to train so as to give order to the inner life or qualitative development of the mind of man (not to speak of an ambiguous "self"). The quality of life depends much on the qualitative state of human kind, not merely the quality of inteliectual powers of man as we have said above, but also the emotional, the attitudinal and the intentional aspects of man's inner realm. This is extremely important in education as lack of emotions, well-directed attitudes and intentions; an intellect is of no use. Of late, we have come across "emotive quotient" as important as "intellectual quotient"; we should further add that any behavioural anomaly in an undesirable person is due to low levels of attitudes and intentions. Often high intellectuals lack in these three things, and for that, matter "inner life" or "mental life" is a bit different from intellectual life. Hence, education should take care of such life. The complete man or the whole man is the one having a complex life in which *integration* of the psychological, the intellectual, the physical and the moral is needed. We are still not sure whether to include "spirituality" to these things; though it is one aspect of the "inner life", not belonging to the "psychic self" rather to the "metaphysical self", which becomes a bizarre proposition at this place.

Still we speak of "self realizing" aim of education. What is "self realizing"? Hopefully, not always in the history of education did we find talk about "self" and its "realization" in metaphysical terms. Hence, the expression may be understood either as realizing the *true nature* or the *real nature* of our being or better said *Being*, which is often found to transcend corporeality to enter metaphysicality or even Divinity, or as realizing the true capacities or powers of the corporeal being having body, mind and environment to live in. This is to use environment, adjust therein, and to find out ways to enlighten oneself to come out of ignorance one encounters in life. However, the realization of the powers of body and mind does not mean an unrestrained growth of human powers, but a harmonious or balanced one. It is the flourishing of the many possibilities of the corporeal being to the fullest. Education should thus aim at bringing out the *best in man*. However, the "best in man" is dubitable if the *moral best* of man is not brought out — the quality of life that educated man has need not be the mere realization of the self as having such and such physical, mental and intellectual powers.

We would like to continue with "man-making" a little farther. Many thinkers believe that man may be made in different ways through education. Some think that when the individuals develop their capacities (physical, mental and intellectual) to the utmost and are cultured (through acculturation), "man is made". Still, we have almost all the elements (except the "moral") about "man-making". Further it is hold that "man is made" when an individual truly becomes "social" (through socialization), that is, they turn out to be a fine blend of egoism and altruism at the social interface. These theories have some "positive" character regarding the tasks or aims of education but socialization and capacity development cannot wholly make a man. Bertrand Russell in his elegant piece of work *Education and the Social Order* (1977) mentions another view of a man-making education without which whole view of a man is not in view. He calls it "the negative theory of education". (He devotes Chapter 2 of his book in explaining this). I would like to bring out the gist of the said "negative task" for its important and interesting aspects, though he remarks that the "negative" conception of education alone does not amount to holistic education. However, he speaks of the negative conception for its novelty and progressive nature. The task of education is called "negative" in so far as its only purpose has been conceived as "removing hampering influences" for growth[5]. We have to find out what these "hampering" or obstructing elements are without removing which we shall not make a man. The first obstacle to overcome in this regard is the necessary bindings inherent in any educational training in the name of *moralization*, discipline, social conformity and the like on the basis of commands, toughness or the stick and rod, and therefore, snatch "freedom" of the learner. Another obstacle to be removed in education is those elements that take off flowering of learners' *originality* and *natural intellectual interests*. Russell notices that there are basic intellectual desires inherent in learners, which are destroyed by the over enthusiasm of educators because their desire to give more outwits the learners' desire and their power to assimilate. The natural curiosity and original ideas of learners are thus destroyed in the name of profound education, which needs to be overçome. It is also important, therefore, to overcome the obstacles in education that snatch basic *freedom* of learners. Freedom basic to pupils are many but not unchecked. We have to get along both freedom and checks when needed. For instance, learners are free to be hygienic and clean, educators are free to tell them the virtue of these things and check them if they are untidy for nothing, but can we not allow them to be unclean at the price of their freedom to be inquisitive, discovering and finding out something they think to be of worth? Surely, we are obliged to allow such freedom. Russell says, "In the matter of cleanliness and hygiene, therefore, although present conventional education involves much too great a limitation of freedom, yet some limitation is necessary in the interest of health"[6]. Almost similar is the case of some *virtues* like, punctuality which is most likely not to be produced in the puritan way we think it may be produced as a virtue in a learner because in that way we need to take out the freedom, the initiative of the learner to become a little savage if needed to find out new things for themselves. Closely related to this is our puritan ways to teach the virtue of a *routine life* because on our part of champions of education we think that rigid and absolute routine makes a man more disciplined and successful. However, the truth is that such virtues are hardly taught in an unnatural way; we should prevent doing so and allow child's own way of taking time while he learns with some care nevertheless that the time taken does not spoil the entire academic soup. This is also true of teaching to be disciplined through education. While we do not disregard the value of being disciplined because that is one way to socialize, cooperate and be constructive, we cannot make it happen with an iron hand because in doing so, we train to be insensitive, foolhardy and obstinate who do not dare to go a little wayward, walk a few more miles to see what interesting things happen around us. Our education need to obstruct becoming too crazy about teaching these virtues in a puritanical sense to convey the value of freedom on our part to not to follow a routine, to relax, to hitchhike, freak out, break all routine for a while and limit our discipline. Similarly, "unnatural" ways to drive home honesty in man has to be prevented in the name of education. In fact, the message with unnatural ways to teach honesty is to teach the opposite, that is, to show what pain goes with dishonesty. That thieving does not pay much is the route to teach to be honest. The problem is when there is no likelihood of an ordinary theft, honesty can never be taught by showing what pays in the real sense of the term. Hence, the puritan would always put the horse before the cart and teach what is not there, or, when something is there (theft); they teach in terms of punishment that it did not pay them. However, the basic theme of *social cooperation* and brotherhood that goes with honesty as positive, need no negative instances. Harshness, punishment and non-payingness of theft are not akin to teach honesty. Hence, education has the task to see that learners remain free for a spontaneous urge to learn at the right time and at the right frame of mind. However, Russell further says, "The acquisition of concrete knowledge is pleasant in most children: if they live on a farm they will watch the farmer's operations and get to know all about them"[7]. This amounts to say that though the task of education is *negative* in some ways, it is not all, something concrete and positive has to be done. It is due to this that though giving freedom, withdrawing compulsions and affording opportunities of self-initiatives are important, something more has to be done. "The negative theory of education, therefore, while it has many important elements of truth, and is largely valid so far as the emotions are concerned, cannot be accepted in its entirety as regards intellectual and technical training. Where these are concerned something more positive is required"[8]. And we have already said something about this matter but not about one "positive" task of education, which is, moralisation. Let us now come to it with the champion of "education as moralisation" in Immanuel Kant.

In *The Metaphysic of Morals*, Kant describes "moral anthropology" which deals with "the development, spreading, and strengthening of moral principles (in education in schools and in popular instruction), and with similar teaching and percept based on experience"[9]. Clearly, Kant favours a pedagogy in which moralisation is required starting from the schools but it has not to be confused with teaching ethical theories or first principles like deontology. On this pedagogic aspect of moral instruction, he is clearer in his works *On Pedagogy* (1803) and "Methodenlehre" section of the *Second Critique* and *The Metaphysic of Morals*. Though Kant stressed on common human experience as basic to understand what is moral and that he was emphatic about instructing right, good, just and so on in the name of moral principles, but the truth is that in "Methodenlehre" and elsewhere, he hinted towards his ethical theory as basic to moral instruction, which is queer for us in school education. Let us explain Kant and Rousseau (in *Emile*, 1762), both precursors of Russell (about whom we have just read), regarding "negative" education apart from moral instruction at a more positive plane. For Kant (and Rousseau) "negative education" is "hands off" approach telling instructors to let the child have natural development until checks are required when it tends to harm the child. Kant's conception of the "negative education" may be found as follows: "the first stage of education must be merely negative, that is, one should not add some new provision to that of nature, but merely leave nature undisturbed"[10]. In addition to what we have seen in Russell here, an interesting point is that the negative education must be at the "first stage", that is, at a tender stage in school, as we believe. Russell needs a back up here when Kant reminds that child's freedom need not be unchecked either, it should be checked when it hurts the child, and more importantly the child "must also learn to work"[11]. And they should learn "only those things that are suitable to their age"[12]. However, when we come to the said "positive" aspects of education or positive aims of education, Kant is remarkably different from Russell. Some of his commentators put his thesis as *species perfectionism*, that is, the main aim of education is not to advance welfare of the individual student but that of the human species as such. In Kant's language, it is defined as "cosmopolitanism". The universalisation of the goal of education is thus in view wherein "human welfare" in its unambiguous "perfectionist" mould comes to the force, which also focuses the importance of moral instruction in education. This is clearer in Kant's thesis in *On Pedagogy*. He first states that the notion of "education" is true to species—specific not intra-species because unlike humans, non-human animals do not need education, they need some training when domesticated or for other purposes. Hence, a talk of aims of education is sensible in the context of humans. In his empirically based theory of human education, it is further necessary to trace the growth and development of human individual because that is necessary for a decision to impart the kind and quantum of education. Any education is not suitable for any individual. He further asserts that "moral education" among other things is needed in education as such, for that is basic to "perfection" of the human race. For Kant education is not a cause of moralisation. In fact, "morality" and "moralisation" are aspects of human culture and not nature, and for that reason, it needs educating rather than leaving to "nature". It is here that Russell and others rightly noticed that "negative education" is more of entirely justifiable than positively good. Going by this "education" being an aspect of human culture becomes key to human acculturation and moralisation. Moreover, moral-talk is essentially human, so is education, therefore, they go along nicely. It is also important to notice that the goal of education for Kant is also to *civilize* the individual being because cultured, social and moral humans need to be civil in nature and habit. It is not that culture, sociality and morality would automatically count to civility. It is due to this that in the *Anthropology from a Pragmatic Point of View* he says, "The human being is destined through his reason to be in a society with human beings and to cultivate, civilize and moralise himself in it through the arts and sciences"[13]. More clearly, according to Kant, human beings are cultivated through school education; they get civilized in social education and moralised through both schooling and social mixing. Education and its aims most interestingly transcend schools and colleges to enter the whole of life we live in society. Yet, as an anti-climax Kant thinks that humanity has kept a long distance off the stage of moralisation—truly so. More intriguing question is how is a leap from civilization to moralisation possible through education?

Kant thinks that three factors are mainly responsible in this regard. First, a *disposition* to be moralised that is unlike habit, a conscious, rational deliberation concerning one's maxims. Hence, internalized principles that lead to morality are crucial. Second, moralisation is made possible not only by internal maxims but by one's own free and autonomous will to *choose only the desirable* or the good. Finally, moralisation is possible through the autonomous choice of what is *universally desirable*, which is for Kant an "imperative". Moral education, therefore, is based not on discipline (negative) but on internal maxims and will to act because if we can, we should. Naturally, therefore, for Kant the aims of education (positive ones) are three: *scholastic-mechanical formation* in the context of skills, *pragmatic formation* in the context of prudence and *moral formation* in the context of ethics. However, we will happily take up all that Kant has said because his internalized maxims and universalized imperatives of duty may be unacceptable. More interesting is to notice that he himself recognized the *teleological* truism that education's aim is after all "human welfare". Anyway as I have said at the outset, we are here interested in bringing out the basic features of what education should be like or what should be the aim of education. We still stick to the moral goal of education because that "should" be its aim irrespective of debates over relativism or moral scepticism. Even moral relativists have conception of education with moral orientation and not without it because relativists are not anti-moral or immoral or morally neutral. They would not like to fix one definition of moral goal of education as Kant has done or what communists, socialists, Nazis and others have done.

At the outset, it should be said that we are here considering the moral or the ethical task of education because we believe that education is inseparable from value-judgements. It is deeply related to the individuals who are moral agents and as such have every possibility to act anti-socially and immorally at their will, which needs some defence mechanisms through proper education for prevention, reform and damage control. Finally, education being capable of empowering man to live a moral form of life, that is, a form of life in which a lot of care is taken about the right, good, just and desirable intentional actions, it should itself be ethical or moral because immoral education or unethical goal of education is of no good, it is bad. Hence, value-judgement is involved in the way education functions within a society. We have to be careful not merely about what *are* the aims of education rather, what *ought* to be the aim of education. It is also important to notice here that the "moral task" of education should not be confused with either educating or instructing traditional or contemporary and moral dogmas, opinions and commands prevailing in societies or instructing one or more standard ethical theories, both normative and metaethical. It is also not preaching moral do's and don'ts and seeing that students get moral teachings of such and such religion from *gurus*, and to find out how moral problems of real life are solved by applying one theory or the other. It is neither imbibing nor making a regular practice to grow certain virtues and values in one's nature as if like regular exercise it would tone our self. However, this does not amount to say that none of the moral virtues and values needs to be spoken about by the teachers in the classroom or in the campus because that is difficult in a campus situation. We perhaps learn the value of tidiness, discipline, punctuality, regularity and so on indirectly while we teach various issues. Not only this, virtues like honesty, non-violence and the like are regularly appreciated in and outside the classroom. In fact, a campus is a form of life in which we teach and thus learn about many things, most important among them are how to live together, how to live in the natural world without plundering it and why *should* we live together and ought to care for the natural world. It is the campus that teaches us the many "desirable" actions we need to do as humans. It is here we come to know value of acting rightly, justly and dutifully. It is the campus that teaches us the intricacies of moral valuation of human actions even if they are not taught in classrooms. The life of the campus is such that through common human experience we come to know the value of honesty, truth, non-violence and the like. It is here that we come to debate about the universality of many virtues and values, the relativism of the virtues and values and the non-fixity of a standard in life. Nothing is as elegant as the campus is because here we spend a lot of time in a cosmopolitan and secular condition among a range of people of different age groups, opinions, religions and values. It is the microcosm in the macrocosm of morality. Hence, the task of education and its intuitions is to see that they are not value-neutral or morally callous. To my mind, hardly any educational institution can be neutral and callous because life here cannot be bereft of the teeming social activity, the various decisions and functions. We cannot rob our teachers off all paradigmatic actions that are good, right and just for the students. It is due to this that our common experience soaks moral teaching here, we do not need a subject called ethics or moral philosophy here for conditioning. It may be that in schools in iron curtains, which run in the shadows of a so-called moral philosophy where moral conditioning goes on, in reality immorality is practiced. Is absolutist moral conditioning the moral task of education? Human history is testimony to Nazi conditioning, Talibanization and religious intoxication in educational institutions, which were the opiate of the masses. But it is education all around the world, which has vehemently and openly come against such conditioning because it was felt that not all tasks in the name of moral task of education are desirable. Hence, we always challenged the so-called moral task of education because we felt that something better should not be done in education. A rage against indoctrination is justified if that means such intoxication and conditioning. A morally oriented education must be itself moral because moral task of education is possible to undertake if education is its own moral critique, its own moral evaluator. The critical study of values should go on within education, and so far it goes on, the moral task of education goes on, or else a curtain of scepticism, ignorance and darkness lulls. It would be a little trivial, therefore, to say that we only 'pick up' or are 'conditioned' in the prevailing social values and virtues when education performs its moral task because all prevailing values are countered for their moral validity, only those grow that turn out to be time tested in the moral panorama. It is thus trivial to say that we are educated but we have no values and virtues. However, that does not mean that one Mr. X taught us to be good and we learnt to be good. The moral task of education is not artificial in any sense, that is, it does not artificially consider to mould or change human characters from the bad to noble to nobler by a group of instructors on the basis of some "theories" like Kantian deontology or Mill's utilitarianism or Cārvāka's egoistic hedonism. Education to my mind does not, cannot and should not take up such impossible task and believe that "the task" of education is thus fulfilled. The evaluative bases of human actions are neither taught nor learnt in our schools and colleges so that we become great people. If philosophers teach and learn such things, do not confuse that all should do that as all of us should not learn and teach quantum mechanics. Moreover, I have never found that ethical theories were taught to us to reform our bad or not so good characters and to spread that wisdom to people. I will come to discuss at a proper place (as I did in all the three earlier volumes in the Series) that ethical theories fail to do any good to us in our real life when we face moral resolutions if they are applied by us thinking one to be true and believe that others should follow the suit. The moral task of education is not to teach us how one moral theory might help us in resolving a moral crisis or moral crises. On the other hand, when we live a campus life, or, if we study many things all by ourselves, we may be equally moral though none of the theories have been taught or learnt by us. Hence, the moral task of education does not amount to "teaching and learning academic ethics". We shall now drop the discussion here because the rest of the book will deal on such matters.

We believe that much has been said on the "nature" of education in terms of its "tasks". However, there is an interesting issue raised by some thinkers. It is said that "education" (as we have said) is a "concept" and, therefore, does not have any "task". What we confuse is that though teaching, instructing and training take on tasks, education has none. We can imagine parents, students and teachers having certain aims but education have none. This is trivial because confusion about "education" amounts to such assertion. At the outset, we have said that to define or determine what is the "nature" of education is not possible in few words. We need to pronounce the aims and tasks, which amounts not to consider "education" as something in space and time. No one thinks that "education" like "philosophy" or "physics" is not a concept but still has tasks or aims. What prevents education having some tasks and thus their clarification amounts to clarification of knowing the meaning of the concept? When we are asked to find out what "philosophy" means we do not search for students, teachers, and books of philosophy rather, we find out the different tasks undertaken to clarify what "philosophy" means. It is due to this that the modern normative way of explaining education is to find out what is expected of it or what it should do, we thus move away from the description of education. We do not describe the concept now but find out the functional components of education as they are and as they should be. We have found in this connection that education has many aims and tasks; we tried to find out what is universally acceptable or what is expected to the least to be called "education". This way we have moved away from the several theories of education, which belligerently fought to prove that only this is or these are the aims of education. In the meanwhile I have, with some welcome risk, moved away from analysis what "*śikṣā*" and "*vidyā*" amounts to because my job was to undertake the nature analysis of 'education", which I did, I shall be pleased if someone takes up the Greek, the Chinese and other conceptions such as "*śikṣā*" and "*vidyā*" used to mean "education" for nature analysis. However, they should remember that it would be a great logical fallacy to analyse the meaning of "education" with the help of what is essentially differently meant by another term or terms.

In the following Chapters, I will take up the nature analysis of "educational ethics". Further, in the second Chapter, I would like to educate the first and the second order tasks of educational ethics. In the third chapter, I will elucidate the value and virtue related tasks of educational ethics. The fourth chapter takes on the practical task of educational ethics in view of a number of value-laden practical problems in education needing resolution. The fifth and the last chapter consider the possibility of the participation of educational ethics to make us people of noble character.

NOTES

1. Peters, R.S., 'What is an Educational Process?' in R.S. Peters (ed.) *The Concept of Education*, Routledge and Kegan Paul, London, 1979.
2. *Ibid.*, p. 1.
3. *Ibid.*, p. 3.
4. Miltner, C.C., *The Elements of Ethics*, The Macmillan Co., NY, 1959, p. 272.

5. Russell, B., *Education and the Social Order*, Unwin Paperback, George Allen & Unwin, London, 1977.
6. *Ibid.*, p. 25.
7. *Ibid.*, p. 29.
8. *Ibid.*, p. 29.
9. Kant, Immanuel, *The Metaphysic of Morals*, Drawn from Academic Edition, George Reimer, 1902, (6:217) (Trans.) by Robert B. Louden in *Kant's Impure Ethics*, O.U.P., London, 2000.
10. *Ibid.*, (9:454).
11. *Ibid.*, (9:470).
12. Kant, Immanuel, *On Pedagogy*, *Ibid.*, (9:485).
13. Kant, Immanuel, *Anthropology from a Pragmatic Point of View*, *Ibid.*,(7:324).

1

The Nature of Educational Ethics

In the Introduction, I have said something about the nature of "education". In doing so I have avoided the study of different definitions of "education", and in its place analysed the important tasks of education or what education aims at. I have said that some of these tasks are universally agreeable, that is, without much controversy we agree that some tasks constitutes the essential nature of education, whereas some other tasks may be debatably included to mean what "education" is. Most important point is that these unavoidable and universal tasks of "education" are desirable, that is, if something needs to be called by the term "education", should include some of these tasks or else something so-called will not be "education" in the proper sense of the term. Among these important tasks of "education" we include the "moral" or the "ethical" task because if "education" needs to be truly so-called, it should undertake the task of ethical orientation of the individuals. First, we should not wrongly suppose that education as education should undertake the tasks of moral teaching and ethics teaching in the name of "moralisation" because teaching moral science, moral philosophy (or ethics) and moral codes and moral ways of a particular society in classroom may be seriously doubted for value because nothing ethically relevant might be passed on to the learners to shape their character. It is important to remember that moralising through academic pedagogy or theory-churning is not necessarily a part of education. Education, as we have already discussed, need not be necessarily and sufficiently considered as teaching a course of morality by paid teachers to moralise them. We have seen that "educating" transcends mere pedagogy in many important ways. Hence, moral formation of the learners does not beg strict academic pedagogy in moral philosophy and moral codes. No one really believes that if ethics is not taught to the learners at all levels (or at some levels) no moral task has been performed in education. Still, we believe that among many other ways to "morally educate", one way is to teach ethics and common morality, but lot of problems emerge in this programme, to which we shall turn at a proper place. For now, we may say that education among other things takes on moral formation of students but that is not the same as teaching academic philosophy or ethics or moral codes and rules prevailing in societies so that we have great moral character. Second, we have to remember that information about ethical virtues and values are important in education, but there are many more virtues and values which needs to be informed as well. Moreover, we need to remember that informing about human virtues and values including ethical virtues and values does not necessarily and sufficiently beg classroom pedagogy in ethics and axiology. Hence, educating and thus moralising differ from our common notion of a teacher teaching ethics, values and so on to pupils. Further, we have to remember that to talk about "educational ethics" is not only to talk about ethical formation through education, rather, to talk about whether it is at all ethically relevant in education, to undertake such task. In this sense, moral-talk about the different tasks of education should come under "educational ethics", and for that matter we can talk about the moral questions regarding moralisation or ethical formation in education and about the *means* through which moralisation is undertaken. For instance, we may raise morally relevant questions about what should be the method of a morally oriented education and whether religious indoctrination should be its part? More interesting is to ask whether it is ethically good to impart moral education in the name of moral character formation, and whether educating about safe sex be its part? It is extremely important, therefore, to unravel the *nature* of educational ethics, which in the main asks us to ponder about what are the ethically relevant issues in education and educating. However, we cannot overlook the importance of the fact that in educational ethics, we have to consider what the ethical or moral tasks of education are because a lot of confusion about ethics-talk in education is really due to the ignorance of the said tasks of education. Some among us asks why at all education as education should have ethical or moral task when it does not have any task like this? This is a serious question because a proper reply to this question justifies the truth that as per nature, "education" conceives of a moral or ethical task, the justification of which further enable us to discuss why moral-talk becomes relevant in this regard. No doubt, the question of ethical basis of moralisation in education is a relevant educational ethical question but beyond such ethical scrutiny, some other justifications are needed to show why education as education should include moral or ethical orientation of students. It is important to mention here that I will not make strict difference between the "moral" and the "ethical" in this context though they are not synonymous. Similarly, for all practical purposes I will not differentiate between "moralisation" and "ethical formation".

The moral task of education, that is, the task of moralisation or ethical orientation of the learners in formal and non-formal systems of education is backed up by the idea of greater social good (individual's good being its part), because greater social evils like disharmony and non-cooperation destructs the social structure. If individuals need to avoid strife and misrule, wants peaceful, harmonious and well-knit social life, then they should have the basic ethical knowledge of the good of social coexistence and peace. Education has the task to promote moral values in individuals, which happens to be crucial for social co-existence. However, "social good" conveys a wide range of meaning, notions like "harmony" and "co-operation" cannot remove its inherent vagueness because we might still ask, when is there an ideal harmony and how do we come to know about it? Or, when is there ideal co-operation and how do we come to know about it? Many among us believe that the vagueness can be removed by saying that production of "social good" is a matter of "material well-being" of the individuals in a society — the freedom from wants and poverty. Only such well-being can bring peace and harmony. One cannot doubt that people having formal education are more able to eke out a living and be materially satisfied to some extent. Some of them might be well-off and happy too. Equally true is that nothing is great in being poor and in pain, and a society having a number of people having no formal education are more in wants and miseries than living in peace because they cannot look after their material good or the well-being of their families. Even if agriculturists or the one in the business of logging has no formal education, they most likely received some education from their peers to conduct their business. Without having taught and thus learnt how to plough, sow and reap, none can be a farmer. Hence, lack of any education ruins individuals' career and robs peace of mind. Such people certainly do not have a good life. Briefly, education of any form puts morally charged people to care for their own and their societies' material good. Hencc, moral task of cducation is justifiablc on thc *non-moral ground of production of material good.*

However, some people believe that educating people to earn something of their own is at best training and not education in the true sense of the term. Hence, in the above examples of learning farming and logging in an informal way, are at best "training", not educating. If this be so, education does not have any moral task to charge up people to come to know the value of their material well-being and act accordingly. This is in fact a "narrow" way of looking at "education" and "educating". This way of thinking is tragic because it takes "education" to be the one that transcends the drab material well-being and embraces higher things like growth of critical understanding, powers of evaluation of the theoretical intricacies, to develop the spirit of inventions and discoveries and the flourishing of the self. We may say that when self flourishes in terms of the non-material or the theoretical-intellectual, only then do we get education, and only then do we come to know what the moral aim of education is. Still better, without being critical, let us accept the truth that a flourishing academic self is good enough and morally charged up education does this good to us. How can it be "non-material" in any case? The greater theoretical-intellectual powers are at best quality improvement of human capacities, which is so good, but surely, it leads to material well-being in most cases than not because such people stand ground independently to earn a decent living and make themselves happy. There is always a danger in thinking that only quality improvement of capacities in formal education is truly education, whereas what a mother does to her child (and thus to the society) to "educate" how to behave and what the basic human values and virtues are, will be deemed mere "training" and not educating the child. This tragedy lies in our intellectual chauvinism to think that only people having home science education are educated and only those having education in agricultural colleges are educated but mothers and farmers are not educated. No one denies the value of having scientific knowledge of managing a child and a farm, but one cannot deny the value of having education to stand on ones own foot from their peers who teach through life and practice. The real difference between the two might be qualitative or even quantitative, but for sure, both fall under "education". It is important to notice that even "training" (vocational) and other things like teacher's training comes under the broad perspective of "educating" because they are *special means* to attain a level of specialization. Nevertheless, "training" a dog for the police squad is not "educating" the dog. However, knowing the intricacies of dog-training in police institution is having a special education. We cannot deny the truth that mere vocational training or learning to do certain things does not suffice to define "education" because there are many intricacies of the theoretical and the practical realms that sharpen our abilities to criticise, moderate, detect, discover and invent many things crucial for the good of man and other beings and things around man. Hence, both educating and training go hand in hand in the production of the material good for man.

It will be a little too much to think that the value of education can be judged on the material basis alone because material good all by itself does not guarantee "qualitative life". It is beyond doubt that the "quality of life" is unimaginable without proper education of the citizens of a state. Little or no education guarantees disharmony, strife, ignorance and all sorts of ills in life rather than quality of life. In fact, those who strive for material well-being through education should be reminded of the truth that quality of life is not synonymous to the material well-being. In R.S. Downie, E.M. Loudfoot and E. Telfer edited *Education and Personal Relationships,* the chapter on "Justification: Extrinsic Aims" (Chapter Four), notes: "Otherwise they produce things which are materially convenient but ugly or inhuman, and which in the end, the community does not want; this is the case with much modern building. Now this reason construes "the good of society" as "what people want", and points out that in the end people want more than prosperity"[1]. One sense in which we do well to the society (and thus to ourselves) is that we strive for altruistic good guarantying quality of life. However, good for others may be material good for others, but we agree that not always altruists strive for material good for others. Even if they do so, they are not averse to the production of a qualitative life, which is more than production of material good. This does not prevent some altruists to speak of production of non-material good of the social members, which is according to the basic presupposition of education contributing towards a qualitative social life. "For education does seem to promote the creative impulses and the self-criticism which are bound up with the good of a society broadly and humanely conceived"[2]. Thus, we cannot deny that the justification of moral task of education is based solidly on the material and non-material good of the individual and the society. Equally true is that the non-material good is not only spiritual in nature, ethical good or moral good of society is an important aspect. "For part of the good of society is its moral tone and morality is also necessary for other social goods which depend on cooperation"[3].

Let us now come to the justification of moral task of education as based on moral grounds. The justification is based mainly on the truth that moral task of education is necessary for moral goodness. Education as such and moral education in particular, is justifiable on the ground of production of "moral goodness" among people. We have to clarify further what production of "moral goodness" amounts to. The moral goodness of education in any case is not to produce some such individual characters that are either strict adherents of traditional morality or traditional moral codes or are so rationally equipped that they know right, good and just through intuitive moral grounds or principles. Hence, it is completely out of way to imagine that moral goal of education is justifiable on the moral ground that education amounts to *fixity* of mind regarding social codes and/or intuitive normative standards of rightness. Yet, we stress the point that education is morally justifiable for its production of moral goodness because it enhances among moral agents, the spirit of non-fixity to moral codes and principles. It is due to this that moral education enables us to stand upright to challenge several customary moral codes and thus show that not all moral codes are morally justifiable, and to show that without having theoretical idea of principles of morality, we intend and act morally as well as evaluate actions for moral value. On the basis of this we may say that the moral goal of education is to enable us to be critical about absolutist views of what is morally desirable, right, just, good, duty, obligation and about what things are undesirable, wrong, unjust, evil and so on. We might be thus able to justify why our views about such matters is morally stronger than the contrary views. We might say that why in cases of moral disagreements, our non-absolutist views have greater moral weight than the absolute views. This is nevertheless, a difficult task as we have said that "fixity" of moral views is not easy to dispel. Still we can say that we should not be obstinate about having one conception of moral right and wrong. The social structures and the mesh of moral disagreements within these structures does not allow us to be obstinate because only those win over disagreement, who are sound on ethical basis not to be arbitrarily intellectual. Later on I shall argue (as I did in all the three earlier volumes) that moral goodness is a matter of judgement on other than theoretical grounds, mainly speaking on practical grounds, when our moral knowledge is put to some real life test in the face of questions of values and disagreements about such matter. Education that produces such moral goodness in us is morally good because it practically puts us along side the social self to decide on several moral impasse, and because it allows us to cultivate many virtues and values, such as, to respect other members of society to resolve ethical impasse and not to be bossing in nature. To learn to be judiciously other regarding in moral matters is one among many human virtues which education as such and educational ethics teaches us.

The education of self-regard and other regard in practical moral matters is not everything because when we come to theoretical morality the regard for my moral opinions backed up by moral reasons are equally important along with those of others. In fact, since our childhood, whether we liked or not, we were flooded with moral opinions, that is, opinions about what is good and right given in our culture or in our form of life, which is highly relative. We like it or not, we were flooded with moral reasons about why such things "ought" to be done in our form of life and why other "ought" commands may not be as good as ours. Such theoretical moral education is carried on in our schools, where we come across 'ought for us' and 'ought for them', 'our goodness' and 'their goodness', 'our reasons for calling us good' and so on. The point is that the true end of education (and moral education) is to empower us to be courageous and free to know or scrutinize why 'our ought' is 'ought', why 'our goodness' is 'goodness' and at the same time why 'ought for them' is 'ought' or why 'goodness for them' is 'good'. Or, much stronger one, 'why our judgement of their goodness and badness were unfounded' and 'why their judgement of our goodness and badness were unfounded' or 'why we wrongly thought we were good'! Moral goodness evolves out of power of critical moral acumen when education frees us of socio-cultural bigotry and thus liberates us of moral fixity. The end of moral education being education of moral goodness has no place for objective values we thought to be so noble but tragically disregarded relative values. The abundance of moral goodness and good people around us is a matter of simple empirical discovery lest education cared for the power to discover such things while living among abundantly varied cultures, ways of life, virtues and values.

It is very difficult to contest the position that we are well placed to act morally if at all we realize why acting morally is desirable and that should we intend to do so. Hence, pages of writing on the education of moral ought and right will not be of much help if we do not know why moral ought is so valuable and if we do not intend and act morally. It is a misconception to think that the aim of moral education as a theoretical discipline has nothing to do with our right intentions and consequent actions. If moral education helps in the evolution of moral goodness, it should be understood as some discipline that practically instigates us from within to do what we know is worth doing. A habit of such practical wisdom makes us man of character, which many among us have. It will be out of way to argue here that uneducated people act morally, much better than educated people at times. The reason is what is "uneducated" becomes difficult to understand. If we mean by it "illiterate" or those having no formal education, they may be morally educated about 'ought' and 'desirable' by their peers, fellow beings, families, friends and even the whole of the natural existence where the person thrives. I have argued at many places (see Volumes 1 and 2) that moral experience and moral knowledge is due to our interactions in the vast ecological community. It is this community in part or in the whole that 'teaches' us in different ways the 'ought' and the 'desirable'. 'Education' and 'moral education' in this sense may not be restricted to classroom education of such and such subjects. The classroom teaching of moral philosophy or moral codes may not make us morally good to the least through its vast repository of theory-laden enterprise if moral education is not understood as a practical enterprise to learn to do what should be done among the human and non-human population. It is this large population where the pressure of 'doing' is felt most, and it is here that what we have learnt from our peers and the environment about 'ought' is put into practice irrespective of our theory-laden academic life. Moral education thus evolves moral goodness when such education is taken as some wisdom coming from our interactions with the numerous existential of existence (see Volumes 1 and 2). The whole of the existence we are placed in is the place where we are educated. Thus, moral education is not education as pedagogy within the limits of space, time, locale and trained professionals. To me, education (and moral education) transcends the said "limits" because our fixed ways of knowing education bereft us of education. For me, all illiterates are not bereft of either moral education or moral intentions to act morally. In fact, moral education is largely educating us through actions in real life situations. Schools and colleges cannot be the only source of moral education, therefore, no one contests the theory that moral education broadly understood as above does help in the growth of moral goodness, and no one is contesting that moral education in schools and colleges does help evolve moral goodness because schools and colleges provides us ample moral experiences and knowledge in unique interactive forms of life.

Let us carry on with the idea that moral education is good because it produces morally good beings in society but for that *expert teachers in schools and colleges are not necessary*. However, we accept that though educating moral matters by teachers is not the only important thing, we cannot disregard the truth that the theoretical knowledge of right, good, ought, just are extremely important when it comes to the making of a skilled intellectual who does not simply churn what he learns rather, *applies* what he learns when it comes to the evaluation of the theoretical knowledge that has been gathered. This might help in the growth of moral wisdom that theoretical moral knowledge is not an article of faith or convention or command or pleasure, but is a matter of value conducive to the evolution of a high moral character who recognizes that knowledge is not merely an instrument of any personal good, it becomes a desirable thing to be constantly tested for validity before acceptance. It is very difficult to deny that moral education is morally good in the *teleological* sense, that is, equips people with some such knowledge, which, when pressed in practical situations is conducive to the good for man (not only to the good of the moral agent). In the *deontic* sense, it prepares characters for us who value moral knowledge as *good itself* and thus strive for attaining such knowledge whether or not such attainment would necessarily allow us to be experts who resolves moral matters and does well to man. Any disregard to the *intrinsic and the extrinsic values of moral education* thus moves us away from the realization of its moral value. Morally good people are those who are educated to see that education of something like, morality has a value and produces value. It is pointless, therefore, to argue that theoretical moral education as imparted by teachers have no value or are detrimental to our growth. However, I do not deny that what the teacher wants to impart should be clearly not his or her value, his or her morality, their moral dogmas and opinions and so on without any idea of appreciation of these things. Equally true is that theoretical moral knowledge given to us by our teachers needs to be tested for validity before acceptance.

Closely related to what I have said just now, moral education and education in general has close connection with the production of several valuable things or goods in our life. Hence, education produces moral goodness among us in so far as it enables us to have access to many 'non-moral good' or 'non-moral value'. For instance, we know how to earn decently for a living. More than that education enables us to know the non-moral value of certain things, which turns out to be most important for the judgement of ethical value of intentional human actions and decision-making. In order to evaluate whether cloning is morally good or bad and whether we should clone humans, we should know what cloning is, what human cloning amounts to and what the impacts of the same on the biological and the social existence are. Without the necessary "non-moral" knowledge about cloning, we are not in a position to morally evaluate the decision to clone humans in our societies. Similarly, without the "non-moral" knowledge of globalization of economy and its various socio-political repercussions, we are not in a position to morally evaluate the decisions to free the entry of private schools and colleges in Indian education. Hence, "education" as such has the ability to impart knowledge of the "non-moral" good needed so much for the moral evaluation of human decisions and in doing so, it helps in making us morally good citizens, who do not evaluate something to be morally good or bad on whims or on the basis of tradition or belief or hearsay. One is non-morally equipped to understand what the impacts of something on social life are and thus knows why on moral grounds certain impacts are good and right or evil and wrong. Education thus provides persons with critical acumen to judge why something is moral or immoral given the non-moral information. However, as I have mentioned before, formal education is one important aspect of moral evolution in men, but it is not the only factor for having morally good people. Closely related to this is our understanding of the truth that education is morally good in so far as it helps in the growth of moral virtues in man, and the most important one in my opinion is to be able to do in actuality what should be done, which is a form of "courage"—"courage" is indubitably a factor in the evolution of a morally good person. Not only this, education develops in us temperance, love, cooperation, tolerance and care for cultural relativism. These virtues make us morally good because we behave as a reasonably self-regarding person who knows that without care for others, there is no self-regard and without self-regard, there is little regard for others. We thus know how to live with people having different castes, creeds, faiths and opinions, though we know how to counter them when they are wrong on the basis of universally agreed upon objective standards. We are thus tolerant towards those who eat beef but we will not tolerate them when they eat meat of cows having foot and mouth disease or when we kill milch cows in large numbers caring little about back up measures. Education thus pours in us (if that is the right expression), the nectar of "ought", which we need to bring into practice, which is however, a difficult task always in real life, but we are from within urged to apply ourselves. Perhaps this is net gain from education. A morally good person through education does not, therefore, become intellectually passionate about theories of morality rather, turns out to be a morally charged person, who is not necessarily a moral philosopher. W.K. Frankena in his book *Ethics* (1980), in the context of virtue ethics asks, "whether being virtuous is not important than following standards of morality and then doing something?" Without much fuss, one has to accept that though being virtuous is extremely important, it does not happen without any personal effort as supported by others. The effort is to go along with the process of educating ourselves particularly when 'official education' is a must in civil societies. So 'being moral' or 'being morally virtuous' needs our sincere educational endeavour. Those who do not have official education are not morally worse, but it cannot be a great virtue to remain officially uneducated. I have said that bereft of official education, one might be equally morally evolved, but imagine a society full of people who would never like to be educated officially because among other things, moral orientations in education (also moral philosophy) makes us slaves to dogmas causing bondage of intellect. In such societies, people are sure to lack in the evolution of one moral virtue at least, they do not have wisdom to know why and how the phenomenal world continues to be such a mystery. Ignorance of why, what and how finishes the inner inspiration of man, the urge to know and discover, and the love towards what is intrinsically good. Even staunch religious persons would not agree that metaphysical—spiritual knowledge of Reality obtained unofficially, is sufficient enough. It is a matter of great tragedy that staunch followers of "no formal education" who are nevertheless, religious would never care to listen to their *gurus* or read the sacred texts or discuss philosophical aspects of religion in colleges. For the non-religious and the anti-religious people things are not different because they too cannot glorify "no formal education" on the basis of glorified common sense and training. Hence, it is immoral to imagine a state of "no formal education".

There is no point in arguing unnecessarily that a school or a college alone teaches us to be social and moral because we know that our life in community teaches us to be social and moral. I have said that in a broader way of looking at "education", there is no harm in accepting this obvious point, but that does not mean that we need not have any school or college and any subject like moral education. There is a lot of confusion in the minds of fashionable modernists opposing education in moral matters that it aims at 'converting' our 'original' nature. There is no fear about such things when we realise that the corruption of conversion can be stopped when we are taught many things but cultivate in nature the most needed ones for our moral growth. School and college education thus enables us to be morally spirited to challenge many attempts of corrupt moral conversion, or else, the "uneducated" remain the best parties to be corrupted through moral dogmas of their age. The lofty goal of "character making" is often corrupted morally when what makes "character" has been manipulated by our masters. Nevertheless, a characterless education is "characterless" when moral experts boss about character from the top. Such difficult people hope to solve all moral crises by virtue of their noble character and teach dogmas without any challenge. Education as builder of moral character grows many virtues and values in us with an eye to moral reason, moral scrutiny and moral debate. An empirically anchored moral education does not, therefore, overlook the views of masses as well as what peers say in unique atmosphere of discipline and method. However, we should never forget that many other goals of education which we have discussed are also necessary for the growth of strong moral character. It would be a little too much to say that philosophy as a mind boggler or mathematics as a teaser does not build character. Character is not a sole affair of moral education. Similarly, moral character making cannot be sole aim of education. Education contributes to many other things.

Something has been said about the moral aim of education and the moral significance of moral or ethical education. However, we are still unclear about what "moral" or "ethical" means and what "educational ethics" means. In fact, if we do not know clearly what "ethical" means, we are groping to understand what "educational ethics" is and why it makes any sense. First, let us discuss about "moral" and "morality" for our non-philosophy readers in particular, who are, however, more acquainted with these concepts rather than "ethics" and "ethical". There is an old dogma that what is "moral" is either sanctions of society or family or groups, or what is permitted in religions, which "ethical" is not. The vision is more blurred regarding the "ethical" rather than the "moral" because we say that in reality "moral" and "ethical" are synonymous. This is no less dogma. I must say that when we listen to people having little or no idea about such matters and thus depends more on what is believed in the common parlance, confusion about "moral" and "ethical" is at hand. Readers might remember that I have myself said in this work that I have no intention to flounder much with the use of "ethical" and "moral" though they are not synonymous. There are reasons for this as well but let me first come to the meaning of "moral" and "ethical" along with "morality" and "ethicality" so that their distinctions are made clear. We should naturally discuss about "ethics" before we consider what is "ethical".

Simply stated, "moral" is that which pertains to "morality" and "ethical" is that which pertains to "ethics", but we have to know what it is to "pertain to" morality and ethics, which is one way to explain what is "morality" and "ethics". When we come to "morality" and "ethics", they are essentially distinct in nature because "ethics" is a branch of philosophy doing something unique whereas "morality" is not a branch of philosophy though "moral philosophy" is a branch of philosophy, which is in reality "ethics" called by another name. This name is, however, self-explanatory; it tells us about a branch of philosophy that aims at philosophical query or reflection regarding "moral" affairs or "morality". Hence, "moral philosophy" or "ethics" is academic inquiry that takes "morality" as its subject and for that reason; it is something about "morality" and not "morality" itself. Ethics or moral philosophy thus cannot be "morality" because it is "philosophical reflection about moral matters or morality". Naturally, we now ask, what matters pertain to morality, which becomes a subject for philosophical inquiry? Though, it is not true to say that moral matters are all matters of social and religious dogmas of human conduct and character, we cannot deny that morality or pertaining to moral matters are those involving unique problems and evaluations or judgements about human conduct and character. Most interesting is that when we judge some moral dogmas to be immoral or unethical as opposed to moral or ethical, we are involved in 'what pertains to morality or moral matters'. Hence, "morality" is not merely, what is sanctioned to us by social institutions. Nevertheless, we cannot deny that it is the social body that gave us the ways of life, our families being chief contributors to pass the same to us. It has thus given us guidance for living, doing, not doing, shunning, abandoning, cursing, and loving and so on. It has given us rudiments of faith of the good and the evil, those to be cursed and those to be commended. In many cases, along with "dogmas" of how life should be lived and how to judge a good and bad life, the power to evaluate on the basis of lists of do's and don'ts that are at the receiving ends of prize and punishment. In this sense, morality or moral matters are means of guiding our social life where we act, influencing ourselves and many others. In this sense, morality passes on "value systems" comprising moral codes and moral opinions to us so that we are guided by them to behave as society wishes and judge behaviours of others. It is not unlikely that in the name of passing these things, society passes religious, spiritual and metaphysical codes to live a proper life. However, it is not always that an individual does not have his own morality or own ways to guide moral life. One important aspect in individual morality is that rather than being whimsical and go-as-you-like character, he or she has decent ways to lead his or her life though that may be different from what many others do according to social codes. Again, we come to know that disagreements about the "value systems" passed to us are one way to transcend rudiments of moral dogmas to come to the realm of the ethical. 'Transcendence' from the moral to the ethical is thus a story of humans transcending themselves and the society with regard to value systems taken to be absolute and sacred. Not only this, I have argued in one of my papers that ethical as different from moral involves 'transversality' of value systems because ethical, unlike moral is disagreement and agreement about good, right, just and so on. When we stick to the periphery of the moral (as given and true), we hardly care any disagreement about moral matters such as do's and don'ts and strive for a consensual agreement on the basis of moral debates wherein relative set of values criss-cross, conflict and converge as a system ethically more desirable than being morally desired or morally believed to be desirable[4]. We can thus hold that moral and ethical are different matters though they are closely related. Ethical scrutiny of moral beliefs, dogmas, opinions, views, habits, customs, codes etc. are basic to what pertains to ethics. In this sense, moral matters are judged for value on the basis of some principles which are never universal in nature rather widely populist among cultures and do not withstand critique of other sources even if something is grossly immoral or, on universally agreeable or objective standards laid in ethics as ethical principles or norms. Such ethical norms are bases of evaluation of the prevalent moral matters and human intentional actions for goodness or desirability irrespective of cultural relativism. In this sense, what is not in accordance with these principles are judged to be unethical or immoral. There is a basic difference in the pattern of value judgement, therefore, in cases of morality and ethicality. The former follows a pattern laid in cultural relativism without regard for overreaching universal ethical bases, and, therefore, subjectivist at the individual and the group levels or better said are relativistic, whereas, the latter follows a pattern laid in universal or objectivist bases at individual and group levels. However, cultural relativism as well as objectivism becomes matters of ethical scrutiny. This takes us to moral reasons, moral arguments and moral debates where truly speaking, "moral" reminds us of what is not non-ethical or non-moral. We can say that there are distinctive ethical reasons, ethical arguments and ethical debates, but there is another side of the coin when moral reasons, arguments and debates are simply taken as reasons provided and prevalent within a culture by individuals and groups and tantamount to sophistical debates wherein chauvinism of expert moralists counts most or best. Ethical reasons and debates being unlike chauvinistic or sophistical are both *formal and informal*. Let me elaborate on this matter. The reasons on which ethical debates rest are 'formal' in nature because an analysis of these debates revealing many criss-cross arguments that reflects *formal pattern in reasoning*, which is a matter of the persons trained in ethics to discover. This does not mean that participants in ethical debates are trained in logic and argument as sophists demanded should be the case. I have argued at length (in volume 1), that ethical scrutiny of matters of value (or moral matters) involving debates, arguments and reasons are essentially "informal" in nature, whereas its analysis, particularly after the consensus in a debate reflects the "formal" pattern. However, in case of "moral debates", amounting to *sophistical churning of moral matters, becomes a class-based activity*, highly artificial, prejudiced, unnaturally formal and wayward. In this sense 'the moral' and 'the ethical' are essentially different but there is nothing wrong in using "moral" in place of "ethical" if that means arguments and debates which are neither class-based nor dogmatic but *pertains to debates about moral good and right*. Moral or ethical debates and arguments therein are not one of "herd" having no pattern whatsoever, they are not cacophony rather, they are most informal ways to bring out our moral experiences and knowledge which 'transcends' individuality and 'transverses' moral views to come to a point which despite our cultural biases and ways, takes on *objective positions* as worth for coming to a *consensus*. It has to be reminded here again that "moral experiences" and "moral knowledge" are truly, what we call "ethical", that is, pertains to right, just, good and desirable human intention, decision and actions. No doubt, our moral experiences and knowledge emerge in our society and our culture, but that does not mean that our experiences and knowledge of good and desirable are what has been given to us and we carry them forward. Our moral knowledge is of no value if we do not press them in demanding situations in social life. It is here that we are pressed in isolation and association to "transcend" the "given sacred" morality and "transverse" our moral knowledge for a real life ethical evaluation of the same, that is, the so-called "moral". It is in this sense that "ethical" is distinct from the "moral" reverence of the codes of conduct, virtues and values, laws and etiquettes. In reality, it transcends them through a thorough rational scrutiny of what is desirable in the given prudence, conduct, rules and etiquettes on *objective basis*.

This does not mean that individuals have no freedom and identity as moral agents in so far as what is moral is also "internalisation" of commands or autonomy of decisions. However, "morality", if it is bound to the individuals, might cause greater danger as their autonomous decisions and actions do not influence them alone. Hence, one has to "transcend" individual morality to objective morality, which is truly the realm of the "ethical". Now and again in this discussion we have found that much misgiving about "moral" and "ethical" and "morality" and "ethicality" are due to the double edged use of "moral", that is, the "conventional" and the "evaluative" (to be precise). Once we understand that the terms "moral" and "ethical" can be used to mean right or good as opposed to immoral and unethical meaning wrong or bad in the same "evaluative" tone so to say, there is no harm in using both. Similarly, if both "ethical" and "moral" means "that which pertains to the evaluative aspects of conventional moral opinions", there is absolutely no harm in using both. It is exactly due to this that I prefer to make no fuss about the "ethical" and the "moral". However, I am fussy if they are taken equivalent overlooking the "conventional" tone inherent in "morality", which needs to be differentiated in the ethical parlance.

There is less confusion about "moral philosophy" but in the common understanding, "ethics" is abused to some extent no doubt.

Without taking much notice about it being a branch of philosophy many people define "ethics" in peculiar ways, most popular among them is to state that "ethics" is "morality" taken in the "conventional" sense. Many among us ask a false question like, "what else can be ethics but discussion of right and good as determined by people of changing societies in changing times?" Others ask another one: "what else is ethics than religion?" "Ethics is what is permitted by God." Even moral philosophers have bad habit to confuse ethics and religion as well as ethics as relativistic judgements of value. Let us not fall prey to such gross understanding of "ethics" because that will do much harm to our understanding of "educational ethics". It is easier now to say that a careful reading of the introductory essay in this book that deals with the nature of education reveals that many concepts need not be defined and thus known. Ethics for its nature analysis does not depend on a definition because most carefully carved out definitions leave out many tasks of ethics. It is desirable, therefore, to explain the tasks of ethics. We can still risk definitions that as a branch of philosophy "it is philosophical thinking about morality, moral problems and moral judgements"[5]. However, thinking about morality and so on is extremely wide conception. To be clearer we need to deconstruct the range of "thinking". One philosophical thinking is to explain theory of the nature of human intentions, to find out why at all humans are led to act altruistically rather than purely egoistically or *vice versa*. This is known as *descriptive task* of ethics or simply "descriptive ethics", which cuts across fields like psychology, anthropology and so on for a proper study. Further, we have the *first order task* or the primary task called the *normative task of ethics* about which we have seen something before. It is to consider the problem of moral evaluation or judgement particularly when we are in a position to find out whether certain intentional human actions irrespective of an influence on me should be called right, good, just, wrong, bad and unjust. Naturally, "normative" thinking involves problem of *bases* of evaluation to find out why some actions are surely good and not bad. Good excuses are always needed for a moral judgement. Then we have the *second order task* or the *metaethical task* of ethics which amounts to consider the problems of meaning and truth of ethical language, which on its turn is a problem of analysis of nature of crucial ethical concepts like "good", "right", "just" and so on, as well as the problem of *justification* of or the logic of the bases of moral evaluation, that is, true norms of ethics. This is, therefore, the 'analytic' or 'critical' task of ethics mainly taking "language" to be most vital for inquiry. It is extremely wise to consider these issues because in want of nature clarification of vital ethical concepts, we do not know how to apply them meaningfully in language. To know that "X is good" is meaningful; we should know at the outset the meaning of "good", as an evaluative moral term is sensibly used in the above ethical language. However, we have to further ask on what grounds 'X is good' is true and meaningful but not false and meaningless. Can we sensibly speak in ethical language that "God is good"? Does it make sense in ethical perspective? Can we say that "wearing a cap in the sun is good" is ethically sensible? Or, can we say that "Helping the poor is good" in ethical context? If we justify any one (may be the last one of the three statements) to be ethically sensible, we need to ask further: On what grounds? How are we so sure about it? Is it true to say so? We have to justify why any one or two statements (as above) are not ethically sensible. These are all "analytic" issues; they involve logic. Similarly, if we say that "Helping poor is good" on the utilitarian ground, we speak of a norm and then we need to "justify" why at all this should be a ground? Can we not say that it is our "duty" to do so? Well, we can, but that too needs justification. However, an interesting analytic point may be that the above assertion is true and meaningful in terms of our "intuition" — we directly experience the truth. Yet, it needs a justification. We may say that the assertion being one of value and not fact, or better, value of a fact, no justification in natural or non-natural terms are sufficient. Hence, these assertions are true and meaningful only if we peruse into the speaker-hearer situation in the moral contexts. It might be speaker's emotive expression to arouse a similar one in the hearer or an attitudinal or a prescriptive expression or all of them and something more. Yet, we have to find the basic logic in such explanations. Not only this, the justification that such and such branches of ethics are really so and not out of it, is a matter of analytic ethics. Interestingly, in this chapter the analysis of the nature of "ethics", "value", "education" and "ethical and value education" are essentially analytic in nature. Hence, we can safely say that here we are doing something within ethics and not out of it.

Our readers should not be satisfied of the tasks of ethics. We have just mentioned the important ones. We further have the "practical" task of ethics wherein main issue is the resolution of the value-laden or morally significant problems in practical life of ordinary people including several professionals. We have to see whether our known ethical norms have any role in the resolution of value-laden practical issues (see Vol. 1). In the field of practical and professional ethics, we have several interesting tasks, which have given ethics an emphatic empirical status (Vol. 2). Not only this, we now speak of ethically significant issues in environmental and ecological sciences, biology and medicine, computing, accounting and so on (Vols. 2, 3 & 5). We should now stop because we have reached ethically significant issues in education or "educational ethics".

What is then "educational ethics" and not educational morality? Putting things together may be one good idea but that is not sufficient because nature analysis of "educational ethics" needs clear statement of tasks of educational ethics and not tasks of education and ethics put together. It should be noticed at the outset that I will not attempt at providing cut and dried definition of educational ethics to satisfy readers because I do not think that a short or a long satisfactory definition revealing all-important aspects of educational ethics may be stated. Naturally, therefore, it is better to analyse the tasks of educational ethics. However, there are some reasons to say that putting what we already have in hand together may be of some use. It is clear from our analysis of the nature of "education" that among other aims or tasks it has the task of moral formation or moralisation, which is however, not the same as shaping a child's character in accordance with the moral opinions and dogmas of the teacher, society and state because it is more important to empower a child to freely and meticulously scrutinise on ethical bases why certain moral dogmas or traditional morality is either commendable or cursable. Education should thus aim at an "ethical empowerment" of the learners at different stages of life so that all matters pertaining to 'ethical value' or 'ethical worth' are resolved without peer pressure but not without the public taken in view, that is, the value opinions of the public has been taken care of. On the other hand, we have seen that the aim of ethics apart from empowering us to know why such and such intentional actions are judged to be good or bad on different basis, it allows us to remain actively engaged in the resolution of value questions about human decision-making and actions, that is, questions about life lived in society. Having made two most important points about the tasks of education and ethics, which brings these fields closer to one another, I have some reservations to say that moralisation through education means moulding or shaping great ideal characters stuffed with numerous ethical virtues and values that habitually and unfailingly put these stuffs to practice. This is an absurd idea, because most mechanical programmed life does not assure us of ethical sanity. In fact, test of ethical sanity depends much on how we respond to value challenges of real life about which this work intends to speak more. Whether we are ethically stuffed does not depend on whether we are goody-goody guys in family, neighbourhood, school, college, functions and parties and so on. Many goody-goody guys turn out to be morally blank when despite sound education they completely or partially avoid value challenges in real life. Even great people of a lofty religious character, which is to my mind tragically confused to ethical character, does not eke out a small pittance for the resolution of questions like whether or not AIDS victim children should have access to free schools or physically challenged children should have the same. Hence, it is a pity to take educational moralisation as teaching how to behave and be a goody-goody guy. It is a pity not to break the ideals in which we were conditioned and became too good persons but did not see the truth that religious hawks as we were made have no care to challenge a religiously coloured history education. We did not see the truth that despite being behaving well, we bribe, take bribe and fall in caucus to elevate the ladder of social success. Being good people we fall back to cut throat competition with our colleagues for a post though we have been great Vedāntins or were moralised like that. Coming closer to people, facing their challenges and resolving crises with them are great virtues as educated and thus moralised man.

Now if we put these findings together, educational ethics should be a discipline that at least aims at value resolutions pertaining to educational affairs. However, this is too trite, it needs more clarification. We shall come to this clarification but with an idea that the term "educational" in this context is "what pertains to education" and "ethics" is "what pertains to ethical discussion" putting them together we get the idea that "educational ethics" is meaningful ethical discussions with regard to the different aspects of education and educating. Why on earth should ethical discussion be carried out in case of education, which is essentially a different category? Why should we unnecessarily borrow ethics from philosophy to educational matters? Is it not a bad habit on our part to discuss something, which is not at all expected of us? If we can find pertinent replies to these questions, we are sure to "justify" "educational ethics" as an independent and meaningful enterprise, and this is *metaethical* in nature because it *justifies* why ethics should take on a task like this one. This discussion is also *metaeducational* because here we *justify* (or attempt to do so) why education should happily allow its ethical scrutiny. There is another problem here, that is, to justify educational ethics as falling within either ethics or education or none. Even this *justification* is basic to "educational ethics" as a "meaningful" enterprise. However, we have by this time considered a substantial part of meaning clarification of "education" and "ethics" in "educational ethics", which has helped us a lot.

Answer to "what pertains to educational ethics" gives us ideas about why ethics should interfere in educational matters (though not in all matters), why education which is itself ethical should include educational ethics and why methods of educating should be discussed with care when it comes to educate in ethics or moral philosophy as well as educational ethics. When we consider these things at one place, we get an idea of *range of issues* in educational ethics, which in turn gives us a near clear idea of nature of educational ethics, which is a good follow up of what we have been doing in this chapter. It is in this context that we also have an idea of which value-laden issues in education need resolution and what ought to be the right way to do so. R.S. Peters in his book *Ethics and Education* (1974) writes: "That educational issues should give rise to ethical questions is not a contingent matter.... That education must involve something of ethical value is, therefore, a matter of logical necessity"[6]. The main reason Peters thinks is that "education" involves the passing on of something good or worthwhile, to improve, better and initiate people for a good life. Hence, the conception of "value" or "good" or "worth" is built into the conception of "education", and therefore, we cannot disregard the truth that the very attempt at educating people shall be tested for what it was expected to do or should do. Yet, there is no compulsion of passing on particular values not even particular ethical values to the learners when we educate them. In fact, attempts to indoctrinate in some values as ethical but not others, is unethical. This takes us to consider whether when we try to pass on what is good through education, it is good to pass only something granted as good and leave out others which were good. If we deliberately do that, the natural consequence is to *ethically evaluate* why such favour should be ethically good at all. Hence, education logically involves what is good and thus involves *ethical evaluation* of whether it has done so in several attempts at obtaining that objective. Education as such cannot at the same time aim at giving us something good with something essentially evil. Education as such cannot at the same time try to do well but does bad. Education as such cannot at the same time improve us, better us, initiate us but either does not *in reality* do so or does what is just the opposite. Similarly, if education as such tries to pass values but *in reality* passes fixed set of values, then we should evaluate such evil acts. But what it is to "ethically evaluate or scrutinise evil acts like these"? The question might take us too far but for the time being we can say that it is simply discussion of the *ethic of education* or finding out what is *ethically justifiable* in one or the other aim or aims of education. For instance, it is to find out what is ethically justifiable in value-indoctrination or in religious-indoctrination or in privatization in education etc. Thus education (and educating) having goals to achieve should nevertheless be careful in answering whether what it attempted to do in some ways were at all *ethically* desirable, just, right and so on. However, the term "ethically" raises some questions. We might say that what is practically desirable, right and just or desirable, that is, right and just on social, economic, political, legal grounds is what is "ethically" justifiable. But this is not the case because things that are practical and right and good may be further asked for "ethical" rightness and goodness. One might say that for a particular religious group, religious value-indoctrination is practically good but that opens the can of worms for ethical judgement or ethical queries. Privatizing higher education may be practically, that is, socially and economically good but we still ask whether that is ethically good? Hence, to understand ethical scrutiny of matters of education or the ethic of education, we should understand that it is not based on *practical grounds* (this is a sweeping expression covering social, political and economic grounds of evaluation). Naturally, ethical scrutiny is "what pertains to ethics" and not outside ethics. This takes us closer to understand what it could be to speak of ethically good or bad or just irrespective of being practically good or bad or just. In fact, what is practically good in private education is evaluated as such on a distinctive practical basis or some practical bases, it may be social or political or economic or all of them. Similarly, evaluation of good of private education from ethical angle is distinctively ethically based or so evaluated on completely different set of ethical theses or principles, which is naturally different from social thesis or political thesis and so on. Hence, what is "ethically justifiable" depends mainly on the distinctive grounds of justification. It is due to this that we give distinctive ethical justifications of matters pertaining to education.

For instance, we might argue that private education is ethically good is to say that it *maximizes individual's pleasure*, which is different from arguing that it does justice to those who could afford money for quality education because they have that right by virtue of their enterprises in life. The latter is an economically based justification, and, therefore, we speak of 'economics of education'. Whereas the former is ethically based justification (such as individual's pleasure theory or egoistic hedonism), much different from social scientific justifications and for that reason we speak of 'ethic of education'. Naturally we have an idea that what is ethically relevant inquiry of education is in the major speaking about ethical grounds or theses that provides sufficient strength to our arguments in favour of justification or evaluation of educationally relevant issues as good or bad. It is to be noticed that such evaluated notions (good or bad etc.) takes on a distinctive ethical tone in this context and are thus "ethically good or bad". Hence, economical "good" of privatization has a unique economic tone than "good" in its ethical tone when it is used to evaluate the same phenomenon but on unique ethical ground.

However, it is a little too much to believe that ethically relevant inquiry of matters pertaining to education is "theory based" and nothing more because two important reactions are: If educational matters are not solved as based on practice, there is no ethical involvement and if educational matters are not inquired as based on virtue, there is no ethical involvement. To this, we may add that educational issues involve metaethical queries and therefore, called ethically relevant inquiry. Now that we know about "tasks" of ethics or moral philosophy, we can follow that certainly there are some "metaethically relevant inquiry about education". For instance, the nature analysis of "educational ethics", "value-based education" and "justification of teaching educational ethics" and "models of teaching educational ethics". Important metaethically relevant queries are about the theories, application of theories and virtues as well. We might ask why at all private education should be judged good and not bad on grounds other than the theory of egoistic pleasure maximization? Isn't the basic theory wayward or unjust? Why should someone not argue that for the *intrinsic value* of private education it is good and desirable? (Deontologists might argue like this). Further, metaethical query might be about why theory co-option in the ethic of education is at all justifiable? Is it not more important to reflect on some basic ethical *virtues* than theories to find out whether private education is ethically good? It may well be that inculcation of altruistic spirit may be ethically more valuable than egoistic spirit to judge that private education is averse to pleasure maximization of all sections of society, and therefore, evil. Then we have to further justify why being an altruist is ethically virtuous than pure egoist. Further, we ought to ask, how should we apply our moral experience to resolve such crises? What is the justifiable model of application? These are some stray examples to show how varied and important "metaethically relevant questions" may be raised with regard to education and educating. If this be true, we have an idea of what is "educational ethics". To be precise, "educational ethics" consists of metaethical inquiry into matters of education, but it is something more about which something has been said above.

Closely related to metaethical inquiry about virtue inculcation is another basic inquiry about virtue ethics itself. An ethically relevant inquiry is to ask which virtues are needed to be cultivated and in what ways by us when it comes to matters related to education like private education? This is not metaethical in nature because here we are interested in the kinds of virtues in the resolution of educational matters but not why such things are justified as ethically relevant inquiry. Naturally, there may be various replies to this inquiry as there are a number of virtues in diverse cultures in changing times and places, which need careful consideration. One finds a discussion of inculcating cardinal and other virtues so that one becomes a person of morally charged character to deal with value-laden educational issues in real life. There is no doubt that without basic virtue of "love" for our own and other people we will hardly care about their education whether provided by the public or private institutions. Without basic virtue of "cooperation", we will deem it necessary to resolve moral impasse regarding privatization along with concerned people. Without the virtue of "loving the nation", we will hardly care to take some pain to contribute in the resolution of the said problem and further to do our bit in the education of our people. The question is how should we acquire these virtues? How should people come to know and inculcate them? These are methodological questions, which are regarding education and educating but with a distinct stress on virtue ethics. However, to discuss what "altruism" as a virtue is and why it is better than "pure egoistic virtue" is a metaethical issue. However, the discussion of whether virtues are at all cultivated through education or education should at all try to do so in any manner are still sensible ethically relevant discussion within education wherein "virtue" is in the focus and not out of it. Still more, "justification" of a model of educating about virtues and to pass them to children and to justify that a set of virtues needs to be passed not others, are ethically relevant inquiries in education but are meta-ethical in nature. However, one can find out easily that virtue ethics and education are closely related, the former has a strong bearing on educational matters, which is also the case with metaethics. Going back to virtue ethics, it is interesting to see which virtues count most for character-making education and for that matter countering real life value-impasse in education. I have said that there are lists (long ones), regarding this matter related deeply to the socio-political and cultural situations. Whatever it may be, taking a cue from W.K. Frankena (in *Ethics*) we might speak of cultivation of egoistic traits, altruistic traits and deontic traits mainly when it comes to educational matters, but these may be supported by others found in Indian wisdom such as, spiritual traits but there might be a lot of disagreement in so far as spirituality is dragged in virtue ethical sphere because they are different categories.

Coming to another by and large "theory non-co-opted" field in ethics that has great impact on educational matters is "practical ethics" or what we call "applied ethics". This part is extremely important for me in this book because I shall approach educational issues, which are value-laden from this angle, that is, the angle to find resolutions of these issues. Applied ethics as we know it is either applying standard ethical norms or theories such as teleology and deontology by expert ethicists to solve questions in education or whatever field which arise distinct value related or ethical problems because they ask not what is done or have to be done but what *should be done* or what is *ethically desirable*. Or else, it is taken as *theory non-co-opted way* to resolve the value-laden educational problems by parties most needed to do so in association with ethicists through a moral debate. The analysis of the debate and the resolution of issues on the basis of consensus reveals further the dynamics our known or unknown ethical theories or norms. In volume 1, I have elaborated why I prefer applied ethics in the latter sense and not in the former sense, though at one place (in this chapter) I did say that the basis of calling something related to ethics is to refer to theories unique to ethics. This may raise eyebrows but certain issues are called "value-laden" or "ethical" in education when their resolutions are based distinctively on ethical thesis and not non-ethical thesis that does not amount to say that therefore, applying ethics in case of educational matters is applying one or many ethical thesis or theories. The reason is that in real life application of ethics, it is our theory non-co-opted *ethical experience and knowledge* are applied spontaneously and not theories are applied "artificially". Thus, applying ethics is not unique to ethicists because they know theories of ethics. Hence, to say that "privatization in education" is a value-laden practical problem is to say that it raises unique questions related to which ethical thesis is suited for its resolution, but that does not mean that expert ethicists or others should resolve this issue, which will be acceptable to all of us because they do so on the basis of theory co-opted ethical knowledge or ethical expertise. This is absurd and impossible on the one hand and undesirable on the other hand. In fact, when concerned people apply their ethical knowledge which they have by virtue of being members of vast moral community, the known and unknown theories are naturally applied which is known at a later stage of analysis of debates and consensus. It is at this stage we come to know that after all educational ethical matters are distinctive in nature for they are dealt differently on moral grounds. Hence, the moral bases as crucial to the educational problems are not forgotten nor have no role; they are very important as are the problems themselves. We have to say many things about this matter in the following chapters because I have persisted in this chapter that educational ethics is not merely a body of theoretical churnings in academic ethics, which has been forcibly dragged in educational issues. It is rather a body of numerous problems in education, which are not (as we now come to know), stark practical problems and/or theoretical problems in the field of education. We have no intention to deal with the management of funds or infrastructure in education, or the methods of mathematics teaching or philosophies of education, but we do not rule out an entry into the ethic of public vigilance *versus* in-house vigilance in public education and the ethic of imposing a philosophy in education as absolutely true and necessary. However, every work has its own limits; I shall consider only some educational issues, which are ethically relevant for not only a careful study but appropriate resolution. We are here poised to take up educational ethics as "doing" something and not as "reading" something worthwhile. However, to compensate to some extent, I shall try to accommodate some ethically relevant queries in education, which are predominantly "theoretic", the first is already in our hand in this chapter.

The range of morally relevant topics in education is in view to some extent. We may now put them systematically as: normative ethical, metaethical, virtue ethical and practical ethical discussions relevant in educational affairs. Among these at least two if not three are basically "theorctical" in nature leaving applied or the practical ethical discussion in education as essentially "dynamic" though it has its own theoretical aspect such as analysis of normative thesis in moral debates. Some of us might argue that virtue ethical discussions cannot be predominantly theoretical either because here becoming virtuous is important than knowing virtues, and that several theoretically important aspects of virtue ethics (as we have seen) belong to metaethical inquiry, which may be taken as theoretical, but most important is inculcation of virtues. As such when we are involved in educating people, we might not have mechanically determined to inculcate a set of virtues, which some learners take seriously. We go on speaking about virtues and values whereas others leave them out. However, we agree that deliberate inculcation of virtues may be well planned and selective. It is a matter to ponder whether doing so is itself unethical in "educational ethics". We have to know that discussion of virtues should be done along with the discussion of values because it is not only ethical and non-ethical virtues that we speak about in education, most importantly, in "value-based education" which is a wider conception where we discuss different values essential for us to take care of while we seek education.

Further, we have to find out whether or not teaching as a profession gives us a set of ethically relevant issues. If it does, we have to see whether in educating, the professionals face some ethically relevant questions needing resolutions. We have to find out why educational ethics involves interesting professional ethical questions unique to the educators or the teachers. In this sense, it can be said that there are meaningful professional ns or independent of both. I would like to write here something regarding this issue of "inclusion". The straightforward question is, whether it is proper to speak of "educational ethics" as a study within ethics or moral philosophy or within education or none of them? In the foregoing discussions we have made it clear that a study of educational ethics is neither synonymous to the study of education nor ethics, it is not synonymous to the study of practical and professional ethics either. The reasons are simple because within the field of education we study many things, which we have clarified to some extent in the introductory part of the book in terms of aims or tasks of education. We did see that education apart from other things discusses ethically relevant issues but that does not amount to say that educational ethics and education are one and the same things. Similarly, when we discuss ethics, apart from its tasks about which we have seen above, it does take up many normative, metaethical and other ethically relevant discussions about education, but that does not amount to say that educational ethics and ethics are one and the same things. We must, therefore, distinguish educational ethics from both education and ethics. However, that does not mean that educational ethics has no relationship with education and ethics, and that educational ethics cannot be safely included within any of these relatively broader fields, that is, within either education or ethics. The problem is that from our earlier assertions it appears that educational ethics may be happily included within both education and ethics because there is something ethically relevant in the field education and there is something in ethics, which relevantly takes on educational matters. Or else, is it not safe to say that educational ethics constitutes an independent field of study, related closely to both education and ethics? This is thus the bone of contention, which are at the brink of understanding.

Let us first see whether educational ethics is within education because in education we take on the task of moralisation as well as ethically relevant discussions such as ethic of privatization in education and many such things. On the basis of the moral aim (or task) of education, we cannot logically hold that educational ethics should be considered within education because education aiming at moralisation is not the basis of holding that, therefore, ethically relevant discussion about educational matters such as ethic of privatization is within education proper. Hence, it is a mistake to say that as education has a strong ethical aim to build ethical character, therefore, educational ethics is within education. Nevertheless, there is a stronger reason for the non-inclusion of educational ethics in education. Educational ethics should be logically included in education proper and nothing else if and only if education proper has enough basis in itself or all by itself to explain that such and such matters in education, for such and such reasons be considered for ethical discussions and be resolved on such and such ethical grounds. For instance, the justification of privatization in education to be *ethically relevant* for discussion is not possible *on non-ethical grounds*. The available "bases" within education are thus logically unfit for proper understanding and resolution of the value-laden educational issue such as privatization in education. Hence, we conclude that to know and to resolve certain issues as ethically relevant in education, we need clear ethical bases and not non-ethical ones, which we find in the fields of education, economics, politics and so on. However, we do not argue that if education draws *non-moral justifications* from fields other than it, as it does from economics, it is logically improper. What we stress is that if it draws from any field other than ethics, it should be "non-ethically based" and thus not to be included in ethics proper or called "ethically based" or "ethically relevant". Hence, the name, "educational ethics" will not be proper in such cases.

It is clear now that educational ethics should not be included within the field of education proper. The reasons advanced for such conclusion enables us to hold that ethics in itself or all by itself has necessary and sufficient grounds to make us realize that such and such issues in education (as privatization) apart from non-ethical intricacies, raises distinct questions of moral ought, right and so on. Similarly, on the basis of ethical grounds proper we are able to resolve these ethically relevant issues in education. Naturally, we are able to 'know' that private education is ethically relevant because despite economic, political and other grounds, it calls for ethical justification such as "general welfare" or any other. It is also natural to depend on practical ethical efforts to resolve such ethically relevant issues. It is important to notice here that though our ability to know why educational matters are ethically relevant depends on axiomatic ethics, which is largely a theoretical enterprise, the resolution of the same is not so because it needs *participation of the public* who have moral reasons to give in an *informal way*. Yet, the practical ethical effort is so called because educational issues are solved on the basis of morally oriented debates, which reflects our known or unknown moral theories or moral grounds. It may be said that even common people 'knows' the distinctive ethical tone inherent in educational matters, which cannot be thus completely "group-specific". Truly, I have said that though analysis of ethical debates and resolutions are predominantly group-specific affairs but I have no hesitation to accept that through our moral experience and moral knowledge, we are in a position to know that on such and such distinctive moral reasons we know that some issues in education are value-laden or ethical in nature and on such and such moral grounds we need to resolve them.

Apart from these basic reasons, educational ethics considers many metaethical, normative, virtue and value related issues, which we have already seen. All these come within ethics proper and not education. For the time being, let us resolve that though educational ethics is a separate branch of study, it is related to education because it owes to field for the basic issues in consideration, and it is related to ethics because the above issues in education are approached and resolved on distinct moral grounds. There is no point to say that being in the broad field of ethics; it is not independent from it because what educational ethics considers is not what ethics as such considers as a whole. Being a part of the whole, educational ethics has to be separately considered from ethics as such because it takes different set of issues though metaethics and other branches of ethics contributes in educational ethical enterprise. It is just like considering metaethics or normative ethics within ethics separately for clearer study of what subject falls within their realms. Hence, separate consideration of educational ethics apart from ethics does not to the least justify that it is not within the broad field of ethics; rather, the truth is that it is within ethics proper. On the basis of the reasons displayed here, we are now in a position to say that though something in the field of educational ethics has close relation with practical and professional ethics, it is in anyway not included in those fields. Even if "teaching" as a profession raises distinct issues to be considered in professional ethics, "education" raises other issues of ethical importance, which are not merely those to be considered in practical or professional ethics. Educational ethics is thus to be studied as a branch of moral philosophy or ethics and not as a branch of education.

NOTES

1. Downie, R.S., *et al.* (eds.), *Education and Personal Relationships: A Philosophical Study*, Methuen & Co. Ltd., London, 1974, p. 95.
2. *Ibid.*, p. 96.
3. *Ibid.*
4. Guha, Debashis, "Transcending Transversal Ethicality" in the *Journal of the Indian Council of Philosophical Research*, Vol. XX, No. 4, 2003, pp. 97-107.
5. Frankena, W.K., *Ethics*, Prentice-Hall, New Delhi, 1989, p. 4.
6. Peters, R.S., *Ethics and Education*, George Allen & Unwin Ltd., London, 1974, p. 91.

2

The First and the Second Order Tasks of Educational Ethics

Let us recapitulate two extremely important points made in the Introduction and the First Chapter. First, we have found that education apart from having many important tasks ought to initiate pupils to do certain things in their life which are of some value or worth because doing something not valuable or worthless or evil is not desirable practically and morally for they produce greater harm than good for man. Second, educational ethics is not another drab discipline to theoretically peel off the intricate aspects of education and educating needing no ethical reflection. On the other hand, it takes us to *ethical reflection about educational matters* that have close relation with the field of education (and educating) and ethics. Now both these findings enable us to speak of the first and the second order tasks of educational ethics, which tasks in turn enable us to embark on the normative and the metaethical aspects of educational ethics. Hence, when it is important for us to discuss in details what are ethically relevant reflection regarding educational issues, we should take resort to the 'normative' (the first order) and the 'metaethical' (the second order) inquiries because as a branch of ethics proper, educational ethics is expected to take on such inquiries. Otherwise, what are "ethically relevant inquiries" in education is not known to us. It is important to tell here that the expression 'first and second order tasks' is neither fashionable nor arbitrary. It is not 'fashionable' for it is not one aesthetic way to put things for inquiry. It is not 'arbitrary' because it is not our whims and lack of reason that we have made something 'first' and 'second' as if that should be the way of understanding the matter.

In fact, calling 'normative ethical inquiry' in education 'first order' and 'metaethical inquiry' in education 'second order' has strong reasons though one cannot deny the truth that history of ethics itself is a testimony to the growth and fixity of use of these expressions. The 'normative inquiry' is not historically prior inquiry because going back to the roots of ethics and educational ethics, we cannot find an instance of one inquiry starting first whereas the other coming later on. It is needless to say that in Socratic, Platonic and Aristotelian thinking both these inquiries went hand-in-hand together. It is simple to understand that old wise people involved in ethical inquiries were logical enough to think that a 'talk of norms' should accompany a 'talk of the logic of the norms', that is, their justification, which is, however, a metaethical inquiry. Hence, it is needless to tax our head on pointless historical priority of inquiries such as these. It is but natural to understand that the normative study in education will thus involve metaethical study of justification of norms. If this be the case, what can be the point of grading normative inquiry as 'first' and not 'second order'? The philosophers championing the cause of language analysis as most important inquiry than any old fashioned synthetic inquiries, did not hesitate in calling this most important task as "second order" though that was to the least intellectually shocking for them. Putting aside the popular notion of "normative discussion" happened much before, and the latter became more robust in recent times, we must say that branding the former as "first order" is to state simply that some discussions in ethics and educational ethics considers *moral agents as the crucial point of reference* to discuss what pertains to their well deliberated actions and their evaluation, whereas the "second order" inquiry states that transcending the realm of agents and actions, when we come to consider the formal aspect of morally relevant discussions such as the *language of morals as the crucial point of reference*, we refer to "meta-study" or "second order" inquiry. I don't think that there is good ground to say that in ancient philosophies (and ethics) there was no "meta-study" because it was cooked after Vienna Circle's esoteric coterie had new *masala*, because the ancient people had all the *masalas* for a "meta-study" but never underlined them as most important as wiser people did later on. So we come to conclude that in educational ethics normative or first order study is so called because in such study the basic reference is "human intentional actions and evaluation of their worth on normative grounds." Some people say that this takes us to the "content" of moral education rather than the "form" of moral education because it is related to find out which good things constitutes education and *why* something is better than another thing. This is exactly the inquiry of *good ideals* that education have or the *norms* of education that enable us to discover its goodness. Hence, the normative aspect of educational ethics considers the problem of evaluating the worth or good of our various activities related to education and educating. Let me thus put the words of Robin Barrow and Roger Straughan to be clearer about what has been just said. Barrow writes: "by definition, 'education' involves 'initiation into worthwhile activities'... anybody who regards the business of education as important, must be concerned in principle to ensure that children come to engage in worthwhile activities. What activities are worthwhile is of course another question, and one about which there may be widespread disagreement.... How do we evaluate any proposed educational activity?"[1] And Straughan tells us, "The question of content is best tackled by first re-focusing upon the subject of moral rules and principles. This is because any attempt to define morality and moral education by means of their content will have to spell out what that content is in terms of particular rules or principles, for that is the way in which the subject matter of morality is expressed... any 'content based' approach to moral education will aim at teaching a certain set of rules and principles to children."[2]

Whatever the case may be, we are at hand other problems. First problem is about clarification of the *nature of norms* at hand which are in good number, needing a critique for comparative value. Second problem is about the "justification" of the number of norms at hand because reasonably we cannot take on anything and everything for their worth on face value. Norms need thorough appraisal for acceptance but that is essentially "metaethical" inquiry as we have seen before. Hence, we need to take on the "formal" inquiry ("second order" so to say), following the normative inquiry. Not only this, the gamut of 'normative discussion' as well as the discussion of moral virtues and values provides a wide range of unique moral language containing important moral statements, which contains important moral concepts. We need to discuss about the truth and meaning of such language, which is going to the roots of sensible use of language, which is again a matter of theories of different kinds. We need to explain and analyse them as well. Hence, in this chapter we will discuss the range of normative and metaethical theories and their merits, which together constitute a considerable portion of ethically relevant inquiry in education.

The first order inquiry of ethical norms is extremely important in ethics because any statement of ethical value is searched for its validity on some grounds that count more than a mere belief. In the statement 'humans tell plain truths, which is good', what I assert is the value of the intentional act of telling a truth. But the basic question is, the value adjudged as 'good' and not 'bad' is not my belief or prejudice or orthodoxy because I have some reasons to show why this must be the case. The basis or bases of value assertions thus takes us to the discussion of moral norms, which has important bearings on ethical valuations found in education and educating. For instance, when we assert that "It is good to impose compulsory measures for universal education", we are evaluating the moral goodness or desirability of 'compulsions' in universalization of education, which cannot be a matter of whims or belief, rather we may ask, why should it be true or valid? Hence, normative ethics is expected to supply us with some good bases for above evaluation, and faithfully it gives us a number of normative theses, each claiming for validity as well as absolute status with regard to such evaluations. For instance, we may justify the above said 'compulsion' on the ground of "happiness" of those who get universal education or on the ground of "well being" or for its "intrinsic value" or because the social "authority ought to be respected" and so on. However, all of them cannot be valid for we like them. Hence, normative-talk in education drags us to a good exercise of explanation and logical evaluation of norms. Nevertheless, in the assertion: 'It is a good exercise to scrutinize value assertions in education', an intentional action is judged to be "good", and it is not judged to be "morally good" as based on distinctive normative basis because the so-called "good exercise" in this context is *non-moral* goodness, which is for instance, based on distinctive academic grounds. Hence, all value assertions in education are not moral assertions and thus do not depend on norms of morality for evaluation of worth.

It is important to notice here that though in most of the cases the bases of moral evaluations are absolute, highly abstract axioms, which are universalizable, there are norms not so basic, that is, relatively less abstract and relative in nature. For instance, we may speak of the non-basic norms such as "absolute right to universal education" which may be treated as an extremely important norm to evaluate the 'compulsion' in universal education, which is not an overreaching norm like hedonism or altruism or the like. In most cases, the non-basic norms are of great practical importance because they are anchored to the value of some major social and political institutions. It may be argued that these non-basic norms do not fall in the category of 'ethical norms' rather, they are 'non-ethical' in nature, which becomes more important for sociologists, lawyers, politicians, planners and so on for practical decision making than ethical evaluation. The idea may be that philosophically (or ethically) relevant norms are basic ones, which are axiomatic in nature. Hence, the idea is that evaluation of moral assertions in education needs basic axiomatic norms only. However, Richard B. Brandt argues, "Actually things are not as simple as this, however. For one thing, we cannot get a well-substantiated set of basic general ethical principles without looking into these more concrete problems, for we do not have reasons for adopting a proposed basic ethical principle until we have seen what it implies for these concrete questions"[3]. In fact, on ground reality, axiomatic norms are neither creations of fertile mind nor do they drop from the blue, they are philosophical generalizations of a few intellectuals who care a lot about the concrete social situations, questions and grounds of evalution. Hence, without having any idea about fundamental rights in a nation and their value with regard to education, we may not be in a position to understand the basic axiomatic thesis that human happiness and welfare as principles of morality are basic to judge why universal education is good. Hence, *non-basic normative* talk is as important as basic axiomatic talk in educational ethics. Naturally, we have to say that "normative ethics... as a philosophical study, is an inquiry aiming to state and defend as valid or true a complete and economic set of general ethical principles, and also some less general principles that are important for what we may call 'providing ethical foundation' of the more important human institutions"[4]. To take a cue from this we have to say that educational ethics as normatively meaningful ethical talk in the field of education should consider the explanation and justification of some basic and non-basic ethical norms, which have great role to play in the ethical evaluation of matters pertaining to education. The term "economic set" is to remind us here that normative discussion cannot be endless or too wide rather, they should be highly restrictive. Even then, it may not be possible for us to consider all basic and non-basic normative theses having deep impact in educational affairs. We shall, therefore, take up only a few of these theses, which count heavily on moral matters in education. However, we have seen before that any normative talk should be justified logically, which becomes a basis for critique of normative thesis and their relative merit judgement. But, this is essentially meta-normative or best said metaethical in nature. We shall try to explain and justify normative theories without less interest in their comparison, but more intently we shall try to find out whether any of these normative bases have really any positive impact on value judgement of educational matters.

I prefer to consider here the *theory of authority, naturalist* (particularly the hedonist and the welfarist) and the *rationalist* (particularly the deontic) normative thesis. The discussion is extremely important when we come to consider the value-resolution of issue in education and the post-resolution analysis of dynamics of ethical theories. Let us first take up the "authoritative" normative theory and its bearings on education. It is common sense to believe that there are many moral grounds "external" to us, which are truly the basis of morality or moral evaluation. Something is an external moral ground when moral agents without caring much about what they feel or reason or will, strictly adhere to them as absolute and binding on them. The external grounds are for them overreaching and sacrosanct, to be followed as commands because they are absolutely valid grounds of morality. We call them "authority" in morality, which may be either in the form of individuals or groups of individuals, or in the form of institutions, social or religious. For instance, our grounds for moral evaluation may be our parents, neighbours, teachers or God, God-like people and even scriptures and religious texts. Truly, they are all external to our own moral autonomy and decision. More often than not, we do say that "I do not prefer friendship with a girl" because "my mother has asked me to do so". Similarly, to judge the moral worthiness of "sexuality education" on the basis that "such and such holy texts commands us to refrain from unholy education such as sex" is based on "authority". In any case, use of "authority" in the evaluation of moral worth is not a bizarre proposition, it needs careful scrutiny.

One important aspect of both the *personal* and the *impersonal* types of moral authority is that they do not appear to us as abstract sources of morality or generalized axioms of morality deemed to be true for humans in general. Authorities do not disregard the truth that cultural relativism might allow different authorities for moral judgement. The theory of authority holds that despite all relativism, there must be an absolute and unchallenged principle in morality, which is good—itself needing no rational justification for validity but which should be followed for its intrinsic and absolute truth. There is, therefore, no role for personal evaluation and understanding of these principles. Hence, authority does not allow us to state that "*I think* it to be just to have sex education because my father said me so", but it does allow us to state that "I always shun sex education because my father *asked me to do so*".

Richard B. Brandt in his book *Ethical Theory* (in Chapter 4) has said that the use of authority in ethics has three important aspects. First, it may be "importantly relevant", that is, in many cases of moral evaluation authorities turn out to be good enough than not because not following it turns out to be bad in many respects. There should be no doubt that parental and public evaluation of the desirable is at times morally good as in the case of "It is just to obey the teachers in the campus" because "that is what our institution asks us to do". This is a good use of authority, which is, in this case, impersonal in nature. However, other authorities are more stringent, they are "infallible" in nature because in case of any moral conflict a particular authority has to be respected for judgement not because it turns out to be good sometimes or it is good for me, rather the authority has to be followed because it can never go wrong even though it may not be fruitful to follow it. We may thus say that "I always prefer sex education because our school authority has adopted it as compulsory". Stronger is "absolute authority", the extreme one which states that our moral knowledge consisting of moral judgement is *solely based* on an authority thus reducing our own moral powers to a non-entity. In fact, this is the method of authority in the true sense of the term. We find them active when we say, for instance, "I know that sexuality education ought to be damned because my holy scripture knows that these are damned things". Brandt argues that though there are thin lines of demarcation in these forms of authority in ethics, we cannot overlook the relatively useful and the infallible authorities in matters of value judgements when we are not sure and safe about our moral powers of judgement. However, to say that use of authority is both *necessary* and *sufficient* in moral evaluation such as in the evaluation of ethic of education needs further evaluation. The extreme form of moral authority that takes what is external to the learners or the teachers necessary and sufficient is deemed to prescribe some such stringent moral codes of conduct which can never be questioned for moral validity. We have seen that lack of intellectual urge to question what is imposed on us as sacrosanct on obvious ethical basis is itself an immoral stance in life. Hence, the prescriptions are in reality imperatives forced on children or adults often with an eye to prize and punishment, that is, essentially external to judge the basic value of the commands. It is not because the sacrosanct verdicts were intrinsically good that we ought to follow them rather, we must do so because the sacred is supported by the good of prize and the evil of punishment. Does it not disvalue the authority? It does so, which is against the basic spirit of morality if authority has to be regarded at all. Straughan rightly says, "The highest moral accolade will probably be reserved for respect for authority itself, as a general rule or principle because it is only through adherence to that percept that such a system can be maintained; conversely, critical questioning will normally be seen as an educational vice rather virtue, as it poses a threat to the status and reputation of the authority"[5]. Often in our schools we find such 'heartless' authorities (as I would say) active in compelling pupils to behave, be neat, polite, truthful and so on whose commands are said to be sufficient. Most tragic is the expectation that in doing so the so-called students are sure to become morally decent. It is greater tragedy perhaps to follow the sacred commands of the state in the fear of punishment and the repugnant idea of prize to either accept sexuality education or refuse it. However, we should not have any doubt about the truth that many among us become authorities in an extremely strict sense when it comes to manage our own children or a class. Brandt and Straughan do say (and rightly, as I believe) that more often than not you have to impose your authority on matters of common morality, particularly when it comes to manage the cases of decisions regarding sexuality for the adolescent. I have argued in *The Primer* (Vol. 1) that ethics is not all about sexuality or guidance regarding sex. It does not take the pain to philosophically reflect about, nature, growth and maladies of sex in humans. In reality, ethics or moral philosophy has no business to enlist directives of authorities about sex. However, it does aim at discussing the moral basis of sexuality education in schools and the *moral bases* of who should be taught what and by whom in sexuality education. Parental and authoritative compulsions, the rude strictures of behaving in the face of challenges of sexual urges might be good for the study of psychologists and sociologists and educationists. However, it is one thing to say that the educationists manage sexual matters and it is another thing to say that they care for sexuality ethics. In case of real life management of challenges in and off the campus where some untoward sexual activity is noticed, the educational managers have a task cut out for them to be strict and authoritative, but that has nothing to do with the ethic of sexuality education because the latter asks among other things whether such education can be justified on authoritative grounds. It is in reply to this we conclude that sexuality education cannot be ethically justified because our strict managers do not like it or they know it as bad and ordered accordingly to avoid in schools. Hence, it is difficult to justify on the ground that as sexuality discipline needs authoritative commands, sexuality ethics begs such authoritative commands.

Nevertheless, many educational psychologists who have also contributed to educational ethics argued that as a matter of fact in the moral development of children and in moral education the role of authority is taken as necessary and sufficient. It is a truism that young pupils depend heavily on what authorities tell us about moral matters. This has been elaborated by J. Piaget in *The Moral Judgment of the Child* (1932) and by L. Kohlberg in *The Psychology of Moral Development* (1984). Piaget, for instance, argues that authorities are taken by young pupils as sacred, absolute and to be obeyed in moral matters as a matter of command or rule. Kohlberg argues that at the initial stages of moral development children take authoritarian rules on moral issues as extremely important because for them prize and punishment have great value. The problem with Piaget and Kohlberg is that something is the case with some people or many of them does so do not justify that the same should be the case. Further, a perfect account of history of ethical development of children across the societies does not suggest the linear pattern *imagined* by these psychologists. However, even if it were true, it does not suffice to justify that, therefore, moral education *should* be in the way of what authorities command or have commanded thus far. The norm of ethical education should not be to follow any authority as sacred. Hence, the so-called moral paradox stated above is resolved by a simple reason, that is, children at some stages in their life bank on authorities for moral guidance, which, however, does not prove what they 'should' do so at some other stages in life when it is expected of them to apply their own moral experience, and autonomy. When we speak of the relevance of moral authority as the basis of resolving impasse in moral matters, we need not be hasty in our decision. Piaget and Kohlberg should be further reminded that most of the time young people are faced with many non-moral experiences so that they are able to gradually face the difficult moral experiences in life. It is for the former that authorities are needed, who tell them that abusive sex behaviours are not good in school or outside because the very idea is repugnant to people who are mature and thus needs to be obeyed, but when it comes to 'why' at all such things were repugnant to mature people, it needs independent reflection on our part because when we mature to find finally that not because we were told not to be abusive in sex behaviour, it is palpable unethical on such and such non-authoritative ethical grounds. Educational ethics enters exactly here to tell us what these grounds other than the authoritative ones are, and why the authoritative grounds lose ground in many instances.

Yet, R.S. Peters in his book *Ethics and Education* (1966) argues that rather than leaving out authority, 'teaching' as an important activity in the field of education suggests strongly the viability of "authority", and that moral teaching is inseparable in 'teaching', it needs to beg authority than leave it out. We cannot deny that in our schools, children progress in the path of moral development through moral indoctrination, which needs some authority on the part of the teacher as does development of other knowledge because that is the way we think moral development should proceed. The crux is that 'teachers' are authorities; they cannot help moral indoctrination to stop. The point may not be so good. Peters does not get the point that even if it were both essential and sufficient, we have been taught to remain free from authorities because we need to scrutinise whether authorities were at all morally just in conditioning us particularly in their *own ways*, which they deemed to be absolutely right morality? Peters should have realized that it is not always that 'teachers' are chauvinists, and truly, moral chauvinism is a repugnant idea (see Volume 1). Whatever takes from us the power of moral scrutiny must be essentially immoral because "My father or mom said so" might turn out to be repugnant for us at a later stage, what to speak of a teacher who said, "I do not like this to be done".

Straughan has raised an important point in this regard. He asks whether our 'call of conscience' be not taken as authoritative in educational morality. This is more popular among the Christian thinkers like Bishop Butler who has explained human nature in his own way and adjudged conscience as supreme in morality. Whatever may be the problems with this theory, we cannot overlook the truth that this is a new idea on "moral authority" because by definition authority was treated as "external", which is not so in this case. Whatever it may be, 'moral authority' in this case tell us that 'man is his best judge' or 'man is his best moral guide'. As such, what our 'conscience' judges and tells us to be morally good has to be done. Immediately, such 'subjectivism' as one would say, has many defects. If whatever is moral to me should be true for all, then Hitler has done well thus far according to his call of conscience. The case is not to be easily teased because Butler says that 'conscience' as our 'inner voice' of morality is not a human organ or like our mind so limited and so faulty. Conscience is voice of God in us or the dictates of God in us, which is in essence, absolutely valid. It should be paradigm in ethical matters, and truly, authoritative. Moreover, being so good in it, we need to follow the dictates, which should be the case when it comes to ethical matters in education. To have a joke here would be fine. Why did Saint's conscience tell them while getting education that 'do not go for a sexual life', whereas others were permitted while getting education to 'go for sex'? Must be that 'conscience' is not universal in nature, and God's relativism in dictates is good as well. When it comes to ethic of sex education (and not sex), saints and others are told by their conscience to be good enough to go for it because that is good (as told by God). Well, God must have omniscience in all matters, including ethic of sex education, but what if many of us decide against it? Are they told by *Satans* and not God? If that be true, it is not that God is a valid source of authority as in our conscience; He is the absolute source of morality with certain absolute dictates refusing any relativism, which is however, against our common experience.

One way to come out of this impasse is to argue that the dictates of 'our conscience' in cases of ethic of education such as sex education, we are not speaking about Divine conscience or even irrational conscience, we are rather speaking about "rational conscience" needing moral reasons. The natural way is to say that in education we should strive for developing rational conscience in our students so that they are able to analyse and judge what is ethically good in their life. This is possible if we come out of the ideas of divinity (which is external to us). However, it is difficult to understand why at all 'rational conscience' should be the same as moral authority. Does it really justify that individual's conscience as based on 'reason' is in anyway unfaltering or sacred? Why should we do what we reasonably think to be moral? It may be that during our education, we were *taught* to be reasonably good to apply our reason and the inner-call for what should be done, but that goes back to our teachers and not us. Hence, authorities external to us are not out. Further, when we turn to ourselves, we must be dead sure of our noble rational conscience to be absolutely valid on moral cases in education, which is nothing but our emotive predilections. A return to subjectivism in this way is to rule out 'authority' as 'external', but again that does not save the case to be unethical because individual's chauvinism in moral matters based on so-called sacred inner reason and glorious education that developed such reason, are not put in abeyance.

Much has been said about authority as the basis of moral affairs in education. Let us now turn to another basis called "naturalistic" consisting of a number of theses like egoism (hedonic or non-hedonic); *altruism* (hedonic or non-hedonic) and the much-touted *human well-being*.

Naturalism in ethical context has different meanings, among which we are considering here in the normative context its special meaning as different from the meaning that emerges in the metaethical context. In the metaethical context, we take it as a theory of truth and meaning of ethical language. It speaks of a "natural" basis essential to justify that ethical language is both true and meaningful. For instance, in the ethical language, "Telling truth is good", the concept "good" depends on the fact that there is at least one thing in nature such as "telling truth" which constitutes its meaning. That it is good and not bad is either a matter of sense experience or intuitive experience. In this sense, there is no ethical concept and thus ethical language which is not anchored for truth and meaning to nature. We are here not speaking about naturalistic theories in this sense. In the normative context where the issue is what consists of moral worth or good of human actions, we are speaking of at least one naturalistic basis without which value or good or worth of these actions is indeterminable. Hence, for the value judgement of "telling truth" as an intentional human action, we must have a basis, which must be a basis understandable on 'natural' terms such as "maximization of pleasure or happiness" or "self-realization" or any other. To be precise, moral evaluation of our intentional actions are based on some naturalistic thesis and not on a non-natural one. Closely related to this is the idea that, therefore, a natural thesis in normativism gives way to a natural thesis in metaethicalism because we can say that asked about instances of what constitutes the "meaning" of "good" (or value or worth), we beg for natural concepts like "pleasure" and "happiness". Hence, in one sense, the normative bases are suggestions of ethical value or good in natural terms, any non-natural suggestion is improper. Naturally, one may say that "Pleasure is good" as a norm of morality is also a suggestion of speaking about meaning of "good" in a natural way. In this sense, we can say that either "pleasure" is a natural example or instance of *understanding or explaining* the meaning of "good" or that "pleasure" is a natural way to define "good". In the first case, we do not logically define the term "good" by a natural equivalence rather cite an instance of what things may be called "good", whereas the other one is the logical definition of the ethical term "good" as "pleasure", in which the definiens must be *equivalent* to the definiendum in meaning. In any case, "normative naturalism" has a close connection with "metaethical naturalism", but they are different too. The former is a thesis of ethical norm needed for evaluation in natural terms; the latter is a thesis of interpretation of an inherent meaning expressed in the normative statement where a natural term is necessary and sufficient for either definition of or meaning analysis of a value term. An interesting feature of "normative naturalism" is that when it answers to the question: which human decisions and actions are ethically good and why? Naturally based answers are not one but many, each of them have the habit to declare that only one answer is proper than the other. This has far-reaching effect on the evaluation of educational activity as good and not bad, that is, to answer why one educational activity should be judged as good and not bad or why some educational decisions are worthwhile and not worthless. The plain speaking naturalists (henceforth take it as a normative case), argues that morality and values therein are neither non-natural nor unnatural matters, they are matters pertaining to humans living in and with nature as important members, whose complex actions and interactions with the social and natural environment are crucial in our understanding of what is morally good or valuable. Hence, bereft of natural explanations, value judgements are not possible when it comes to humans living in natural settings, acting and thus influencing beings and things. Naturally, therefore, why certain educational decisions and enterprises are right and good are known on natural basis. However, we have seen that there are a number of natural ways to say what is good for man, for instance, what is good for man in the enterprise of education.

Naturalism of this kind has a wide appeal because it has a natural attraction on our common sense morality, most of them are not of philosophical nature because they take recourse to human nature or psychological or physical or sociological factors. Many such popular theses are, therefore, uncritical in nature, mostly non-philosophical argues many. It is due to this that the non-naturalist holds that more often than not humans by nature do *not* base their moral actions on non-moral grounds. Whatever the case may be, the naturalists do not understand the significance of any non-natural basis of moral evaluation, and for that matter, moral evaluation of educational matters is but naturally grounded for them. The gist is that naturalism is an ethical theory that takes "factual description" as the basis of morality which applies to moral issues in education as well. The range of naturalism is extremely wide because there are a number of 'factual descriptions' relevant to the ethic of education. Let us come to some of these descriptions.

Taking a cue from what is crucial in normative naturalism, namely, argument from the 'human nature', we find that many people conceive of 'nature of children' unique to them, who are also the most important party in education. It is due to this that in educational theory as well in moral education, children have been put at the helm of affairs and ideologies of education built up keeping their unique 'nature' in mind. Ideally, the 'nature' of a child is conceived as amenable to specific education, be it morally based education, which has to be kept in our mind who have the responsibility to impart such education. Quite likely, therefore, a search for what child's nature is, leads the naturalists to argue that children naturally tend to be averse to compulsions in education, punishment and bondage owing to petty guidance over the way they should lead their life. Naturally, therefore, a serious ethical consideration in education is to find out methods to educate such pupils who by 'nature' have own ideas about what is good for them. It may be put as the hedonists would say, by 'nature' children want "pleasure" without any fuss. Hence, it is crucial for us to consider in ethical education, whether morally good education is the one that goes by the 'pleasure seeking nature of the child'. We shall come to this shortly but before that I must say that Rousseau wanted some kind of "negation" in early phases of education to very young children. He asked not to intervene in moral formation through do's and don'ts or prize and punishment or indoctrination because the child will surely find its good independently according to his or her 'nature'[6]. This is emphatic in the words of A.S. Neill in another pioneering work *Summerhill* (1968): "Only under freedom can he (a child) grow in his natural way — the good way"[7]. Naturally, Rousseau and Neill thought that moral indoctrination makes a conditioned child, morally bad because adoption of values alien to him or her through pressure and/

or compulsion is essentially immoral. Hence, the ethic of education calls for 'natural inculcation of values'. Only in this sense much to the unhappiness of supporters of theory of divine conscience, Neill thought that the care for nature rather than being evil, is good for the child whereas, care for divine teachings is in the name of morality essentially evil. However, the naturalists have been thoroughly objected for their uncanny habit of confusing the factual with the evaluation of the "moral". Even if it is true that some or many children is by 'nature' averse to moral conditioning by adults at early stages, how does that logically justify that, therefore, what they "desire" by nature is "desirable", that is, "morally good"? How can brute facts, which are by nature neither morally good nor bad, that is, are essentially "value neutral" be the basis of "value judgements?" Hence, to say that moral value judgements of good, bad, just etc. depends on the fact that we naturally desire egoistic pleasures at early stages in life or, if we believe Freud, we want to kill our fathers, but does that justify that, therefore, such things are "desirable"? Let us not confuse a value judgement about facts with factual truths as basis of value judgements. All that does not prove that moral indoctrination is a must or religious teachings are needed because only these provide us proper bases for moral evaluation. Let us now consider some remarkable naturalistic theories having impact on ethic of education.

Take the case of the theory of "pleasure as the only good" that is, pure hedonism, which may be of egoistic or altruistic types. Simply stated, the theory holds that pleasure for me or others or both, and the correlative diminishing pain for the same agents are morally good, which should be true in case of education because it involves human activities which should produce good rather than evil (that is, pleasure, rather than pain). When we come to pleasure as an end of educational activity, it is needed not only for an individual but for other people, and for that reason an individual and other people needs to act in ways conducive to maximization of pleasure and minimization of pain. We ought to be watchful about those activities, which have indirect bearing on the said maximization of pleasure. Leaving out all intricacies involved in the calculus of maximum pleasure, we have to say that if educational activities needs to be judged on the basis of this theory, one cannot sensibly support production of pleasure for a child rather than for many others, thus preferring both egoism and altruism but neither pure egoism nor altruism because that would be against the moral agent's own pleasure maximization. Normative naturalism in the hands of the "hedonists" (we may leave out references to pure egoism and pure altruism to stick to this expression or, we may substitute "utilitarianism" because it is neither pure egoism nor pure altruism but combines both), has a strong point to make in the educational context. If we accept the truth that some activities have more contributory value than many other activities in so far as the maximization principle is kept in mind, then we should be encouraged and encourage participating in such activities. As education and educating are some such activities that maximizes pleasures or that we do find pleasure out of them as a matter of fact, it is desirable to participate in such activities. Similarly, educational activities should be of such nature that rather than pain, it should, morally speaking, contribute to encourage people to take pleasure in life while doing something for the maximization of pleasure of the community as a whole. If education is truly of moral value, it should prepare us to see the value of pleasure in life and to see that such pleasure is obtained through education as well as through imparting education. Robin Barrow says, "Through education we can be initiated into and come to take pleasure in activities that we would not otherwise have taken pleasure in. The task of education is, therefore, broadly speaking to develop people in such a way that they will be enabled to take pleasure in life, while contributing to the maximization of pleasure in the community as a whole. What is educationally worthwhile is whatever will contribute to that end… it is the task of education to initiate children into those activities that seem most likely to contribute directly or indirectly to pleasure, discounting the immediate pleasure of the agent"[8]. Barrow further suggests that though education should morally speaking, maximize pleasure of the moral agent and other moral agents, it is important to find out which educational activities are more amenable to the growth of some such "desirable characteristics" so that they take more and more interest in maximization of pleasure. This is a problem of choice of 'means' towards the realization of the end, namely, the maximization of pleasure. Barrow feels that some important characteristics to be developed through education are the attitude to know the proper reason (or why) of some effects or phenomena; the development of the power of coherent reasoning and the sense of empathy in a community life[9]. The crux of the matter is that the ethic of education calls for these desirable activities not for their own sake but ultimately for the higher end of maximization of pleasure. Hence, hedonism as a theory including the value of self and others should be the basis of or norm of judging which educational activities are good or worthwhile. It is interesting to notice that the basic activity as mentioned above are like "rules" or "cues" of morally good activities which are necessary for realizing the end but they are not sufficient. The *rule utilitarian* approach of Barrow gradually emerges out of his arguments.

What he tells us further in the way of logical establishment of his said thesis is more important because we have a good critique of some important normative theories in this regard. He discards the deontic position that certain activities in education are intrinsically good or worthwhile needing no reason (inductive or deductive), for intuition is sufficient to know the intrinsic worth of these activities. Barrow quotes N. Postman and C. Weingartner (1971) in this regard to show the way deontologists argue. We will come to this position shortly. The main point is that educational activities are of worth not for any end extrinsic to it like maximization of pleasure because "what they are talking about is literature *qua* literature, grammar *qua* grammar, and mathematics *per se*"[10]. Barrow thinks that such position has its inherent defects because it is not always that many subjects were taught to us because they were good themselves rather for the reason that they were good as means to produce pleasure in our lives. We do decompartmentalize mathematics from its brackets of formality to show the ways in which it is materially useful for us and because it gives us immense pleasure. For me, it is a repugnant idea that my students would gracefully tell me that 'Sir, I have studied Philosophy for its sake. In fact, I did my duty.' You always do not like people who find it graceful to do their duties particularly when they come to meet you in hospital when you are sick or when they tell you why they found philosophy to be interesting. It may not be that like Barrow I would settle for a hedonic position because that has its own problems, which we shall find out after seeing problems with other normative theories.

Is it proper to say that educational activities are of some worth because children "see" or "think" like that? If that be the case, children may not "see" or "think" that all educational activities are of equal worth. I am sure that during childhood, I 'saw' mathematics to be a marauder of my fanciful dreams and thus palpable evil. Hence, all those who taught it were bad for me, and all those classes were best for dreaming a plot for my next play until someone caught me by my ear. Frankly, I did not have any "pleasure" in mathematics but a lot of pleasure in English and Bengali literature. But does that justify that mathematical activities are bad and only pleasurable ones (for me) were good? Certainly not because child's own education of what is worthwhile in education is not the basis of such things. If we mean to say that a child is unable to see any value of anything, it would mean that there is no basis of worthwhileness for a child, which is unacceptable as well. Hence, what is subjectively relevant for me is merely attitudinal; it cannot be a norm of moral judgement of educational activities. (Of late, I found great value in mathematics). We may further ask whether proper *needs* of children are bases for moral evaluation of what is good as educational activity. Noticeably, both the conceptions of "seeing relevance" and "having needs" are non-deontic in nature; like the conception of "pleasure", these views are essentially "teleological" in nature, but with a difference. The proponents of "need" as norm holds that factually speaking, in educational activities all things which are needed, are of great value. Such need is either of the children or their peers or both, which is however, a matter of careful analysis. However, the moot point is that needs are not one but many and if we leave them to anyone of the above, it may be too confusing than comforting. Truly, some of these 'needs' are basic but that does not go to justify that, therefore, 'need' should be the sole guide of what is good in education. An important point in this regard is that a good list of basic needs does never complete what is desirable in education, which is also the case with subsidiary needs. Hence, a complete set of 'needs' in education is unavailable to us for many reasons, one being the relativism in the contexts in which educational activities are carried on. However, we cannot deny that even the basic need in education is itself good because in the end they produce happiness for the learners and those associated to them. It is difficult to say that among other things education need not aim at fulfilling the need of job empowerment that gives some pleasure to the learners. How far would all of us think that we were educated for the sake of being educated without fulfilling the requirements of jobs that might lead to pleasure? It might appear that the basis of judging what is worthwhile in education is, therefore, "fulfilling needs" of people. We cannot avoid the truth either that without having some "interest" and without fulfilling interests of learners, nothing is good in an educational activity. To imagine that education should be based on pleasure, we have to imagine that we must take some interest in things like having pleasure out of education. However, this is 'ambiguous' to Barrow because a child's "interest" may be understood as what is thought to be of their interest or what in fact interests them. It may well be that what a child 'thinks' of his interest does not turn out to be so necessarily, that is, in fact, it does not become something of his interest. On the other hand, what in reality turns out to be of someone's interest was not thought to be so by the person concerned. There is no doubt that the teachers should take care of the interest of children as well as their interest but that does not justify that in doing so, the judgement of value of education is possible. The judgement might transcend interest because we might ask ultimately, what is the most desirable thing to do in education that is of the interest of the students and the teachers? Barrow thinks that a reply to this question takes us to the norm of value of education, which he thinks should be "maximization of pleasure". Barrow thus says, "Once again the utilitarian will say that it is in the child's interest to equip him to find happiness in life in such ways as contribute to the happiness of others and cause no misery"[11]. Barrow is extremely careful to underline that the worth of maximization of pleasure in education should not be taken for particular moral agent. He is also emphatic in saying that utilitarianism as normative educational theory does not necessarily justify that it is the sciences rather than humanities, which will be worthwhile in education because physics gives us physical pleasures but philosophy has failed to do so. The utilitarian do not indulge in comparing the value of teaching game of cricket and listening to Ravi Shankar either. What it suggests is that in education we need some such curriculum and procedures, which instigates us to value pleasure in life and strive for our and other people's pleasure. For this, the learners should be in an atmosphere of choice among a range of activities wherein educators and they discover what is amenable to the end in consideration. However, one has to discover all this in view of the "rules" one needs to follow and the "consequences" which were available to us for the necessary calculus of pleasure.

However, the normative thesis of utilitarianism raises many questions. Foremost is that why should we consider "pleasure maximization" as the *only* intrinsically valuable end or good in education? Further, we must answer why the utilitarian should assert that "maximization of pleasure" in education is alone intrinsic good. Does it amount to say that at least seeking pleasure is our 'intrinsic duty' in education? Many other questions might follow. For instance, why should such and such "rules" be conducive to the production of pleasure in education? And how do we come to know that such and such consequences of educational activities did really produce pleasures for all? Finally, the question that was asked before, why should non-moral ends like "pleasure" be the only basis of morality in education? Let us start from here before going to problem of possibility of "transcending", "pleasure" as an end in education. A utilitarian being a naturalist (as well as a consequentialist) should realize that facts are extremely important to pass a judgement of value *about* facts, but facts are not important to judge the value of facts, some other *non-factual* bases are needed. The deontologists argue that they are better placed in normative thinking because they have justified a basis of moral evaluation (in education or in morally relevant fields), which belongs to the field of ethics proper. The conception of "duty" or "intrinsic value" of activities as crucial for the determination of what is right and good in education are conceptions within ethical discourse or within ethical vocabulary. Hence, they do not need any conception like "pleasure", which is in fact, a "feeling", and thus alien to the ethical vocabulary. It is not logical, therefore, to speak of a norm in ethical parlance, which is basically non-ethical. This is "confusion" about how norms in ethics ought to be justified. They have to be justified on ethical grounds and not on non-ethical or factual grounds. A fact cannot justify a value, is the gist. In another way, what is good ethically cannot be derived from the fact that we strive for pleasure and as this is the case, we should strive for pleasure. No 'should' can be justified on the basis of what "is' the case. Coming to what 'is' the case, even if it is true that most of us seek pleasure for us and others, does not to the least justify that all of us ('we') seek pleasure, always, and that all *should* seek pleasure. That some of us seek pleasure cannot logically justify that all of us should, ethically speaking, do so. Even if it is true that sane people should see that educational activities need not aim at producing pain for any person, does not go to justify that as a corollary, these activities should aim at the production of pleasure and nothing else. Why we are only left with this option and nothing else? It must be an absolutist conception, a subjective whims or an intuitive idea regarding what is 'intrinsically good'. If the last point is taken up, that is, the norm is an intuition regarding what is intrinsic, it amounts to state that for the inherent value of pleasure, pleasure has to be sought in an absolute way, which is the point stressed by the deontologists and not the utilitarian because the latter, unlike the former, are consequentialists giving stress on factual aspects. For the utilitarian the conception of inherent value of pleasures for all, which is basis of desiring such a valuable thing, does not beg any intuition because it is our common experiences that tell us that to call "pleasure" desirable there must be at least one person who desires it. However, the person's desiring does not make pleasure "desirable"; rather its "desirability" is intrinsic to it. The circle is complete when we ask, but how do we know that only "pleasure" is desirable? This takes us to consider that though educational activities might have one aim to seek for pleasures, how can it be the only aim of educational activities? How can it be proper to say that pleasure is the only aim of education when there is at least one person who on earth aims at being educated for its inherent value? Utilitarian might argue that people tell plain untruth because in the name of duty and doing something for itself, they hide the truth of seeking pleasure and nothing else. They further argue that none can deny that we 'should' seek pleasure in educational activities. Critiques do not doubt it because they too believe that sane people 'should' have pleasure in such things, but that is something they deserve or something they have as a matter of fact. This cannot be the basis of participating in the process of education. Moreover, educational activities results into pleasure production, is a matter of calculus. Which educational activities really amounts to pleasure-production is not *a priorily* known to us. It may well be that some activities did not produce pleasure at all, and then those cannot be inherently valuable. Naturalists hold that this "chance of error" (as R.S. Peters calls it), shows that nothing is objectively or intrinsically valuable as duty or "pleasure production". The moot point is that in many cases it is desirable that educational activities ought to produce pleasure, but if it did not, the ideal is not degraded to the least. Yet, if we are steadfast to say that objectively "performance of one's duty" is good in education, if it really did not turn out to be true in some cases, we should still believe that was expected but not fulfilled. But, for the deontologists this risk of 'error' is too serious than the naturalist's risk because they are committed to the view that all educational activities have intrinsic value, and, therefore, needs to be pursued. R.S. Peters thinks that what is strong about the naturalists is that for them there is a natural chance of 'error' though something is taken to be of great value. If we think properly, the strongest point that emerges from the above defects of the normative thesis is that it is difficult to justify that objective value or good in education is pleasure alone. Hence, the naturalists of the later period extended the notion of "naturalism" itself. Now it appears as a thesis in which the bases of value judgement are ideals that transcends the hedonic ideal in essence because human activities, such as educational activities are judged for their goodness on other useful conceptions such as "well being" or "welfare" but not "pleasure" or "happiness". We may speak of "self-realization", "God-realization", "liberation from ignorance" and so on in this regard. It is a matter of debate whether a change of name of the "teleos" (purpose) at all changes the basic naturalistic stance of these new moral ideals. We might say that they are surely non-deontic, teleological bases of morality which may be either naturalistic in a broader sense including "welfare" or metaphysical in another extended sense including self-realization and so on. With this, however, the deontic stance is not completely outdone because the hedonic and the non-hedonic naturalists are not able to answer properly why the ideas of *intrinsically valuable ends* and their *realization for their value* is not important as duty of moral agents. One might ask another interesting question, why should the performance of the intrinsically valuable duty of benefit maximization in education be not taken as the "purpose" in moral life?

Let us take up the norm of "human welfare" as the basis of value judgement because many naturalists find it one good way to transcend the older version of utilitarianism as a theory of 'pleasure of happiness maximization'. Traces of transcendence could be seen in J.S. Mill's *Utilitarianism*, which was called, "qualitative utilitarianism" for its favour of "quality of pleasure" that has to be maximized at the cost of some diminishing "quantity of gross pleasures". Mill proceeded further to mention that the conceived quality of pleasure depends on well being of non-human existence as well. The idea of well-being or welfare, though as old as Aristotle in the west was perhaps given a fillip. The ideal of *eudemonia* which has been translated (wrongly) as "happiness" because of sheer convenience of English knowing people had its own problems for ambiguity and mix up with the utilitarian "happiness" or better said (the parallel), "pleasure". Certainly, for Aristotle and for many others, including Mill in the true sense, "well being" or "welfare" is neither pleasure nor happiness, but apart from other things, includes both. What these "other things" are is important to know. Hence, welfarism as an ideal need not be taken synonymous to either hedonism in general or hedonic utilitarianism or even non-hedonic utilitarianism. There is no need to imagine that "well-being" or "welfare" consists in everything other than "pleasure" as good for man. Hence, welfarism should not be understood as a theory of maximization of good over evil (utility) without care for pleasure maximization. Human welfare should not be taken as a purely economic theory either though there is no way to disregard the truth that "welfare" consists of "economic good" for man. However, the idea persistent is, "there is something more than that". One cannot deny that welfare of humans depends on social, political, economic, physical and (arguably) on spiritual good. However, the old-fashioned argument is to assert that these elements basically produce "pleasure". The contestants hold that "happiness" and not gross pleasure is produced, which is something like "bliss". Others hold that they produce "good over evil". The welfarists think that the conceptions of "pleasure", "happiness", "bliss", "good over evil" may be comfortably and without much ambiguity rolled in the conception of "welfare" or "well being" meaning thereby a near ideal order or state of what is "ethically and pragmatically desirable" for man. Humans are said to be in state of well-being when they do not have all or many benefits or rewards or desired objects like pleasure, happiness, economic or other goods and so on, rather they have what they *should* have as humans for their good. The "naturalistic" conception of "welfare" cannot be dominated by any 'non-naturalistic' element, therefore, as such, it is very different to justify why "well-being" should consist of a state of metaphysical good. There may be a debate here because given the inherent vagueness of the notion of "welfare", why should it be a 'naturalistic' conception is difficult to say. Naturally many thinkers prefer to scrap the term "naturalistic" with regard to "welfarism" because well-being of humans is a matter to be explained on the production of some "non-natural" good. However, some others do not find any difference when welfare consists of production of non-natural good because in essence, for naturally existing humans, any good for them is essentially naturally grounded. The conceived metaphysical or spiritual good for humans may be taken as a different kind or quality or degree of natural good. What appears to be non-natural or beyond the corporeal world is thus not a matter to be debated, that is, questioned whether or not they really exist rather, they are *thought* or *imagined* or projected to be *useful* or *beneficial* for *us*.

Taking a cue from this, we find that "welfare" is not a vague ideal if we do not lose sight of its natural anchors which comprises use, benefits, wants, desires, interest and so on of humans. As such, human welfare as an ethical ideal or standard in itself needs some clarifications; the best way is to conceive of a state of maximization of what is pragmatic and desirable for humans as humans, which is however, a matter of careful social consideration and subsequent agreement. "Welfare" as an ideal is not an absolute conception of good for man which has been determined by an individual or a group or some intellectuals on the basis of dogmas and opinions. Human good as contributed by a number of elements naturally existing or beyond it is a *matter of fact*; it has nothing to do with non-factual states only to be imagined to be real. What is as a matter of fact ethically and pragmatically valued should be thus termed "good". Or alternately to explain the meaning of "good" we need factual terms whether natural or non-natural, if we stick to the conception of "good" explained in welfarism.

Welfarism nearly sidesteps the problem of utility-calculus because it accepts the measure of pleasure or happiness to be difficult, if not impossible. Whether good has been produced over evil is no less ambiguous for a matter to be computed. Whether human welfare has been made possible is clearly known through our experiences of ways of life, and lists of good things produced, which are materially, emotively and ethically valuable or good for man though "welfare", therefore, cannot be a matter of "prudence" because prudent people know welfare by virtue of *their* prudence, and prudence as a virtue is to know what is one's welfare. The clarification of "welfare" as an ethical ideal is not without problems until we state simply that "welfare" as an ethical ideal is the one advocating the production of greater pragmatic worth for humans on the basis of a number of experienced and imagined things which humans had as matter of fact deduced from the simple idea of *holistic benefit* for themselves. The entire conception of "welfarism" as an ethical standard thus boils down to a "non-ethical" idea causing critics to charge the fallacy for confusing the ethical with the non-ethical or the natural. The supporters hold that there is perhaps no way to *explain* and *analyse* the meaning of the notion in a non-factual way, and this is not to commit a fallacy. Hence, welfarists are bound to accept a naturalistic explanation of "human good". With this, one comes to realize that not always do an explanation of "ethical norm" need the help of a non-natural or what is called proper ethical basis like "duty for intrinsic value of duty". An ethical norm as such can be *explained* on non-ethical basis. Welfarists argue that it is not that an ethical norm has been replaced by a non-ethical fact because the stated norm remains very much ethical, the only point is that as a matter of meaning analysis, the 'ethical' conception of 'welfare' needs the 'non-ethical' conception of holistic benefits.

In the recent times ethical debate has centred around the significance of "human oriented" ethical ideal of life, the point is why should it be so without welfare of other *beings and things*? Truly speaking if the ethical ideal of life ought to be *holistic welfare* not "human welfare", the whole conception of "welfare" in "ethical welfarism" needs overhaul. In the recent times, a spurt in environmental and ecological ethics has given fuel to discuss the ethic of man-centred welfare. In fact, humans cannot live a life in isolation; they live in natural and built-in environment with a number of people, other living and inanimate beings and things. It is difficult to conceive of welfare of man on the whole if other beings and things are completely neglected for their welfare. Hence, it is argued that human welfare cannot be an ethical ideal as such, it needs other conception of welfare to make some sense. However, the welfarists argue that such misconception is due to confusion between 'welfare of' and 'welfare through'. Welfarism as an ethical norm is based on the idea of 'welfare of humans' and not that of animals and other things because in case of other things and beings, we do not have the notion of "welfare" rather, "protection", "restoration", "safeguards", "nourishment and nurture", "sustenance" and so on. However, it is undeniable that a talk of human welfare is related to or largely possible through the basic safe keep and betterment of other living beings and things. Human welfare is the sole objective of welfarists though it is possible 'through' the necessary good of other beings and things. Every non-human good need not be welfaristic measures in the true sense of the term. Doing "welfare" is essentially a "human oriented" concept, it is not sensibly used in "non-human" contexts. Undeniably, "ecological sustenance" can be ethically good or an ethically sensible norm when we speak of normative eco-ethics, but in the context of normative ethics *per se*, which is a human oriented discourse, welfarism is a different norm. In fact, welfarists believe that whatever contributes towards the welfare of humans such as ecological sustenance, safe keep, betterment and so on, are valuable as means towards the highest ideal of human well being. Nevertheless, normativism in ecological ethics does not fully agree with the view of welfarism because they refute the idea that "welfare" is a "human centred" conception and makes no sense for non-human existential. Broadly speaking, "welfare" should include well-being or maximization of benefits of non-human existential in the universe. It is a different matter altogether whether in doing so ethical norm should, therefore, include on the whole "welfare of existential" and thus not human-centred. Hence, the evaluation of "right", "good" of human actions are possible on the basis that human-regarding and other-regarding maximization of benefits is crucial in morality, and that should truly be holistic welfare though not forgetting the three major elements of the material, emotive and ethical well-being of man.

We would now like to go through the impacts of this thesis in educational matters, that is, on matters of educational decision-making and actions. Most of the welfare states in our times such as India, has nurtured at great cost what we call "public institutions", on an extremely broad basis at the primary, middle and secondary levels. The idea behind a painstaking and cost-ineffective way of broad-based education is the concept of "welfare". Hence, welfarism as a norm, even if it is "human centred", stands as the only ground for evaluating ethical goodness of our educational plans and programmes. The conception of welfare of the human population of our nation is based most importantly on basic economic activities (though this is one way of looking at welfare). Among these economic activities, education falls under the "tertiary" activities such as providing many services for the human population. Hence, "education" in our notion is based on the ethical conception of providing economic empowerment to our people, which is one way to their well-being. Not only this, education is not merely linked to eke out a living and knowing several things rather it empowers us to know how to 'live well' and what 'ways of life are ethically good'. Hence, education is based on the ideal of human well-being, which provides us the vision of other regarding virtues and values. It is urged by the welfarists that broadly as well as narrowly speaking, education is expected to impart the value of "considerateness" or what I call "other-regardness", that is, welfare is possible when through education we come to be considerate towards others. One problem pointed out by the critics with the welfarist conception of the utmost value of 'other regardness' or 'considerateness' is that it tends to overlook the utmost "intrinsic" value of duties and obligations in the face of considerateness. More often than not, we ought to perform such duties and obligations that 'other-regardness' turns out be a curse. We cannot be considerate to all students despite their poor status. When it comes to quality teaching in higher education, for the well-being of all students of poor status we cannot afford free education. We cannot be considerate to a large number of such students and forget our duty and obligation towards other students who are axed financially though all of them are not too well to afford benevolence at high price. The greatest problem, therefore, is to overlook the deontic considerations in being considerate as welfarists. Correlative to this is the production of pleasure and happiness to all as a matter of welfarist measure is problem trodden, when we come to education because we need not satisfy everyone else in our crucial decision-making in education. The issue is when justice, self-esteem, honour, integrity and other values are so important in complex educational scenario, why should the value of pleasure and happiness be overriding? In reality, broad based education is possible when conflicts owing to providing pleasures and preferences to some are taken off as unethical measures. Straughan reminds us of the truth that welfare as the so-called basis of educational good is grounded on the bare fact of 'individuality', that is, the value of pleasures or well being of *a person* and not on the conception of the "collective" as it is touted. Much talk of universal welfare camouflages individual importance in the conception of welfare. The *distribution of welfare* cannot be ignored as a stark truth in the face of a noble universality. The point is, we cannot be sure about individual regardness for many practical reasons, some of which we have seen, and another one is that a lot of calculus and computation is involved in distributive measures of welfare which poses greater problematic issues for the utopia of universal welfare. Other-regardness might face more stiff challenge when we come to 'holistic welfare' because in such 'broad based' welfare, the utopia appears bleaker in the face of larger issues of distribution. Hence, welfarism as an absolute norm either in a narrow sense or in a broader sense has its own problems when we evaluate its impact in the field of education. If the aim of education is to provide human welfare in the name of happiness or satisfaction or benefits, it is clearly a restricted aim, most of us being ready to contest it on other moral grounds. We are sure to ask, why should benefits of humans be so good when many good things are open to us?

We hope that the readers will take care of the important teleological theories and their bearings on education. We urge the readers to find out what is the logical strength (if any) in these theories because that will be important in order to analyse the moral opinions of the participants in a moral debate amounting to resolution of some value laden educational issues.

Let us now have a look at the *deontic* or *the rationalist* norm, which is essentially non-teleological in nature and analyse its impact in the context of education and educating. First, a few words about the nature of the deontic thesis in ethics and the reason for calling a 'rationalist' norm. Deontology states in opposition to the teleologists that though intentional human actions have a purpose or a definite end, it is not the *teleos* or the purpose whose value determines the value of the action under evaluation. The truth is that the act itself must have some value, which should determine its worth, or else all our intentional actions lose their good or worthwhile character. There is no doubt that telling a truth is good but it is not so on the ground that it produces a good result or is beneficial, rather, in itself it is of great worth. Hence, it is an imperative or duty on our part to have regard for such intrinsic values or intrinsically good actions. The deontologists argue that it is not by virtue of bare facts that moral values of actions are judged; rather such actions should be judged on proper *moral grounds* thus justifying the case of moral basis of a moral action and not non-moral basis of a moral action. If this be the case, the moral basis properly so called ensues from our pure practical reason and not from any contingent element such as pleasure and other things. The intrinsic worth of human actions is thus a matter of rational intuition or to be precise, "reason".

There are ample instances in Immanuel Kant's *Grundlegung* that moral philosophy is required to have both *pure* and *empirical* parts. It is required to have a 'pure' part in so far as there is a strong need of *a priori* principle as the basis of morality, whereas there is need of a 'practical or impure' part in so far as *empirical* considerations or principles are the basis of practical curricular obligations such as in education. In the *Grundlegung*, Kant often attempts at equating the pure part of moral philosophy with form of knowledge and the 'empirical part' with matter of knowledge obtained by the senses, but he thinks that it is a great confusion in our minds to view the 'pure part' as merely formal or bereft of content. The said part is thus not "completely separated from reality" and pure practical reason is not "complete abstraction from all content". In any case, the pure part remains concerned with the universal and necessary aspects of moral reality rather than contingent ones. Barbara Herman observes that the "purely formal principles do not have no content, they have non-contingent content"[12]. Nevertheless, the pure part of moral philosophy does not provide us with content to know what needs to be done in specific situations. Hence, it is one thing to have *a priori* moral basis of judgement and another thing to apply them in real life as sharpened by real experiences. It is interesting to notice here that what I have stated above as basic feature of a rationalist or deontic norm is in Kant's terminology, *a priori* or pure part of ethics, which has "non-contingent content" and it has an application as based on empirical principles such as in education. Kant is explicit regarding the *a priori* basic principle of morality with regard to judgement of human actions. For him, as humans, we should conceive of the principle applicable in general and not in particular cases because the first principle is true irrespective of class, species, gender, race and so on. He says that this "principle of duty" when viewed from particular individuals does not truly constitute the 'metaphysical first principle of a doctrine of virtue'. Hence, ethical first principle of intrinsic worth of duty considers what is common to humans as such. Most interesting is to note that this scheme of 'pure ethics' which is for him *metaphysic of morals* comes within the system derived from "reason" in which empirical principles are not included as integral parts of the system. The applicative or what Kant calls the anthropological aspect of the principle does call for empirical principles as basic. This is perhaps his scheme of fittingness in the ideal of the rational and the empirical. In his work *Kritik der praktischen Vernunft* or *Critique of Practical Reason* (Academy Edition, 1902). Kant observes that Ethics requires a normative standard or touchstone by means of which "one must test the moral content of every action"[13]. And in the *Metaphysik der Sitten* or *Metaphysic of Moral* (Academy Edition, 1902), he observes that 'appeals to cultural aspects are needed to find how these standards find their way into society'[14]. It is expected, therefore, of Kant that his normative conception has deep impact on practical concerns in education, particularly when Kant categorically states that "moralisation" is one of the goals of education. However, he states equally emphatically that we are certainly not living in an age of moralisation (this is a stunning truth today). But we should move towards that direction unfailingly which is, however, a matter needing application of the 'pure part' of ethics, that is, the first principle itself. Nevertheless, Kant observes that the transition from civilization to moralisation, though difficult not impossible does not demand our instantaneous or natural picking up of the principle of duty because this artificial scheme is preceded by experiences of moral issues, interactions with moral facts and moral attention. Kant is careful therefore, to state that the impact of the *a priori* principle of duty in any anthropological context, as in education is not a mechanical job of picking the theory by any one of us to resolve matters of value. Education thus includes "world knowledge" and "knowledge of moral interaction in the world" before any sensible application of the norm. Louden notes that for Kant "human beings cannot simply jump unaided into pure ethics; background knowledge of their own empirical situation is a necessary prerequisite"[15]. Hence, for a deep practical impact of the principle of duty in the scheme of education and educating, moral agents needs to be in a strong state of cognitive development or what Kant calls "the natural progress of human knowledge". Hence, impact of norm on education cannot be without sufficient moral development of a person in terms of real experiences with regard to the realm of education. This aspect of moral anthropology as completing the whole system of moral philosophy along with the basic principle is well noticed in Kant's thesis of "moral catechism" and "casuistry". The former lends able support to students so that they are able to exercise their moral judgement in view of moral significance of actions in similar and dissimilar contexts whereas the later is what interests us, that is, development of higher principle in actual cases of moral resolution. Despite all care taken for confusing application of pure part of ethics in education, Kant is equally emphatic in the *Metaphysic of Morals*, that moral anthropology is expected to "deal with the development, spreading and strengthening of moral principles (in education in schools and in popular instruction), and with other similar teachings and percept based on experience"[16].

Kant has written profusely on the matter of the role of the *a priori* principle in education in his pioneering work *Pedagogik* or *On Pedagogy* (edited by F.T. Rink) and in the *Metaphysik der Sitten* or *Metaphysic of Morals*. In his works on education, Kant states clearly that the ultimate objective of education is *not welfare* of individual students but *moral perfection* of the human beings as a whole. The perfectionist scheme spells clear refusal of the welfarism we have just seen. This is to remind us that moralisation, as a goal of education does not amount to welfare of the students. However, education does take care of species-specific care, discipline, skill production, and pragmatic formation and of course civilization apart from moralisation. It has been for Kant some kind of dilemma to find out what exactly it amounts to moralise through education; one point is to consider whether in academic institutions teachers have sole role to moralise by teaching principle of duty or maxims of morality; or, to consider whether students themselves have the sole task to find out the principle of which they ought to act. L.W. Beck and W.K. Frankena believes that Kant's scheme of universal education and the destiny of education, that is, moralisation demands teachers having a duty cut out for morally perfecting students through teaching basic principle and maxims of moality[17]. However, Kant says in *Metaphysic of Morals* that "it is a contradiction for me to make another's perfection my end and consider myself under obligation to promote this... it is self contradictory to require that I do make it my duty to do something that no one but the other himself can do"[18]. Robert B. Louden remarks that there is in reality no dilemma in Kant's writings because he is conceiving moralisation of others through ethics education of basic principle and maxims for children only, whereas for adults such things are not needed. This is evident in Kant's lectures *On Pedagogy* where he states clearly (and repeatedly) that the moral character formation in students consists in the "aptitude of acting according to maxims" because acting on maxims are "grounded in and derived from concept of duty"[19]. Kant states clearly that for teachers it is extremely important to draw the attention of students to "certain laws and follow exactly". This is thus far a clear statement of what deontic or rationalist norm in case of education is like. We shall not jump to criticise Kant because we ought to see what the modern proponents of the Kantian theory have to say about the deontic normativity in the field of education. We should consider the view of R.S. Peters in this regard though both Hirst and Rawls have something to add in this regard. Let us consider Peters' view for its obvious relevance in the field of education.

R.S. Peters in his book *Ethics and Education* (1966) holds that ethical judgement of educational matters call for "practical reasons". For instance, any judgement regarding right and ought of an educational decision making and subsequent action calls for the basis of such judgement, that is, it demands a "norm", which is for Peters, "reasoned justification" of the right and ought. Peters' view amounts to justify that among reasoned justification of right and good, comes the principles of fairness or justice, which is much like what John Rawls supports in *A Theory of Justice* (1980). Justice as fairness is a rational principle of right and ought because it recognises the value of equal treatment of people on the ground of their basic equality provided the fortunate are not deprived of what they should legally get. Peters thinks that "practical reason" is the basis of deducing the principles of freedom, altruism and respect for others as well because these principles are cues to what is morally desirable for us to do. Similarly, "truth telling" is a deduced principle because one who seeks an answer to what is good or desirable, is seeking a faithful or true reply in this regard. In the same way, rationality demands that we should be non-interfering, caring for interests of other beings and considerate towards the self-esteem of other people. Peters hold that "practical reason" does not provide us with a moral ready-reckoned to draw right and ought in particular situations; the principle is rather "general" in nature. However, Peters have no hesitation in providing reason in favour of what impact the "principle of reason" has in the matters of education, particularly, "moral education". The basic problem in moral education is, 'what ought to the basis or reasoned justification of teaching moral matter to children such as teaching children to be good?' For Peters, moral education must have strong "reasons" for its ethical desirability. Peters thinks that the "strong reasoned justification" in favour of the ethic of teaching children to be good is the need for the development of "autonomous" persons who he notes: "follows rules in a rational discriminating manner… to know what is in general right or wrong; he must also go beyond the level of what Plato called (*doxa*, or opinion), so that he sees why such rules are right and wrong and can revise rules and make new ones in the light of new knowledge and new circumstances"[20]. The objective of moral education is thus for Peters the development of human character who moves from the realm of mere belief to the realm of true knowledge of or formal knowledge of "good" or "good itself". Such beings are good, do good and revise what is not good. The basis of "practical reason" thus enables us in moral education for instance, to have "moral autonomy" to know and be good. Peters thinks that there are certain obstacles in the way of such education as young pupils are not autonomous in essence, and thus do not base their actions on "reason". Hence, to be "autonomous" as based on "rationality" demands intervention on the part of the adults, particularly the teachers for formation of habits as essential part of moral teaching to be good. Naturally, the intervention towards moral habit formation *on the part of the teachers* is a *rational process* because the teacher needs to *instruct and justify* some "basic rules" to the children so that they see the "reason" behind them for adoption. This is the initial "reasoned justification" of children as supported by the adults. Hence, "reason" is basic to ethic of education.

Peters takes some pain to elaborate further what these 'basic rules' should be which are so needed for habit formation. Much like Rawls, Peters thinks that it is a matter of sufficient agreement among rational agents who reflect on this matter to form the rules, which are not one but many. Unlike the Kantian stress on duty and Rawlsian stress on justice as fairness, Peters speaks of basic rational rules such as respecting contracts, property, to care the young and to refrain from pain and injury.

Peters' rationalism as a norm has its own problems. The first is an inherent circularity in saying that the principle of "practical reason" is needed when we justify what is desirable of us to do and to explain when we sensibly ask the question of desirability. It is important to notice that it is not always that we necessarily and sufficiently beg practical reason for justifying what should be done because the ethic of decisions and actions might be based on the purpose or *teleos* of the actions. Another serious question is whether there is anyone principle or many of them, which is necessary for morality? It appears that in the context of social interactions Peters' rational principle is overreaching, but may not be absolute and necessary because a moral agent in dire isolation in a spacecraft might need some basic rules of morality which are other than the overreaching principles of rationality then it comes to what should he do in the face of a severe technical snag, should he eject or try a heroic damage control exercise, which is likely to be fruitless. Coming to the reflective method of Peters and consequent discovery of moral codes through agreement obviously falls short of expectation, most of the time unpragmatic in case of young people in educational institutions. Moreover, not always do we agree in the reflective process that such and such rules regarding contract and property are good enough. In a democratic society like ours, one might think it morally good to have as much private property as fortune favours us, whereas others would like to live in a commune without caring for much private benefits. Which moral code is good enough for the moral development of a child is difficult to tell. Interventions in such matters at a tender age as "official ethics" are common in the capitalist and the socialist systems since long, they are no less irrational though are deemed to be "rational" only on arbitrary grounds. Hence, the general thesis of 'practical reason' may not be good enough to provide us with reasonable set of moral codes (all rational; therefore), which needs to be taught to our children at tender age. Peters' project of moral education opens a can of worms in reality. We find it difficult to reconcile whether a gamut of rational principles be at all ethically grounded simply because they are "rational" in nature, and whether we can teach them to young people so that they become good. Rationality *qua* rationality does not imply ethicality or the other way round, which is then a standing imbroglio as to why should we teach these principles at all.

Much like Peters, P.H. Hirst in his essay on "Liberal education and the nature of knowledge" in Dearden, Hirst and Peters edited book *Education and the Development of Reason* (1972) argues that the basic aim of education, which is ethically just as well, is the development of the "rational mind". He thinks that education should initiate students into the *eight forms* of knowledge, all of them develops "rational mind". Hence, whether educational efforts are ethically grounded is based on the idea whether they develop 'rational mind', the latter being the basic "norm", therefore, for Hirst, it is queer to ask for the justification of this "norm" as "the justification of any form of activity is significant only if one is in fact committed already to seeking rational knowledge. To ask for a justification of the pursuit of rational knowledge itself, therefore, presupposes some form of commitment to what one is seeking to jutify"[21]. The "deontic" tone in Hirst's passage is clear when he conceives of the intrinsic value of rational knowledge, but what is of greater importance for us is that Hirst has an inherent anti-rational attitude towards justification of "reason" as the norm of ethicality because it is a redundant effort. How can justification of first principle be theoretically and rationally redundant? If that be the case, the 'second order task' in ethics is deemed to be irrational, which is not the case. As such, why moral education should be taken as *intrinsically valuable* is not known to us because there is no need for us to know why it is so. This would take us to the position that there are some people on earth who give great inherent value to reason but are not in a position to state why they do so. The truth is that people do not have faith in the ethical norm, rational or whatever, rather, they try their rational best to justify the norm, and it would be undesirable to say that they do not involve in such theoretical pursuit. Stranger is to argue that evaluation of reason-based actions as "good" implies that some people do act ethically for they are initiated by the principle of reason, which they nevertheless, do not care to justify as having intrinsic value. Hence, the principle of rationality as intrinsically good and, therefore, to be followed does not guarantee that all of us does follow and act likewise or that all of us need to necessarily follow and acts likewise. It is also not the case that those who act ethically do the same on the basis of rational principle. In fact, many among us do not even care to ask for what should be the basis for my good action now. If we proceed a little farther, the ethical basis of moral education cannot be reason alone because asking for a justification of moral education and not morally blank education, we are not committed to the intrinsically valuable principle of reason, and rather, we may argue that apart from other things such education gives us such and such good fruits. To ask, how do we come to know that such and such fruits of moral education are good and not bad, is a question not related to moral value but factual value, and for that matter does not beg the principle of reason. It is due to this that without seeing any intrinsic value in moral education, it may be still valuable for us on non-deontic or teleological grounds. Hence, it is logically absurd for Hirst to argue that though we need not bother about logical justification of rationality, it does not justify a higher teleological worth of education and moral education. Equally questionable would be the initiation of people through any form of knowledge conceived by Hirst even if they are said to be based on reason. It would be perfectly logical to inquire why should we pursue moral education in schools with subjects like mathematics, economics etc. though they call for rational exercise, and thus have their value as parts of knowledge. Robin Barrow notes, "Valuing rationality is not the same thing as valuing the pursuit of various studies that happen to involve rational procedures."[22]

With these remarks, we close the discussion on the content of moral education, that is, on the first order normative task. We found that though norms are plenty in number, none may be logically so sound to be absolute basis of morality and moral education. Ethic of education does not stand on absolute norm; it does not stand on norms having relative values either. This point might be crucial for us as we proceed to a following chapter to discuss the point of resolution of values in education through dialogue. However, we have the "second order task", that is, the *metaethical* task cut out for us where we discuss the theories pertaining to "moral language" and their bearings on moral education. I will not discuss the theories of "moral justification" separately as something has been already said in terms of "justification" of norms of ethics. We shall here concentrate on theories of language with a difference that deviating from our known pattern to consider *cognitive* and *non-cognitive* theories, we shall consider four important theses in this regard two of them known to us as "non-cognitive" whereas two others are not so popular among ethicists but extremely important, which in some way is "cognitive" in nature. The first among these is the one provided by Aristotle and others stating that the language of morals, particularly the "normative", is the language of "principles and their need for application". This is in relation with what we have just seen during the exposition of the "first order task" of educational ethics. The normative task is directly related to find out what impact ethical norms have in the sphere of moral education. Now we have to see *what bearing the normative language has on moral education* because our discussion of norms of ethics is closely related to norm based ethical evaluations or judgements, which are in turn expressed in "evaluative language". We have to see the nature and logical status of such language as proposed by some theories and their impact on the moral education or educational ethics. The "principle" based theory of Aristotle and a number of thinkers starts from the truth that one important aspect in education being "ethical evaluation" of educational decision-making and correlative actions, it is based on norms on the one hand and on the other hand ethical evaluation itself projects a body of language unique to it, that is, "evaluative language", which needs to be true and meaningful but the problem is on what bases is such language true and meaningful. If we do not peruse into this issue, which is metaethical in nature, we are hardly in a position to say that normative theories as well as application of these theories for evaluation of matters in education makes any sense. We ought to find out the reasons for calling the evaluative language in education meaningful or sensible, or else, educational ethics does not make much sense. Hence, far different from bases of ethical evaluation in education, here we are concerned with the bases of calling evaluative judgements in education meaningful. The "principlistic" approach holds that the basis of calling evaluative judgements in education meaningful is *in fact*, drawing our attention to some such *moral ways of life* of *moral agents* or drawing our attention to see what "a man of principle conceives and applies in real life". For instance, this metaethical theory argues that the evaluative judgement in education such as, "corporeal punishment to young children is wrong" is a statement true and meaningful on the ground that there is at least one person in the world who 'in fact' conceives corporeal punishment as *undesirable* for different reasons available to that person (the normative ground) and that he applies what is a valuable ethical principle to him because he is "a man of principle". Hence, the evaluative statement in consideration is meaningful on the *factual ground* that "a man of principle" thinks and does accordingly. We may classify it under the "cognitive" theory of meaning of moral judgements. In other words, the above judgement makes sense if and only if what is said is believed to hold well and is acted on or followed by rational beings. Otherwise, a drab value judgement appears to be subjective in nature, which has many problems. One problem is that subjective statements lose their "general" nature, whereas evaluative judgements should not lose "generality". The advantages with the principlist theory is that it recognizes the general status of evaluative assertions as the one in which what is believed to be the case, must be suggestive of a definite course of action. This evident truth can be known (cognized) in reality in the ways in which moral agents think and do what they think to be worth thinking and doing.

An interesting problem with this less popular cognitive theory in the field of education and moral education is whether we can practically and sensibly teach young people (or older ones) that the several value assertions in education, which they constantly come across or use them, are grounded on factual experiences, which needs to be discovered by them and thus taking them to be valid, they ought to further follow what has been asserted? Is it possible and sensible to say that the young people taking a cue from their class teacher's way of thinking and 'doing', like 'systematically refraining from most provocative cases of corporeal punishment', think and do accordingly in life? Can instances of moral agents' patterns of thinking and doing as asserted in value statements be the surety of ethic of non-corporeal punishment or no punishment in education? Can a metaethical theses like this have any direct impact on policies of moral education? Is it not true that unless the "normative basis" available for the teacher who thought physical punishment to be bad on such grounds be taken as absolutely valid, the *assertion itself* does not convey anything as a matter of fact and, therefore, has no impact on moral education and policy-making by students and teachers? There are a number of important questions which principlism has to answer. In my mind, the study of instances of moral agents (teachers in this case) who thought and acted what has been expressed in value statements will be insufficient for the *justification* of the thesis that factual experiences of students leads them to think and follow what some peers thought and followed. The statement in essence must be bereft of a general evaluative feature, and may be at best subjective assertion or purely suggestive in nature, which may not be needed or possible at all to verify by any of us for validity and thus initiate us to state, believe and follow the same. If statements of value does not have a cognitive status and are purely subjective or emotive exhortations, even if they bear an inherent suggestive appeal which is universal in nature, none would in reality care to refrain from physical punishment to their pupils when they grow up and come to teaching. The inherent suggestion in an ethical assertion to follow a course of action and not another one is thus supported not by the mere sound or the words written or spoken by an agent rather what is supported by the moral agent in reality as based on an ideal in life. Well, the debate may be a raging one in metaethics, but here we are more interested in finding out the implications visible in the field of education is unavoidable for a close scrutiny. However, a critique of principlism should first proceed from the basic problems of the theory itself and then move on to the impact in education. The main problem with this is the conception of an artificial scheme of moral education called 'practical syllogism' advocated by Aristotle which amounts to the acceptance of a universal moral *norm* and then the *instances* of intentional human actions for evaluation on the basis of the norm and finally, a *conclusion* that is nothing but the statement of evaluation. Passing from instances to conclusion as based on an assumption is thus a strict logical process inviting fallacies at any stage, most importantly the unquestionable acceptance of the norm itself which though justified on intuitive grounds mainly, such as *eudemonia*, is not sacrosanct morally speaking. If this be the case, a moral agent cannot be good just because he or she believes that something as norm is true and instances of actions are in accordance with the norm. 'A man of principle' who also 'applies' it in life cannot be morally a saint for either having a norm believed to be true or following the norm in real life decisions and actions. Hence, the conclusive 'value statement' is in essence inconclusive regarding the core issue of "value". 'A man of principle' may be a man of wrongly conceived principle. Naturally, the model has no pragmatic value in teaching pupils about one or more values as found in one or many value assertions even if it is the case that pupils see for themselves that there is one man who is 'a man of principle'. Problems are about "seeing". What can we (teachers inclusive) 'see' in such cases? Can we really "see" a "man of principle"? We can see that one Mr. Temporal reaches his class at the stroke of 9 a.m. as per his routine. He is seen to walk a mile exactly at 8 p.m., goes to bed at 9:30 p.m., and always keeps his time in any engagement with people. What next do we 'see'? Is Mr. Temporal following a universal norm of morality such as "well-being" or "flourishing" or whatever? It may be that he is a man of a principle called "unconditional promise keeping" whose instances are his acts done in time but does it help us to reach the 'conclusion' that "punctuality is good", that is, morally good, and for that reason should be taught for its value to pupils though it demands pupils to "see" one Mr. Temporal doing all his punctual acts? The problem is, any degree of 'seeing' Mr. Temporal doing all his acts regularly does not help us to 'see' that he is following a basic norm and on that basis what he is doing is good (morally). Hence, a statement of value is not meaningful on the ground that the value of an act can be seen or shown to hold good because a moral agent did certain things because he valued certain norms to be valid. What can be the sound basis of applying this metaethical theory then in the sphere of education, including moral education? There is perhaps no sound basis in doing so. This point may be further strengthened on the ground (as seen in *The Primer*, Vol. 1) that a statement of value need not be a conclusion of a simple exhortation of feeling or emotion or suggestion or attitude and so on. To imagine that a value assertion is linked to a fact and then to a norm is to forget that facts and norms do not help *impute* "value" to a value assertion because "value" is a different category. The "good" of "punctuality" is not imputed by virtue of one Mr. Temporal respecting a norm and following it up in various actions. The goodness of punctuality though related to facts and norms is itself non-factual and non-normative. In the above value assertion it *acts* as a qualifier as used by a person in a moral context for some purpose which is the core issue to be noted. What function does "good" have in "punctuality is good" is an inquiry of language use of people in unique moral contexts. What at best we can 'teach' our students is that "punctuality is good" and "truth telling is good" are ways in which we sensibly use "good" in moral contexts for different purposes and we can teach them that "Mr. Temporal taking a walk after dinner is good" is a different use of good in another context, which has nothing to do with the *meaning* of "punctuality is good". Similarly, we can teach that "Mr. Temporal is so good to follow the principle of flourishing" is another way to use "good" which has nothing to do with the *meaning* of "punctuality is good". Hence, to assert that "punctuality is good" is to "see" that there is use of the word "good" in unique moral context along with a fact having a description in term of acts of doing things in time recognizes at least one person who "uses" the term properly in a moral context as understandable to others, but that does not prove there is one Mr. Temporal who follows a norm and deduces a value, which we should "see" and 'do so as well'. Even if do not 'see' anything like that the force of "good" as used by a person might instigate me to be "punctual" but for that I do not have to 'see' Mr. Temporal doing all nice things day long. Interestingly, Bertrand Russell (and myself) would love to see students not to be told to see at all what one Mr. Temporal does and then become frantically and fanatically punctual or what is "moral" because the child may not have the time not to do anything in time because something he wanted to do sometime was so important for him to do (Take my case of planning a drama in mathematics class when I was a young school-boy). Anyway, the metaethical thesis in essence has little bearing on education. It is useless when there is conflict among principles.

Coming to the impact of the thesis in education we have commented that what is expected of the thesis to teach cannot be taught and what might be taught cannot be taught at all levels. The metaethical intricacies we just talked about are safely to be reserved for interested parties in technical ethics and not for all. Then do we not teach or should we not teach the value of goodness of "punctuality"? Yes, we do. We should do and we will go on doing that because that is a value assertion conveying strong moral suggestion to fall in one way of life and not in another way of life but the teaching has nothing to do with metaethical thesis of principlism and application. This I say with the risk that the value assertion "It is not good to be fanatic about time" does not lose a small ground in conveying it to our students because it has strong appeal as well, not immoral in any case because the appeal itself is neither moral nor immoral because it does not ensue from a pattern of moral deduction or practical syllogism. In fact, many noble souls in moral education were worried to teach moral values to students on the basis of deducing what should be done on the basis of either norms or cases of people following a norm or both. What is more important to note in this regard (see Volume 1), the 'artificial' method as I call it is practically and ethically undesirable in real life. The intricate moral evaluation in the face of moral dilemma, decision-making and actions should never follow an artificial deductive model because it encourages absolutism of norms by moral experts and thus end up in moral chauvinism. It is equally important in education to not to stress on moral expertise of this kind as it may pass many odd ideas to students resulting into unnecessary moral conditioning. If it is important to show how great Mr. Temporal is, it may be equally important for pupils to have their own ways to manage time by just not artificially following Mr. Temporal. In fact, when we are shown or when we by ourselves start seeing what people like Mr. Temporal does we apply our reason to decide what course of action was good enough. It is our judgement rather than deduction, which is in play in real life situations of moral development. However, we find that our judgements are too inadequate if we do not act likewise. This does not mean that a child should be left to his own predilections in the name of judgement and teachers should shut up when child has to find his own morality. What is said is not, value assertions need not be the only suggestion of good life, nor does it beg a norm and a norm following person for justification. It is a great mistake on the part of R.S. Peters, John Wilson and Lawrence Kohlberg to suggest that moral education must fall back on a method of passing select principles as based on overriding norms until they are too good to rationalize and choose their own ethical norm. I will not straightway come to the elaboration of defects of these esoteric thinkers because I reserve it for discussion in a subsequent chapter. What I remark is Kohlbergian conception is in essence *a priorism*, a kind of *a priori* construction of moral development. Why at all should moral education beg conception of definite stages of moral development when that education is principlistic, is not known to me. For me, moral education is completely misconceived as obsession of the *gurukulas* that “we must show examples of following noble ways of life on the basis of principles”. Principlism as a metaethical thesis of meaning of moral statements does not convey much to what should be done concretely in moral education, it is purely formalistic or an edifice of principles found by fertile brains.

Let us now come to the metaethical theory of emotivism with regard to meaning of moral assertions and find out its bearings on moral education. The traditional principlistic theory is a representative of metaethical cognitivism, more clearly stated, it appears to be a naturalistic theory within cognitivism. We have seen that its basic position, like all cognitivistic theory is to justify the truth and meaning of moral language on the basis of some objects, facts, qualities and relations or in other words, on the basis of some "matters of fact" which are experienced or cognized by us whether through our senses or through our intuitive capacities. Hence, the language of morals is in essence "descriptive" in nature, that is, the moral component of the language of morality, "good", "right" or other evaluative notions are meaningful to us in terms of what they describe. For instance, "punctuality", "honesty", "truthfulness" and so on, each as matters of fact are "known" to us to be true. As such, what is in moral language is not alien to nature, that is, in space and time as objects, facts, qualities and relations. Moral terms are thus meaningful to us in the context of what they describe or, what natural descriptions are available to us that make them sensible in moral usage. We can ask for "natural proofs" for whether "punctuality is good", as we saw that one Mr. Temporal stood exemplary for us who did what was to be punctual and that was known to be good and not bad by either our sense or our intuitive experience. The naturalists think that our sense-experience is good enough to 'see' that what people do like doing things in time turns out to be "beneficial" or "pleasurable" or "advantageous" or "flourishing". Hence, we could "see" the effects of our actions and assume that something like punctuality is good for the benefits it provides us. Things are not so simple for the "intuitionists" because we cannot simply "see" with our senses that "punctuality" is "good" because what we call "good", is in itself unlikely to be naturally explained. It is rather a *non-natural* concept, waiting for intuitive knowledge. However, it is not out of the way to use "good" with "punctuality", but we should remember that "punctuality" is *not* good itself, that is, they are not synonymous and for that matter, punctuality is not the description of "good" because "good" as a value term is indescribable as it has no properties, it is a "simple" notion. The problem is why are we still using "punctuality" with "good"? How are we so sure that the expression makes any sense? The non-naturalists have to take recourse to "intuition" to justify that we "know" (cognize) "punctuality" to be *intrinsically* good and not bad. Anything we value as good or bad must be 'intrinsically' so is a matter of intuition that enable to us "see" (or prove) *directly* that it must be the case. However, we have seen that principlism as a naturalist theory have problems and it is no less problematic to say that 'intuition' enables us to 'see' that something is intrinsically good though 'good' itself is not to be explained in natural terms. The basic problem lies with 'intuition', which is enigmatic, unclear as a notion and begs another intuition to make some sense. It rules out the case of relativism in value judgement because another conflicting intuitive claim cannot be equally true, and surely, Mr. Bertrand Russell (and I) has intuition that Mr. Temporal was always not so good because he did not have any fun to be not in time. Hence, "cognitivism" has its own problems. Can we think of another justification of moral judgements or moral assertions to be meaningful?

Yes, *non-cognitivism* is the reply. This theory states that moral language is in essence non-descriptive in nature, that is, it does not describe moral terms on the basis of objects, facts, relations and qualities, whether natural or meta-physical. In fact, the language has no purpose to explain speaker's state of mind, his emotion, attitudes, likes, dislikes and so on. This is important for us to understand because naturalists most of the time take moral language to *describe* speaker's feelings, emotions and attitudes. When we say that "punctuality is good", we *describe* our feelings etc. towards "punctuality" through "good", in a *positive* or *approbative* way. Thus, naturalism as a cognitive theory does not merely assert that moral language 'describes' states of affair rather, it 'describes' *states of mind* of the speaker of that language, where "states of mind" is a sweeping term.

The subjective forms of naturalism as propagated by Hume, Westermarck, Russell and Perry had deep impact on some thinkers who later on joined the *non-cognitivists* but owed much for their rise on these subjectivists. Our contention being emotivism and its impact on education, we have to find out why emotivism rose from the ashes of subjective naturalism or simply *subjectivism*. Subjectivism in both *personal* and *social* forms supported mainly by Hume and Westermarck respectively holds that moral or evaluative language discribes state of mind of either the speaker of the language in particular or, some or many speakers of a community in general. Hence, "punctuality is good" may be stated as "For me (or for us), punctuality is good", meaning thereby, "I or we have a positive or an approbative or a commending feeling or emotion or attitude or inclination or desire or taste for an act called punctuality". This further amounts to say that "I or we recommend punctuality as a desirable action or action of personal and/or social good" is *not* to describe this act as good rather to describe that this act (punctuality) as something that evokes a feeling of approbation in me, hopefully it does in others when I say so or others say so, and for that reason, in saying so I am "describing a peculiar state of mind" or "state of mind of many others" when they say so. The statement thus does not have any point to be verified for truth and meaning beyond 'us' (or subjects), and therefore, "subjectivist". The crucial point to be noted is that moral assertions are sensible because they describe someone's state of mind (who is eventually the user of that language). Hume in his work *A Treatise of Human Nature* (Book III), Westermarck in *Ethical Relativity*, Russell in his "The elements of ethics" and Perry in *Realms of Value* advocated such ideas. The advocacy, however, supports cognitivism and thus naturalism because of the idea that moral assertions are *descriptive* in nature and their truth is determined or justified through sense experience. Moral assertions are 'known' by us to be true by virtue of our interactions in nature and they are meaningful because it is evidently known or in principle can be seen as meaningful because user of the language describes in unambiguous way his or her mental state towards an intentional act. To be remembered here is that the theory in principle accepts the truth that the value assertions *are* most likely to have a positive or negative impact on the *hearers* because it is "suggestive" in nature. In fact, the inherent 'suggestive' and evocative nature of moral statements was picked up later on by the non-cognitivists, the emotivists in the particular. However, the qualification being the careful neglect towards certain 'subjective' elements such as "description of state of minds of users" and "naturalistic bases of truth and meaning of moral statements". The former became necessary as it is a palpable ambiguity to state "description of person's state of mind" inherent in moral language. The language really does not *describe* any such thing, though it might describe what is commended such as "punctuality" because without its descriptive meaning any speaker or hearer does not know what is in consideration. This became necessary because *verification* of moral language for truth and meaning on natural basis boomerangs on the naturalists and turns out to be a bundle of confusions.

What was established by Hume or before that by Berkley in his *Principles of Human Knowledge* was challenged, revised and modelled afresh as non-cognitivistic "emotivism". The use of the term in popular parlance owes to C. Ogden and J.A. Richards in their work *The Meaning of Meaning* (1923) and later forcefully supported and gradually developed by A.J. Ayer in his *Language, Truth and Logic* (1936) and C.L. Stevenson in *Ethics and Language* (1944). The new turn in metaethics was a sharp one as the subjective flavour was gone, so was the naturalistic one, which amounted to a thesis that the language of value (moral) is true and meaningful because it is *expressive* of emotions of both the speakers and the hearers of the language, as well as *evokes* emotions in them either like or dislike in nature, and suggests and persuades hearers to have the same emotions that speakers have or changes if hearers have dissimilar emotions. Retorting back, the hearers' valuations are equally expressive, evocative and persuasive in nature. In fact, moral assertions are dynamic or functionally sensible; they do not describe states of our mind. Hence, we do not 'know' or 'see' truth and meaning carried in the moral language by any of us either through senses or intuitions in natural or non-natural ways. Moral language is, therefore, "non-cognitively true and meaningful". It is futile to search for the truth and meaning on descriptive basis because such language does not tell us anything about facts and qualities or relations rather they "express" our emotions about something, the description of which is known to us to a considerable degree, which is relevant in the analysis of moral assertions. Another important point to notice is that emotivism does not recognize the value of rational arguments in favour of moral assertions because they are beyond rational justification because whether or not the meaning of these assertions are justified is unimportant than whether or not they are successful in working moral emotions. In this sense, moral statements being not factually verifiable or rather being non-verifiable are not cognitively true or false. Unlike factual statements, they have no truth-value as based on verification. However, this does not mean that emotivism is like subjectivism because moral assertions according to the emotivists do not describe subjects' states of mind rather, they express emotions and arouse emotions, which are evident in the context of a *moral discourse*. The meaning of moral assertions are never clear when in isolation rather when they are in association, spoken, heard, reacted, refuted and so on, that is, when they are functional. No doubt, here the functions emerging are evocative, instigative and suggestive. C.L. Stevenson thinks that such assertions are, therefore, "causal" in nature because they have deep impact on our psyche resulting into either agreement or disagreement not about facts but about value. Precisely, moral assertions are those which cause disagreement (or agreement) among their users which are in reality disagreement (or agreement) in attitude and not merely in belief, though, there is likelihood of disagreement in attitude about belief. The language being suggestive or persuasive, in disagreement there is a likelihood of reaching an agreement depending on many things among which one important thing is dispelling evident misconceptions about the descriptive meaning of basic notions expressed in moral language. For instance, in case of "punctuality" one may have palpable misconception about "punctuality". If "punctuality" does *not* describe 'a state of necessarily and unfailingly doing certain things which needs to be done at a definite time by people like Mr. Temporal', we are able to persuade believers opposing the value of 'punctuality' (as good), to see their mistake and subsequently agree to our disapprobative attitude. The question is whether in the midst of "persuasion" there is relic of rational arguments, which emotivists overlooked? This question may lead to yet another direction but we shall not consider it now. Ayer was not as eloquent as Stevenson in analysing the nature, truth and meaning of moral assertions in the context of moral agreements and disagreements. Stevenson showed that following 'patterns of analysis' of these assertions we get several important components that consist of the nature truth and meaning of the same. He showed that there must be a descriptive component, approbative or emotive component and suggestive or persuasive component when moral assertions are in function. For instance, "Punctuality is good" ought to be analysed as: "Punctuality is something, which I approve and suggest that you (who happen to listen to me) do so as well". Hence, "good" as a value term contains both emotive and persuasive dispositions in so far as they are used in moral context, that is, while evaluating human intentional actions of some worth or no worth. However, one cannot do so without having any idea of what one intends to evaluate (in this case, "punctuality"). Hence, the descriptive features of what is evaluated as good in a statement are extremely important. It is possible however, that in moral dialogues one's approbation does not work, and it fails to evoke similar feeling in hearer. In any case, once the hearer retorts in moral language, it is sure to have the same features. There are several missing points in emotivism, which were picked up by R.M. Hare. Without going into an elaborate criticism, it will be sufficient to mention here that the dynamics of ethical language does not merely express ability to evoke emotion and persuasion; it may have other functions as well which should be considered seriously for a complete analysis of the language. P.H. Nowell-Smith puts it succinctly in his 'Janus headed' feature of ethical language in his work *Ethics* (1954). We shall come to know later on when we will discuss elaborately application of ethics that moral conflicts in real life decision-making demands more checks on the "emotive content" of our moral valuations, appreciations or disapprobation and rely on reasonable agreement on sound *rational basis*. In public morality, the emotive power of our assertions is challenged by stiffer ones and often both have to shut up reasonably. Can reason play a different role here, in persuasion and in moral decision-making? P.H. Hirst notes that "Much moral debate is engaged in with the deliberate intent of removing the discussion from concern for emotional responses to a concern for making judgements on rational grounds"[23]. We shall come to this when we consider R.M. Hare's theory in this regard, but we have to now find out the impact of emotivism on education and educational ethics.

Roger Straughan notes that though R.M. Hare has taken some pain to elaborate the effect of the metaethical theory of prescriptivism in the field of education, the emotivists have hardly taken interest in such things. Hence, we have to read many things between the lines to see what emotivism really contributed in this matter. Nevertheless, Straughan remarks that "It is not too difficult, however, to detect traces of an implicit and unexamined kind of emotivism among those parents and teachers who are uneasy about the very idea of moral education, on the grounds that 'morality is just a matter of personal belief' and that 'if you feel its right for you, then its right'"[24]. To start the query, our readers must be warned of taking emotivism as anything like this, and Straughan rightly thinks that it may be "dubious" to extrapolate anything like this from emotivism because emotivism is not subjectivism. However, one can imagine that ethical considerations in education includes the important aspect of impact of "moral convention" in an institution where most of the time when students and teachers are talking about "moral" matters or when there is an official moral teaching or when students are engaged in moral appreciations and evaluations, we cannot doubt that some party might be better placed in championing emotive force on others and thus impress on moral matters. This may be particularly true in case of teachers, who as I have said before, have great liking for moral chauvinism and thus in the wake of moral assertions press on students their own values or persuade them to pick their values. Hence, a strong point of consideration at the metaethical level may be whether educational ethics should consider an inquiry into the ethic of moral teaching, moral persuasion and moral chauvinism on the part of the teacher who happens to follow 'one way traffic' (see Vol. 1), that is, in moral education teachers spread gems of values when all others shut up. What is ethical in ethical education when moral language is a vehicle of pressing moral feelings on others by following persuasive tactics?

If we follow Kohlberg's model of development of moral reasoning, which is nevertheless, fraught with *a priorism*, we have to accept that moral discussions among children and teachers is not merely mental gymnastics involving intricate ways of reasoning rather dealing in human feelings and emotions. This is so because moral matters immediately attract our attention because as emotivists think, those matters when expressed in unique language have *magnetism*, that is, the language positively or negatively expresses and evokes emotions. This amounts in most of the cases to follow one course of actions rather than another one. Hence, emotivists might say that the ethic of educational ethics is to encourage moral discourses in our institutions so that through the language-dynamics pupils are left to adopt a moral way of life. However, it is difficult to imagine how a programme to give moral freedom to pupils to interact in moral matters would be as simple as following a course of action by the sheer 'power of emotive language'. It may be that the assumed "causal" disposition of the language which does not lead us to moral actions, rather, moral actions are possible when emotions are transcended by the power of reasons which tend to favour benefits which are humane. Emotive forces inherent in language my be true, but they do *not* "cause" a moral way of life in our educational campus, the way of life is possible when we socialize and moralize by keeping powerful subjective emotions in a limbo or, *corroborate* them in association through rational scrutiny of why our emotions about certain decisions and actions should get prevalence over others. To be honest, reasons need support of matters of fact or, the descriptive features present in the language of morals. Popular conception about greatness of "emotive quotient" of people, especially students, which has become popular in contemporary times is of some importance because bereft of human feelings and emotions, a human is not truly so called, but the point is that a care for human emotions alone cannot be the guiding force in moral life because we cannot and *should* not necessarily care for emotions of individuals always. Why is it so? Because there are 'good reasons' for not doing so. Our being emotively conscious demands that we should be emotively judicious as well. The demand is to be rational in the face of rogue emotions because only that way can we be 'judicious'. Hence, teaching and educating can never predominantly rely on letting our emotions fly in freedom in garbage of language among teachers and students, where none cares to harness it and be rational. Bereft of rationality and checks on emotions and emotively charged moral arguments, it is a mere "grunt" says R.S. Peters because it rules out the possibility of a moral dialogue among teachers and students about several value-laden issues in education. We ought to be careful in educational ethics to inquire about the validity of moral teachings to young people in schools in particular and of moral debates in schools, which does not guarantee rationality and thus avoids chauvinism. The educators and the 'pressure groups' among students who overwhelm by virtue of emotions and *their reasons* are worst, they are unfit people in education as well as moral education. It is difficult to see, therefore, what emotivism as such, as a metaethical thesis has to contribute to educational ethics. One contribution I can find out is that it provides us a subject for thorough metaethical critique, which we are considering right now.

Going back to the roots of emotivism, we find basic problems in Stevenson's 'causal' thesis. Is it acceptable that moral language causes emotions? Is it true to say that as we listen to "punctuality is good", we 'feel good' about "punctuality" and start doing what we feel good? Or, is it the other way round, that is, we practically judge punctuality as a good act on certain basis, may be normative ones, and therefore, when we listen to such language, we approves it as good or we show positive feelings towards it? Suppose in our world there were no Mr. Temporal, who did things in time, would there be any judgement of value or disvalue of "punctuality"? If Temporal did things in time, and we judged them as good and bad, and if judgements were emotive exhortations, the emotive exhortations still plays a second fiddle to the acts of Temporal and the bases of judging the acts. This has a far-reaching impact on educational ethics. The subject needs to take care of this issue for thorough analysis whether moral teachings in schools or elsewhere should give prime importance to evaluate act of Temporals in our society to find out what is the value or disvalue of being in time always than analysing moral language to find out which emotion towards the punctual Mr. Temporal were more favourable in our case. It is better to indulge into the query of the ethical value of emotions, but that is a deeper non-emotive issue; it takes us back to the judgement of value on some bases. Rightly, no child can be taught or should be taught the value of a particular emotion of any individual.

No child should be ever conditioned in certain fixed values of emotions. We need not try to persuade and advertise in our schools to be kind or punctual or whatever by uttering language of persuasion because that is to do the opposite of what we should do first. We should find out the ways in which we can find for ourselves the cases in which cruelty and punctuality are either bad or good, and why approval or disapproval follows in the natural course. Moral teaching needs an overhaul in educational ethical curriculum if it has been wrongly framed. An element of feeling should be still there in us to take care of teaching difficult things to children, which might do more harm than good if done in a wrong way. The language expressing "badness of wrong methods of moral education" does have an emotive content that attracts us to respond to it, but that is not all we need to do. Straughan aptly says, "So although emotivism performs the service of attending us to the importance of 'feeling' in some areas of morality and moral education, teaching children to be good need not be so uneducational an activity as emotivism implies."[25]

Perhaps we have reached a climax in considering the second order task of educational ethics because we have to move to one of the strongest metaethical analysis of moral language and its impact on educational ethics. We shall now discuss *prescriptivism* propounded by R.M. Hare in his work *The Language of Morals* (1952) and in many of his writings. Hare's metaethical thesis known as *universal prescriptivism* aims at establishing an ethical theory that answers questions like what is the meaning of the terms and sentences used in moral discussions. What is the nature of concepts used in moral discussions? And is there a rational way to settle a number of moral issues or shall we have to take recourse to facts, feelings and things? Hare thinks that to call his ethical theory non-descriptive as opposed to descriptive, and non-cognitive as opposed to cognitive in the way we normally use these terms in metaethical literature is unfounded because he claims that the so-called non-descriptivist or the non-cognitivists might successfully hold that ethical language is "true or false" in some sense. We have seen in our earlier discussion that a non-cognitivist or a non-descriptivist can comfortably hold that ethical language is true and meaningful because the theory *per se* is *about* the *justification* of ethical language as true and meaningful, but on completely different grounds, that is, *not* exactly based on the grounds on which cognitivistic truth claims stand. Hare thinks that much confusion in the minds of ethical thinkers is about an *ontological* difference between cognitivism and non-cognitivism as if the former holds that there are moral qualities, things, facts and relations in real world, which the latter denies. Hare reminds us that both these ethical theories and his own theory which certainly comes under non-cognitivism on different reasons, are *semantical* in nature, not 'ontological' in nature because they are *about* "meaning and truth" of ethical language and not about ethical facts or things. Hence, in metaethics, what is cognitivism, and for instance, "naturalism" is semantic thesis, much different from "ontological naturalism" which answers what is or is not right or true as a matter of fact. Normative thesis that claims rightness in this sense as does utilitarianism, is not a "semantic" theory though it deals with the "truth" of moral claims like, "maximization of happiness is good" because it aims at justifying what *is* the case in fact, and therefore, "ontological". Yet, when we ask "semantic" questions like, why is "maximization of happiness good", irrespective of whether it is or is not the case as a matter of fact, true and meaningful? We ask why the assertion is sensible at all? Does it make any sense to use value term "good" with "maximization of happiness", which is essentially factual in nature? In this sense, cognitivism and descriptivism as different from non-cognitivism is a theory that fixes definite *truth-conditions* for moral statements which are imagined to be true of all such statements irrespective of the ways in which these statements are used or the ways in which the terms in the statements are used or the ways in which moral language is used in actual moral contexts. Hence, non-descriptivism or non-cognitivism is an ethical theory, which Hare intends to support as a metaethical thesis about truth and meaning of moral language which has no "purely" stipulated universal ground or truth-conditions for justifying the truth and meaning of the same rather, finds out which flexible use (the non-truth conditional), the language has. Precisely, non-cognitivism unlike cognitivism is an ethical theory about truth and meaning of ethical language in which semantic conditions are not *purely descriptive* and fixed, though moral language does have a *descriptive element* (which we saw in Stevenson but that does not mean something verifiable as facts, which Ayer believed), and a *evaluative element*, which is the testimony to the 'functional' aspect of the language (which we saw in Stevenson, but Hare adds something new in it, which we will see). The crux is that moral language is semantically sensible in so far as it has a descriptive meaning and a evaluative meaning, the former, determinate, whereas the latter, indeterminate. Hare thinks that the emergence of the 'evaluative meaning' owes to the 'evaluative functions or uses', which is not merely what the emotivists in the past believed as emotive use, rather, prescriptive use is important as well. It is here that Hare starts contributing substantially in his semantic thesis. Hare is extremely appreciative about Immanuel Kant, who enabled him to see that moral language is, apart from being descriptively meaningful, prescriptive or in Kantian words, imperative.

Hare deviated from Ayer's and Stevenson's "emotivism" mainly on the ground that the theory is predominantly "irrational" because even if they rightly recognized the truth that moral language has a function to express our emotions but they argued wrongly that such expressions are non-rational or irrational attitudes of those who approves or disapproves of evaluation of some actions. Emotivists wrongly thought that reasons can be given only on factual affairs but not on evaluative affairs. He also did not allude to the idea that moral assertions cause any emotion in us. Hence, he concluded that "Prescriptivists, on the other hand, have reacted in a more positive way by looking for a kind of non-descriptivism which would not be open to the charge of irrationality .... They claim to have found it by showing that these were rules of reasoning which govern non-descriptive as well as descriptive speech acts."[26] Interestingly, much of the functionality based analysis of moral language is influenced by the views of J.L. Austin, such as his view on "speech acts."[27] Taking a cue from Austin and Kant, Hare thinks that in moral language for instance, in moral imperatives, there is hardly any proof of deriving their meaning on the causal theory. If someone says "we ought to be punctual" or simply, "Be punctual", the imperative is not meaningful either on the ground that someone like Mr. Temporal demonstrates punctuality or on the ground that the imperative or the command has caused effects on someone like the one who gives the command or people who follows them as Mr. Temporal. Hence, the fallacy of putting the horse before the cart (which we saw in case of Stevenson) has been corrected by Hare because the imperative is used after we found the rightness of punctuality and not after the command has instigated a feeling in us to follow it. Hare reminds us of Austin who said that there is a difference between what one is *doing by* uttering something (*the perlocutionary act*) and what is one *doing in* uttering something (*the illocutionary act*). Moral imperatives are not uttered to do something, that is, to cause an effect, rather in uttering it, something is *done*. We prescribe someone to follow a course of action. Hence, commands do not 'cause' an action (punctuality) rather prescribes or suggests an action for its commendable features. Naturally moral imperatives carry some *reason* with them, that is, justification of why or on what commendable grounds; an action is commanded or prescribed. Moral assertions are *not* "irrational" or "non-rational", therefore, Hare notes that it would be too simplistic to think that moral judgements are like simple imperatives like "shut the door", rather they are more complex than these non-moral orders, having different logic. It is these complex imperatives that have direct relation with "reasoning-rules", rather a combination of the rules. Prescriptives are thus to be found in a combination of some such rules that govern simple imperatives as well as a set of rules that govern modals such as "ought" or "must" (in the moral sense). However, we must note that these modals are not unique to moral sense, and for that reason, the use of these modals in moral sense needs further reasoning—rules.

Coming to this aspect of the specific rules or combination of rules, Hare states that *universalizability* is an outstanding one. Hence, 'universalizability' gives 'must' and 'ought' unique moral features in moral context. Hence, normative and evaluative ethical sentences containing 'must' or 'ought to' have the distinctiveness of 'universalizability', which it does not have in ordinary or non-moral imperatives. This is the distinctive feature of *universal prescriptivism*. It is due to this that "I must keep promises" and "I must keep clean" are imperatives containing the modal "must" but its use in the former is different from the later, as in the former in the context of "promises" it has distinctive moral use and thus expected to be "universalized", which is not the case when we speak of non-moral use of the modal. In the moral use, we find that without involving us into any contradiction we are not in a position to hold that what is expected of me, that is, to keep promises irrespective of any conflicting conditions in my duties, does not apply to another person like me, who is situated in a *similar situation*. It is due to this reason that "Mr. Temporal must be punctual in his class" but I must not be punctual if I am not put to duty of Mr. Temporal. In any case, an ethical imperative contains modals of universal features, that is, applies for all situated in a 'similar situation'. This is one strong "reason" (which Stevenson did not give us), why moral judgements are true and meaningful despite having no causal effect on moral agents who used them or listened to them. Imperative status of the judgement is not enough, we need enough "reason" to show why the orders or commands or prescriptions conveyed sense. The moral judgements being universal commands (of duties) provide us the reason for its being non-cognitively meaningful. Hare thinks that though being situated in similar conditions is one important aspect of universalizability, it calls for considering the characteristics of the people situated in it and their desires and motivations as well. Hence, the rule of universalizability should hold good in moral contexts for moral agents who are similarly situated in important respects which characteristic deviations does not effect. Next, there must not be any confusion about universality and *generality* because it does not profess the truth that what is generally applicable for moral agents is what the universal principle is. In fact, modals in moral contexts have extremely specific use, for instance, "*Never* be a liar except when it is needed to save your nation". Hence, there is no reason to imagine that it should be necessarily as "general" as "*Never* lie" because we have to take care of specific reasons (exceptions). This is another example of how important it is to consider the 'situations' in which moral judgements occur. Further, the principle of universalizability does *not* mean that what is binding on me as a moral agent as a command such as the duty not to lie or the duty to keep promises applies to another person who has his or her duties correlative to what I have and, therefore, both of us should be obliged to perform the duties of the other person. Hence, even if two of us must keep time in class as teachers, the imperative does not imply that apart from my duty, I have to look after the other who has a correlative duty because we are similarly situated. It is a simple point of consideration of not merely hypothetical identical situations rather consideration of actual identical situations in which having deontic commands does not imply one person fulfilling the duty of other and by that the principle becomes universal.

From this Hare draws the conclusion that universal prescriptivism is a thesis about truth and meaning of ethical judgements which considers the aspect of use of moral terms in moral contexts as very important, and that the specific use of command or imperative draws our attention of being accused of "insecurity" if we do not follow them as necessitating or binding on us as duty, provided we are situated similarly. Hence, to use modals in moral language is to accept that we accept them as necessitating commands and for that reason, we are moved in a certain way. Hare calls this basic to an "internalist theory" of meaning, which unlike the "externalist" theory holds that for moral judgement to be true it is not necessary to be motivated in some way rather, one can accept a moral judgement to be true independent of *one's motivations*. But equally true is that "to accept some moral judgement is *io ipso* to be motivated in a certain way."[28] Nevertheless, this is not a causal theory as Stevenson advocated because here we do not say that the meaning of moral judgement depends on what effects it produces on us, rather it depends on how it is used, that is, as a necessitating universal command. And it is natural to say that if commands are accepted, they involve us in a certain way. Hare says that despite these features of moral judgements, we are not in a position to say that all of them have truth values in the sense in which "factual judgements" have truth values. For Hare, it is not impossible to imagine that a normative judgement may be true or false in so far as following an ideal or norm is directly related to it, which is not in the case of "imperatives". Clearly, all moral judgements are not universal imperatives. Imperatives are true in a highly qualified sense, that is, the non-cognitive sense. Their unique "use" in moral contexts among participating people in those contexts determine that the commands are *accepted to be true* and such acceptance amounts to a course of action such as necessitating performance of duties, but that does not amount to say that motivated people proves the truth of imperatives. Hence, acceptance of truth of deontic statements and following them as commands is one thing, and verifying such statements as true on the basis of followers of commands is yet another thing. Prescriptions are *not in fact true* when someone follows it rather, it is true in moral contexts when *we* (in similar situations) follow what it *expresses and implies* and thus *accept* them of worth following.

Given this extremely scrappy account of in the depth study of Hare regarding moral language, we are in some position at least to find out what are its implications on education and educational ethics. This becomes easier for us as Hare has clearly stated that what prescriptivism as a metaethical thesis means in education, particularly in teaching children. He must be equally influenced in this regard by his mentor Kant, to whom he owes much. In the *Language of Morals* Hare takes up this issue briefly and more fully in his essay "Language and Moral Education."[29] He states: "I am convinced that if parents first, and then children, understood better the formal character of morality and of the moral concepts, there would be little need to bother, ultimately about the context of our children's moral principles; for if the form is really and clearly understood, the content will look after itself."[30] What Hare says is not alien to emotivism either, but we have seen that the impact of emotivism on educational ethics is not so encouraging. Let us find out what a *formal* thesis like this one has to contribute to the task of educational ethics, though we must not forget that emotivism has already partially established the truth that ethical inquiries in the field of education should not overlook the value of human feelings and emotions as expressed in moral language, and moral education (if that is needed), must take care of the fact that moral language by itself need not persuade students to accept what is 'given' to them because rationality is at stake if we did such things. However, Hare seems to be extremely encouraged by the prescriptive force in moral language, which he thinks does more than a verbal cacophony. It in fact *guides actions*, which is what is expected of our *teachers* of morality to do in our schools (or may be in colleges). Well, even if moral language does have that force in moral contexts it is only in the context of 'moral education' that the force is felt by us. However, institutions need not necessarily take up this noble task of "moral education". Hare might argue that nevertheless, institutions 'should' do that for the obvious good results. So he must be a teleologist whose formalism is not blank, it has a good follow up in practice. This is good but one wonders what "moral education" is and what if our institutions did not go for such exclusive education and still have "moral atmosphere" in the sense of a teeming life of interaction where many intentional acts and their evaluation are simply an obvious thing to happen, which does 'educate' us, may be without a teacher or teachers because many of us are teachers in such atmosphere. It is very interesting to note that even if our institutions did not have a moral education class (which is often seen as a breathing space among mathematics, physics, and economics classes); we can still have moral education in all the classes which needs fresh approach. This is something unique to consider: How do we educate moral virtues and values "officially" in dealing with different subjects? I will take up this question when we come to the following chapters. Let us now find out what Hare had in mind when he advocated "moral education" wherein moral language is uttered "officially" (to morally blank pupils perhaps!). It must not be something like ethics-education I suppose because in basic schooling that may be too much or even laughing. Well, let us allow it to higher education from class IX onwards, what do we teach there? Moral language cannot be taught; it can be uttered but not in chatter and clatter because ethics is not chattering and clattering. Do we teach all the tasks of moral philosophy or ethics in 'moral education' which does need language, but certainly not 'private' language in ethics? If it be like that, Hare would have to speak out a number of sentences bearing prescriptive modals with a hope that those will "guide" our actions. Will it be really so? Do we learn morality in that way? Let me drop it now with a clear indication that it may not be the case. Hence, in our institutions we cannot teach morality through prescriptive language discourse. Moral education through an unclear proposition is still impossible in an artificial way Hare imagines. It appears that Hare did not come out of his "formalism" in education. Education need not be formalistic; it has every defect, which Platonic scheme had. However, it may be that Hare did not imagine ethics education at all; he was interested in teaching common "morality" which does not need ethically oriented appreciations and evaluations. Still, we ask, will it be possible for teachers to achieve this notoriously difficult goal by uttering *prescriptive specific moral language*? This is a must for Hare because for him ethical language is just this and "prescriptive-specific language oriented teaching" is the key to moral education. It is this language which when uttered to students in similar situations will "guide" them to be good or noble. I must say that all this is completely artificial, imaginary and chauvinistic. Most important to note is moral education (if it be sensible), is one thing and prescriptive-specific language discourse is another thing. The former does not logically depend on the other. In fact, the *disposition* of the prescriptive language *to guide* us to do in a certain way is one thing and *using it to guide* others in a certain way is another thing. Equally different is the *surety element* in Hare's thesis that it *does guide* and *will guide.* The force of modals in prescriptive language is true to a moral discourse very often but that is in most of the time at an agreement level (of Stevenson), whether it guides us to do what is expected of us to do further on, is yet another thing, which is not in the language *per se*. There is a gap in 'having a force' and 'forcing it to have'. Hare cannot be successful in his scheme if he really did not happily commit the error of Stevenson to 'force to have it' and thus be artificial, imaginative and chauvinistic not in language discourse but in forcing a thesis about language in a field alien to it.

Now keeping these basic points in mind we may further evaluate what Hare thinks are the advantages of 'prescriptive specific moral teachings'. He thinks that such teaching leads students to realize that what is taught in morality is not about what 'is' rather what 'should' be the case, and thus adopt a course of action which 'should' be done. Further, the students realize that moral statements are statements of universalizing prescriptions, and thus, if some people are like me, situated in similar conditions, we should be caring about them when we do something, which is sure to affect them. Every now and then Hare reminds us of Kant who took it very seriously that if moral agents should do something, which is an imperative and universal, it can be done as well. No doubt in that because mere thought of 'should' but no accompanying 'can' does not make morality a fertile field. The point remains to be seen is how can we really do that in education. As I have remarked, it does not seem so easy with a prescriptive specific programme of teaching. It is very difficult to understand how love and care for other people who I 'know' are similarly situated be conveyed to them through specific language use. However, Hare has no doubt that if we go for such a programme, students are sure to follow what their teachers and others have conveyed to them in rich language of morals. Interesting is to ask whether following them would be at all necessary and sufficient and even moral by 'their' perspective? Will it not stop our urge to debate, disagree, charge and change what were conveyed to us as sacrosanct? Our schools and colleges have tended to sermonize 'from the top' at all costs to accept what we thought was 'given' to us in the name of 'universal principle' or in the name of 'prescription'. Does it not make some sense to keep the doors open for arguments about the validity of universalizable principles of morality?

In any case, we need not forget the merit of the discussion here because if there is something sensible called "educational ethics" and it has to take care of the *metaethical task*, certainly serious consideration about the role of moral language is needed. We need to consider whether moral teaching is needed for moralisation, whether education needs moral teaching and whether prescriptive and emotive language has anything to contribute in this programme. Thus far, I think, I have not found anything substantive in what Hare imagines as contributory in education because of its artificiality and lurking chauvinism of teachers as moral experts. In any case what is still commendable in what Hare says is that if ethical values are so important to be grown in students in our schools in particular, even if we are not considering classroom or formal teaching, we need to be careful as teachers to use some such language in our campus life, even when we teach mathematics or arts or whatever which does not merely care of what happens around us but what things should be open for our consideration to be valued and adopted. The language of a teacher is extremely important as an exemplary peer group, without being prescriptive-specific, he or she can still be effective in campus life when he or she cares for others and speaks about that openly when needed. It is not that teachers should not utter what they think is ethically good but they should not only utter but do something, and most important, let others utter if care for others is so valuable. It is the free-flowing ethical interactions in campus that makes language so meaningful and effective, but in the midst of it, we must notice that every talk is not prescriptive-specific. The defects in Hare's proposal reminds us that it is extremely important to be careful about 'similar situation' in universalization because to find out a 'similar situation', is a difficult job. It is not intuitively known. Even if we are decisive in sorting out that some of us are in a similar situation that does not guarantee that we start "loving" each other. What it is to love each other? If we understood Hare properly, in his scheme of things in the institutions, the *affective* is replaced by the *imperative* with a masterly stroke of "universalization" of commands. Hence, participation in a prescriptive-universal talk in campus (love others), does not logically imply that therefore, we participate in an ambiguous act of "loving others". If this be really the case, Hare reminds us of one truth that moral language encourages us to be "benefit" oriented and "altruistic". It may be that Hare's neglect of the "affective" under the pressure of "imperative" encouraged him to care for it later on when he wrote *Moral Thinking* (1981), where he argues that *moral education should involve teachings related to moral feelings*. However, this is much in abeyance with his thesis that moral education is prescriptive-specific and universal. Whatever it may be at the end of the discussion we have interesting things to consider. One point is to consider whether moral teaching is needed at all in our institutions. We shall consider it in more details but we have to consider another important task of educational ethics in the next chapter.

NOTES

1. Barrow, Robin, *Moral Philosophy for Education*, George Allen & Unwin Ltd., London, 1975, p. 156.
2. Straughan, Roger, *Can We Teach Children To Be Good? Basic Issues in*

Moral, Personal and Social Education, Open University Press, Philadelphia, 1991, pp. 72-73.

3. Brandt, Richard B., *Ethical Theory: The Problems of Normative and Critical Ethics*, Prentice-Hall, Englewood Cliffs, NJ, 1959, p. 6.
4. *Ibid*, p. 7.
5. Straughan, Roger, *op. cit*., p. 76.
6. Naturalistic conception of J.J. Rousseau can be seen in his pioneering work *Emile*, Dent Pub. London, 1961.
7. Neill, A.S., *Summerhill*, Penguin, Harmondworth, 1968, p. 108.
8. Barrow, Robin, *op. cit.*, p. 159.
9. *Ibid*, p. 160.
10. *Ibid*, p. 164.
11. *Ibid*, p. 168.
12. Herman, Barbara, *The Practice of Moral Judgement*, Harvard University Press, Cambridge, 1993, p. 217.
13. Louden, Robert B. quotes Kant in *Kant's Impure Ethics*, O.U.P., NY, 2000, p. 20.
14. *Ibid*, p. 20.
15. *Ibid*, p. 22.
16. *Ibid*, p. 27.
17. For details see L.W. Beck's, *Essays on Kant and Hume,* Yale Univ. Press, New Haven, 1978, and W.K. Frankena's, *Three Historical Philosophies of Education: Aristotle, Kant and Dewey*, Scoft Fresman, Chicago, 1965.
18. Louden, Robert B. quotes Kant in *Kant's Impure Ethics*, *op. cit.*, p. 56.
19. *Ibid*, p. 58.
20. Peters, R.S., *Psychological and Ethical Development*, Allen & Unwin, London, 1974, pp. 253-4.
21. Hirst, P.H., "Liberal Education and the Nature of Knowledge" in Dearden, R.F., Hirst, P.H. and Peters, R.S. (eds.), *Education and the Development of Reason*, Routledge & Kegan Paul, London, 1972, p. 403.
22. Barrow, Robin, *Moral Philosophy for Education*, *op. cit.*, pp. 170-71.
23. Hirst, P.H., *Moral Education in a Secular Society*, University Press of London, London, 1974, p. 38.
24. Straughan, Roger, *op. cit.*, 1991, p. 35.
25. *Ibid*, p. 57.
26. Hare, R.M., "Universal Prescriptivism" in Peter Singer (ed.), *A Companion to Ethics*, O.U.P., Oxford, 1991, p. 455.
27. For detailed view of J.L. Austin see his works, *Philosophical Papers*, O.U.P., Oxford, 1961 and *How to Do Things with Words*, O.U.P., Oxford, 1962.
28. Hare, R.M. *op. cit.*, p. 458.
29. Langford G. and O'Connor, D.J. (eds.) *New Essays in the Philosophy of Education*, Routledge & Kegan Paul, London, 1973, pp. 149-66.
30. *Ibid*, p. 164.

3

The Value and the Virtue Related Tasks of Educational Ethics

We have seen thus far that education has its own value, by any fertile imagination it cannot be a disvalue. Equally true is that educational ethics as a field of study within ethics has its own value, it cannot be a disvalue. However, when education in general, or educational ethics in particular, is used by a person or group of persons for ends inherently bad or of disvalue, it is a completely different issue because using something badly does not necessarily justify that the thing so used is itself bad. In any case even if education and educational ethics have their own value it is not proved that educational ethics has a 'value related task' because among other unclear things, one is not sure what this 'task' amounts to and what if it did not have any. We may start from any point, but it is better to find out first what if educational ethics did not undertake this task. If it did not do so, it will be difficult to understand what it consists in without doing that. Similarly, ethics is not properly so-called if it did not undertake the metaethical or the normative tasks. No doubt, educational ethics, if it did not undertake both the second and the first order tasks (as mentioned in the previous chapter), it would not be properly so-called. This does not mean that if ethics perform only two tasks like educational ethics, it would be sufficient for them to do so. The truth is that it would be insufficient and unsatisfactory to say that these subjects perform only two tasks and none else. What if educational ethics did not undertake its value and virtue related tasks? The simple answer is we are bereft of something called 'educational ethics' in the true sense of the term. This may be true if educational ethics did not perform its practical task.

This is to say that value considerations in education are not merely expected rather, it is *desirable*. This amounts to say that if educational ethics is to be a sensible study within ethics, it should take up certain things or what is desirable or good or of great *worth* to do. Hence, there must be something *worthwhile* or *valuable* in educational ethics to do, and among many things (like the first and the second order tasks), it is of 'worth' to perform the "value related" task and 'virtue' being a value, is included within the discussion of values. In one sense, if educational ethics remains of some worth, it should consider something related to "worth" or "value". We have seen at different places that educational ethics, simply stated, is ethically relevant inquiry of issues in the field of education. In this sense, one ethically relevant issue is to discuss about ethical values and virtues which education should be concerned about because education should initiate us to something worthwhile or something valuable, which ethical values and virtues surely are. The question is whether values and virtues can at all be taught? Or, whether values and virtues should be taught and/or imbibed through education? Well, we may argue that value and virtue teaching or imbibing are all pointless and hopeless efforts, they do not make any sense, but we cannot argue that we do not have a valid reason to argue on such issues. We do have one but we hope to listen to logical justifications and not whims. Once we indulge into it, we are in a lively debate within educational ethics. We cannot avoid this because educational ethics has already encouraged us to take up the *justification* of its value and virtue related tasks. Hence, to say that value and virtue related tasks are trash jobs for educational ethics, invites the proponents of the view to consider the job of justifying their view strongly, which shows that they are already in the area of 'virtue and value' related tasks of educational ethics. The flip side of the coin being that those who strongly refuse these as trash, should nevertheless, justify the same, and thereby show that the educational ethics makes a lot of sense. We should not be emotionally disturbed when sceptics put their challenge because sceptics are good people; they allow us to realize that certain tasks cannot be undertaken in educational ethics by mere whim.

Next step is more difficult. Sceptics might ask, 'what is the *way* in which we can teach virtues and values even if discussion of virtues and values are arguably sensible within educational ethics?' This is another serious but sensible challenge because "methods" of teaching values and virtues need great care. Who should be allowed to do such things, to whom and in what ways? These are important queries. We have to face them because in that way we justify that educational ethics does have important tasks to take up. It is important to notice that a relevant ethical inquiry in the field of education should involve inquiries about virtues and values because apart from teaching moral or ethical virtues and values, we ask, whether several non-moral virtues and values should be taught? We inquire whether the values of health and hygiene ought to be taught and whether truthfulness and honesty ought to be taught as great virtues so that most expectedly pupils are encouraged to pick them. Hence, educational ethics should not send us a wrong signal that it only inquires about teaching moral values and virtues rather it inquires about teaching value of material, ecological, spiritual and many other values as well as a number of non-moral virtues like cleanliness, punctuality and so on. Hence, educational ethics relevantly inquires how far teaching about "non-moral" virtues and values are *ethically* relevant. It may well be that many people strongly feel and justify that spiritual values and virtues make us truly human, and education must consider them as valuable for further teaching and/or imbibing. In educational ethics we inquire whether it should be *ethically justifiable* or desirable to teach these values. Hence, educational ethics should consider virtue and value related discussions enthusiastically because it penetrates the realms of a number of non-moral values and virtues for ethical scrutiny.

However, one cannot overlook the fact that without having clear conception of the nature and meaning of "value", "virtue", "value and virtue related discourse" and "value and virtue based education", ethical inquiries regarding teaching these matters are useless. This is nevertheless, a metaethical task, which we should perform. Hence, let us first consider what we mean by "value", "virtue" and "value and virtue based education". The notions of "value" and "valuation" have extensive use, which falls for an in-depth study under *axiology*. However, more confined or restricted use is found in economics and other social sciences. It is extensively used in philosophical literature as well, particularly in ethics, aesthetics and logic. Literally "value" means "worth" and "valuation" or "evaluation" means "judgement of worth" or simply "worthwhileness" of something. Evaluation of subjects or fields of study, things, facts, events, notions, beliefs, behaviour, intention, decision, idea make us believe that many things around and beyond us are said to have "worth" or "value", that is, a number of things are "worthwhile", among which are "education", "educating", "ethics", "educational ethics" and so on. This extremely broad field of axiological study of value was popularised by a number of Austrian and German thinkers before British and American axiologists did well to take interest. The credit mainly goes to Alexius Meinong, Christian Ehrenfels, Franz Brentano, Max Scheler, Nicolai Hartmann and Edmund Husserl, from whom we could know many things about *philosophical usages* of "value". The term "value" is used in philosophical discussions as an *abstract noun* either in a *narrow* or in a *broad* sense. In the former sense, the term "value" means what is "worthwhile" or "desirable" or "good", which is common in the ethical and the aesthetic parlance. The same usages may be seen in the metaphysical, religious and spiritual discussions. In educational ethics, the term "value" is more often used in this narrow abstract sense to tell us about which things in the field of education and educating are good or desirable or worthwhile. We have seen that "education" itself is valued as worthwhile because it initiates us to achieve many things in life, which are worthwhile. Similarly, "educational ethics" initiates us to achieve the goal of ethical valuation of educational phenomena, which is worthwhile, and therefore, it is itself of worth. However, the abstract noun in a *broader* philosophical usage covers the sense of that which is right, duty, obligation, *virtue*, truth, holy and so on. These usages of "value" apart from being extensively found in ethics, metaphysics and other branches mentioned above, are found in epistemology and logic. In "education" and "educational ethics", we use "value" to mean what is our duty or obligation or virtue. It is important to note that the term "virtue" has great affinity with "value" used as an abstract noun. In educational ethics, as we have seen, we do speak of value of teaching ethics as a part of our duty or social obligation or contributing to formation of virtuous character. Similarly, we speak of the *ethicality* of teaching ethics in the sense that it is our duty or obligation or contributing to virtue formation.

In the philosophical usages, the term "value" is also used as a *positive* parameter, the *negative* of which is "disvalue". In this sense, "nuisance" cannot be a value of a person because however useful he or she can be, it is a "disvalue", whereas its negation amounts to mean what is good or of worth. Sometimes, we do speak of 'having *neutral* value', that is, bereft of both the above parameters. Hence, teaching *about* Nazi morality to students does have some 'value', but its systematic use for character formation is a 'disvalue' in "educational ethics", though teaching Nazi-age school uniforms might be "neutral" in value when it comes to educational ethics but *not* so in "education".

Hence, things that are of value, disvalue and neutral value in educational ethics are not the same in education. Philosophers like R.B. Perry used the term "value" in an extremely wide sense as a *generic noun*, that is, as *critical* or *evaluative predicates*, which are in contrast to the descriptive or factual ones. However, C.I. Lewis used it in a much restricted sense, that is, true of some *pro and con predicates*. The sense in which Perry philosophically used the notion "value" amounts to "realms of value" or a "genus of value", which includes numerous 'pro and con predicates', not factual in nature. The narrower sense of "value" can be well rolled in the evaluative term "good", which is extremely crucial in ethical writings, as well as in educational ethical literature. Though as a generic notion it covers arts, science, religion, politic and many other things. The genus "good" naturally covers many "forms of goodness", for instance, "what is useful" or simply "utility" or "duty". This further takes us to what is *intrinsically* good, what is *extrinsically* good and *contributory* good. Education as *good* may be thus seen as either having either "use value" or "intrinsic value" or "extrinsic value". Educational ethics as *good* may be understood as a good itself or good for such and such reasons. In ethics, we often use the dichotomy to mean what is *good as an end* and *good as a means*. Educational ethics as good may be thus justified good as end or means or both. Nevertheless, John Dewey who has contributed substantially in educational philosophy disagrees with the dichotomous classification of good as end and means because for him the "value on the whole" or "goodness on the whole" is of greater importance. Hence, education as well as educational ethics may be well conceived as "good on the whole", when we consider all relevant aspects of the desirable or worth. However, not all would agree with Dewey because they argue that distinguishing goodness of certain things is of great importance. Hence, there may be a separate consideration of *technical good* of vocational education, *utilitarian good* of engineering education or medical education, *welfaristic good* of environmental education and so on. In this sense, (much like what Von Wright advocated), different consideration of good of a thing helps us in understanding the distributive sense of "good" than the more generic sense or the "whole of good". D. Ross would prefer to concentrate on *human values* in particular, when he speaks of values in terms of moral values, value of being a virtuous person, value of having good motives and intentions and good character. Educational ethics viewed from Von Wright's perspective might have a utilitarian or welfare value. However, from the perspective of Ross education and educational ethics is not teleological or to be clearer, utilitarian good rather they must be intrinsically good. However, any consideration of value of an educated person should refer to his or her moral goodness, deontic virtues and good intentions and character.

More than this, the term "value" is used in the philosophical parlance as *concrete noun*, that is, a specific thing judged to be valuable or thought to be valuable or *desired*. It is in this sense that cultural relativists would speak of different *cultural values*, of our, their and so on. It focuses the goodness of something within specific cultures, which people think or desire to be of worth or value. However, not always in our cultures do we speak of what we think or regard as good rather, what has value irrespective of cultural prejudices. This asserts what things in *essence* are good or valuable or desirable. When we consider the cases of "education" and "educational ethics", we may have opinions of cultures of such things regarded as valuable or are good. To think that educational ethics is good as per our cultural trends is one thing and to think it good irrespective of such trends, is another thing. This tension between what is culture dependent value and what is not conceals the truth that for some of us value or goodness is relative whereas for others it is absolute. For some of us it is *subjective* whereas for others it is *objective*. People like Plato, Bradley, Kant and many others have imagined something in or outside this world, which are absolute values or are objective in the unique "ontological" sense, as if, they "exist", and we are able to *know* this truth by virtue of intuitive experience. However, thinkers like J.L. Mackie thinks that there are "no objective values" in the sense that nothing is ontologically a value. Nothing in or outside the world "exists" which we "know" as valuable and nothing but valuable. There are other thinkers like Hume and Westermarck who argue differently. They hold that all values are nothing but *objectification* of our attitudes, emotions, feelings, desires and so on. Hence, *all* values are "subjective" in a unique psychological sense. Despite such differences, people like R.M. Hare reminds us that we tend to forget a simple truth that something can be valuable both objectively and subjectively. Much like this has been argued by James Rachels when he justifies that though there are culture dependent values, which broadens our mind, there are still objective values, which we need to respect. Extending this to education and educational ethics we get that though there is nothing unethical to believe that religious communities should hold on to the programme of religious indoctrination in their institutions for they have their needs and reasons to do so, others are equally ethically grounded to believe that religious indoctrination is a matter for serious ethical scrutiny in our societies full of non-religious people or even if people are religious, such teachings in institutions should be ethically challenged. Hence, we can either accept that something is absolutely valuable in religious teaching or that is not the case because cultural relativism would not allow us to stick to any such value. However, we may argue differently to say that though religious teachings have absolute value in religious institutions, they need not forget the cultural truth that not all are religious, not all institutions are religious and not all religious people prefer religious institutions for studies. Hence, something is both objectively as well as relatively valuable in education and educational ethics. Those who hold on to the view that "value" need not be objectified by whim has a strong point to make because any amount of our wish or desire does not turn something to be desirable or valuable. Moreover, as Scheler and Hartmann have said "value" is like "colour", it does not stand *as an* object rather used to *qualify* an object in unique way. In this sense, something *carries* a value but is *not* "value". As such, "education" *per se* is not value rather "a value" or, it *has* a value, which is a simple evaluation of "education" on certain basis. Similarly, "educational ethics" is not embodied as value; rather it is found to be of some value by us. If this be true, both education and educational ethics open a can of problems for us because both may be logically evaluated by us on other bases as "disvalues". This challenges our earlier assertion that by any fertile imagination both things cannot be "disvalues", which we should still hold on to because without calling them as embodiments of value, we may argue that "value" itself loses any significance without concrete reference. So when we call them valuable, it is not that we objectify them as such (wrongly so) or that we evaluate them absolutely as such on whim (wrongly so), rather be explained in terms of "education" and "educational ethics". Still we have strong natural as well as non-natural evidences, which weigh more on logical strength than the same evidences available to the relativists, who argue that "Education and educational ethics may be disvalues at times". Hence, to say that these are values and not disvalues by any imagination is an absolutist opinion of such things, which demands whim than evidences. Well, we cannot overlook the fact that many people do argue that education and educational ethics are disvalues because educated people often exploit other people who are either uneducated or educated, which is itself a bad thing to do. Therefore, these things as means to exploitations are disvalues (or evil or bad). Similarly, educational ethics is a disvalue because many evil questions are put by it, for instance, whether religious education is at all ethical? There may be a number of such arguments in our mind which we imagine counts heavily against education and educational ethics having a value. It is due to this that our evaluative assertion: "education is *per se* good and not bad", is invalid. Interesting is to note that when educated people do not exploit or do not put anti-religious questions necessarily and always, following the same argument above we prove that the assertion: "education is bad and not good" must be invalid. If the assertion is a flexible one accommodating some value it would be like this: "education is not always a value, rather a disvalue as well." In this case, any evidence in favour of education as valuable or not, will be redundant for an absolute claim. Following this, all evidences which are commonly provided in favour of any absolute evaluation of education in reality justifies the last claim, which is a relative one. Hence, taking clue from what Hare and Rachels says, education must have *a relative value*. However, I still say that on natural and non-natural grounds we can justify that "education is a value and not disvalue" because the strength of our justification as based on evidences weigh more than those having a relative value claim. Hence, not everything should be said to be both valuable and disvalue if we believe Rachels in particular because what Rachels says finally is that not all things have relative values, there are absolute and objective values as well that outweighs relativism. The question is what are our so-called outweighing evidences? The simple evidence is that what some educated and illiterate people do (for instance, exploit people), does not necessarily and sufficiently justify whether education (or educational ethics) is in fact, disvalue because *natural events* testifies clearly that it is not education, educating, receiving education and having enough education which exploits or aims at exploitation or things like that rather, those who claim to have received education *use* their educational skills *unethically and anti-socially* to exploit and so on. Further, non-naturally speaking (that is, not drawing from natural events), our common sense and our ordinary rationality justifies that education and educational ethics *per se* cannot be disvalue because all by itself it never aims to do certain things which are evil. Rather going by its nature and subject matter our common sense and rationality tells us that what they aim at are valuable and never valueless. It is due to this that first of all I discussed in details the nature and aims of education and educational ethics. It is a matter of great tragedy, therefore, to imagine that when we become bad, education becomes bad, that is, education does not have good value all by its nature and tasks rather it depends on what educated people do, as if when they 'do good', education *gets a value* and when they 'do badly', education gets *a disvalue*. Can colour be bad if some people splash notoriously harmful hues in the event of *holi*? Thus, we shall maintain that "education and educational ethics *per se* is good and never bad". This is an 'objective value claim'. Yes, in nature, some conglomeration of events called educating outweighs other evidences that make it relatively valuable. Education is 'out there in the world' as *a value phenomena* (the same is with educational ethics). It is also important here to note that in value judgements such as "educational ethics is good and never bad" is not without a reason. Hence, the desirability or worth of educational ethics necessarily begs some bases of evaluation, which we shall turn shortly but before that let us see briefly about the kinds of moral or ethical judgements, called 'moral value judgements'.

Some moral judgements may be called judgements of moral duty or obligation or simply, *deontic* judgements, whereas some others are judgements of moral value or *aretaic* judgements. The first type of moral judgements tells us that some actions are morally obligatory on us or are our duties and therefore, they should or should not be done. Whereas the second type of moral judgements does not consider particular actions for evaluation rather evaluates moral agents, their motives, intentions, characters and so on as morally good or bad, virtuous or vicious. The crux of the issue is that in both the judgements, we need some bases for evaluation. They are essentially different evaluations as in one, we are concerned mainly with *intentional human* enterprises for moral evaluation, whereas in the other we judge humans for their moral worth. Both these moral judgements have in common the need for specific "moral" grounds for evaluation. This is, however, not the case with judgements of non-moral value because in this case, on several grounds other than the moral ones, we judge or evaluate different things, facts, experiences of simple natural things for their worth. In this regard, if we judge for moral worth of several things like books or pens or pleasure, we call them judgements of non-moral value, and when we judge particular or common obligations and duties like suggestions for going to classical concert or walking a mile after dinner, they are called judgements of non-moral obligations. In any case, all non-moral judgements beg basis of judgement or evaluation. Hence, moral, and non-moral judgements too cannot be non-rational or irrational or without a point. Coming to educational ethics, judgement for its worth is judgement of worth of human enterprises. Evaluating educational ethics as good in the "deontic" sense, gives us suggestions about what we should do or what is obligatory on us or what is our duty. It tells us that though humans or moral agents are involved in a specific academic activity done with some clear aims and intentions, it primarily judges worth of what is done in educational ethics that is its deontic moral value. Only derivatively we can say that aretaic moral worth of persons involved in such specific academic activity is also important. It is very interesting to go through what W.K. Frankena puts succinctly in his work *Ethics* (1989). Frankena holds that we call something as having 'moral value' when that thing is good on moral grounds, whereas things good on non-moral grounds, that is, non-moral values should clarify which things are they. Frankena names at least six of them, such as *utility values*, that is, things that are good for their usefulness; *extrinsic value*, that is, things that are good as means to an end; *inherent values*, that is, experiences of contemplating things that are good in themselves or good owing to their own properties; *contributory values*, that is, things that are good in so far as they contribute to the inherently good life and *final values* or *end values*, that is, things that are good on the whole not in parts[1]. In this sense, a "pleasurable life" has non-moral value when it is called good, whereas a "morally good life", which may be a life of performing unconditional duty, is different from it. An "educated life" must be called valuable or good only in this non-moral sense if it is merely useful or good as means to yet another thing or experience of contemplating it is rewarding or contributes to inherent good life or good on the whole. More often than not "educated life" is valued on such non-moral grounds. When we come to "education", we value it differently on non-moral grounds, for instance, education is usefully good and so on. The same may be true of 'educational ethics' as a part of the enterprise called 'education'. Hence, "educational ethics" as intentional human enterprise may be judged on moral grounds though it is not awkward to judge them on non-moral grounds. Nevertheless, we have still not justified the moral value of educational ethics, that is, value of the enterprise on moral grounds, though we have some idea that the enterprise is valuable or good on different moral and non-moral grounds. For instance, it has been said that educational ethics is good because it is a highly useful enterprise or it is a good means to achieve the end of a flourishing character and so on. Hence, no one can really prevent us from non-moral evaluation of "educational ethics" even if it not a thing but an intentional human enterprise, but we can still evaluate it as good and not bad on ethical grounds, or moral grounds; for instance, we can say that "educational ethics is good" because its goodness is based on the ground that it is obligatory or duty on our part as humans to participate in such an enterprise. In this sense, even if there are tensions in showing why the enterprise is non-morally good, to which we largely disagree; we say that irrespective of these, the enterprise is valuable *per se*, that is, given its aims and tasks, it is good itself on deontic grounds irrespective of the purposes and benefits it may have. It is extremely important to justify the goodness of educational ethics on moral grounds, therefore. This is one way in which education and educational ethics is "morally good" but there may be other grounds as well. To repeat, no one can prevent us from judging the goodness of educational ethics on teleological grounds and even on non-moral grounds.

There are two ways in which we can further discuss about "value" and evaluation. In the example, "educational ethics is good" something is interesting when we see that a theory of "value" and "evaluation" is needed here to find out *what has a value* and why, and the much needed theory is *normative* in nature, that is, it speaks of an ideal or a standard taken to be valuable on its own, most of the time as ideal of human enterprise. In this sense, educational ethics as a human enterprise is valued as "good" if and only if we have an ideal or norm, which is supposedly paradigm for the said enterprise to attain. In the same statement is implicit the need of other theories which become the basis of answering different set of questions. These theories answer the queries of meaning of "value", "valuation", "good", "desirable" and so on. For this, we need non-normative or rather *metaethical theories*. It is interesting to note that thus far, we were engaged in analysing the meaning of "value" and "valuation" but we might take up other metaethical tasks regarding the statement in consideration. If we take this seriously, the justification or logic of the bases of evaluation makes great sense. Then we do not worry about why "educational ethics" at all 'has a value' or why should we pass such an evaluative judgement, we are rather worried about a basic thing:

Does the language as stated above make any sense? If it does, why at all? We are worried to know what "good" means than what it is. If this be the case then the problem about justification of "educational ethics as good than evil", is seen in a new light. Rather than falling in the controversy that evaluation of educational ethics as good on *naturalistic norms* can be replaced by a *deontic norm* to call it good, we can say that both the evaluative statements may be analysed for their truth and meaning on non-normative bases. We may say that these evaluative judgements do not justify anything in reality or in fact because they simply tell us how differently the concepts of "value" or "good" and "disvalue" or "evil" may be used in relation to another concept "educational ethics" and still be meaningful. It tells us why on earth "educational ethics" may be logically used with both "good" and "evil". Another interesting point is to justify that "educational ethics is a disvalue", is meaningless because the *use* of "disvalue" with educational ethics is improper whereas the *use* of "value" with it is proper. To state this is to argue that certain notions expressing the sense of an intentional human enterprise as 'educational ethics' cannot be sensibly used along with some notions like 'unworth' or 'disvalue' because using them is not against any grammatical convention rather, against the simple logical rule that two things need not be confused if they belong to different categories. "Disvalue" belongs to a category which should not be used illogically with something (educational ethics), which belongs to the category of "value". Hence, "educational ethics is a disvalue" is a *grammatical expression* not conveying logical necessity. It is a logical fallacy to confuse these categories. Rather, the expression "educational ethics is a value and not a disvalue", does not involve category confusion. But two questions remain — even if this explanation appears to be good we may ask: How *do* we *know* that "educational ethics" belongs to the category of value and thus, using "disvalue" with it is a confusion? Is this a mere presumption, which is itself confusion or does it have any basis? We may ask, even if we come to see that the statement is true, do we see why at all it is meaningful? To answer the first question, the metaethical theory of *intuitionism* states that we may directly know the 'truth' of the above statement. Or else, we may say that the intrinsic goodness of education (but not evilness), is intuitively known. However, many people do not want a queer presumption in the name of intuition. Hence, the argument is that we have to fall back on *human nature* toeing the position taken by Hume and Westermarck to hold that the "truth" of educational ethics as value and not disvalue is not an objectively true assertion rather humans in accordance with their nature, *describes* their *states of mind* in evaluative assertion like these which are thus subjectively true and meaningful. Through these assertions they do not mean to prove anything valuable or a value rather describes what they feel about an enterprise such as educational ethics. This is one form of meta-normative *subjectivism*. However, later on thinkers like Ayer said that truly, the truth of such evaluative assertions are neither assertions of objective values nor are they subjective predilection or description of emotions of users of that language, rather they are *expressions of emotions* of users of such language. Stevenson thinks that evaluative assertions are *causative factors* for *evoking emotions* of others who listen to such language or disagrees or agrees with them. Further, Hare said that not merely expressing emotions, such language *prescribes* us to do certain things than other things. In one way, they are imperatives in an evaluative discourse. Hence, we have many ways to justify that "educational ethics is good and not bad" is a not a mere presumption of intrinsic nature of a value and thus rules out the category of 'disvalue' rather it has nothing to do with any such objective presumptions. The language is true and meaningful on other than grammatical conventions though use of components of language in evaluative contexts is the key to its truth and meaning. The language is true and meaningful under the *speech acts*. This covers both the questions raised above and avoids intrigues of category confusion. In this sense, irrespective of whether "educational ethics is bad and not good", the assertion is true and meaningful on what function the language performs in evaluative context. However, we cannot deny that improper description of "educational ethics" might lead us to wrongly 'use' disvalue with it for expressing emotions and/or prescribing a course of action because it is crucial to understand the *descriptive meaning* of "educational ethics" very well before we express or command or whatever in evaluative language. A proper "description" of the subject is thus vital to realize why "value" rather than "disvalue" should qualify "educational ethics", and this is possible when the tasks of educational ethics are clear to us.

The use of "value" as verb in case of evaluation as discussed above provides a hint towards the treatment of "value" as concept, which, when used, influences us in choosing things which are good as means, ends, useful and so on. In this sense, we find the behavioural aspect of "value". It is important to note that value as influencing choice focuses two important factors, the "individual" and the "alternatives" available to individuals. Clearly, if something is morally or non-morally valuable or good or desirable, it has its own power to suggest some conscious beings that rather than neglecting them in the course of one's life of choice and action, they should be preferred and picked up so that quality-of-life and quality-of-work-life are guaranteed. Values thus enable us to behave as sane individuals. Even young children, gets a chance to activate their common sense and reason to find out why doing something is good or valuable and thus better than doing the opposite. However, the glaring problem is, how sane people with common sense (particularly younger ones), know that "This is a value" or "These are disvalues"? Further, the problem of choosing a course of an action comes to the fore. There are several answers to these stiff problems of which most important is the *agent-centred solutions*, that is, we may say that a value does not itself compel us to behave in a way through a choice among alternative, it is *we* who do so. Hence, the 'behavioural' reply needs to be agent-centred. The crucial issue of our choice must, therefore, boil down to our intuition or practical reason or conscience or the Voice of God in us or common sense or will or wisdom. If this be so, our internal dispositions (any one or more) enable us to behave as we should or to choose a good (a value) and thus demonstrate that we act in accordance with our unique dispositions while we choose a good. We thus have many theories of choice of moral value or other values, which are bases to justify why an individual is incited by an idea of a value. On the other hand, there are theories which do not believe that individuals' idea of a value are expressed in behaviour, that is, behaviour testifies an idea of a good. The *non-agent centred view* holds that something is itself capable to incite in us an idea of its value or goodness, which we pick up naturally for our reason demands to pick them up or simply we are compelled to do so or we think it is prudent to do so or it is beneficial to us or it is appreciated. Hence, individuals themselves do not discover value in something and thus choose and behave properly, values are 'telling on them' all by themselves and they thus choose and behave properly. In any case, "behaviour" remains an empirically observable fact to testify either that we had an idea of a good or that we were given an idea of a good. Inherent in this controversy is whether values are *subjective* or *objective*, though "subjective" does not necessarily imply that we create value. We cannot disagree that in many instances thinkers believe that we create values or objectify values owing to our *nature* or *wish* or *desire* or *feeling*. More problems crop up now. Are values truly so-called when we objectify them? Do values depend on moral agents? Many people ask who else will find them other than the individuals? Values, they hold, are surely discovered or found by individuals. There are thus as many values as we discover them, none of them can be disvalue. Or, disvalues are also our discoveries and they are like that as we found them to be. In such cases, my values and disvalues are only mine, they cannot be *their,* and their *values* and *disvalues* are not mine, and that both of us have found them, we cannot question each other. Alternately, values are *given to us* so are disvalues. We just cannot question their absolute truth because they are not ours. In this sense, it is not my reason or wish that has 'made' religion valuable; it is a religion, whose value enabled me to accept religion. But how do we know why religion is epitome of value or genocide is disvalue? Because without this knowledge we just accept values and disvalues by whim and that bereft us of our free will and rationality, which are so important in active life. Answer to this might take us right back to our *intuition*, *wish, and conscience and so on*, which is again a return to the individuals. Another way may be that certain values and disvalues just influence us, for which no justifications are needed, they are *sacrosanct*. Religion in this sense is a 'sacrosanct a value'; it cannot be an 'opiate of the mass'. Or else, if no justification are really needed, it is a palpable evil being an 'opiate of the mass', we need not ask further.

If choice and actions are testimonies to 'a value', how do we really prove that this is at all true? This is to ask: Why at all should there be a logical relation between "a value" and "patterns of human behaviour"? Why should conception of "value" *imply* "patterns of behaviour"? On the other hand, we may ask, why "patterns of behaviour" does not imply "value"? Let us take the first case; even if we accept for the time being that "educational ethics" is good or a value, does it imply that it evokes us to adopt a pattern or patterns of behaviour? There must not be any logical necessity to find one on the basis of the other. Even if education or educational ethics were good, many people are not evoked by its inherent suggestive and/or compelling power to start getting educated or indulge in educational ethical enterprise. Though we were clearly 'seeing' that educational ethics is a good for us, critiques argue that it will remain so even if we were not indulged in taking it up. However, others say that the "desirable" nature of educational ethics does imply that there is at least one person in the world who *desires* the desirable or the good, that is, *does something* as testimony to the existence of the good. Hence, behaving in one way is implied by a value. Still, many others refute this logical claim to say that though none knows beforehand that educational ethics is a good, as we were not told before attending a course or we did not have least idea about what it really meant, we cannot imply patterns of behaviour from desirability of educational ethics, its desirability is a matter for our scrutiny and gradual discovery. Then, the other way round, patterns of behaviours must imply a value, that is, in this case, *choosing* educational ethics as a serious enterprise and *doing* what is required thereafter implies that such chosen enterprise is a good. In this sense, our desire justifies that the desired thing is desirable or a value. Critique says that it cannot be the case because any amount of our choice and action cannot logically justify that the chosen and the done is good. Hence, the behaviourist analysis of value has many epistemological, ontological and logical questions to face. It may well be that a concept of "value" for its *meaning clarification* does not at all depend on what mental effects the concept produces on humans or what physical effects bear on the concept. Trying to know what "value" means (as different from what values are), depends on its various changes in different fields than making the concept human centred or a queer object. In fact, many among us nurture a palpable misconception that "values" are for "value orientation", that is, the concept of value is the *causative factor*, which has its impact on human mind. This is to forget that a concept cannot be a cause *per se* that orients us to pick up what it presses on us. Stevenson earlier had this notorious idea that moral language causes emotional changes in us. The truth may be that the proponents of this idea have in mind not value-concept rather *a thing called a value* or something which has been labelled as a value. It is in this sense that educational ethics designated as a value (as an enterprise, not a concept), which is thought of as having effects and *orients* us to pick up things which are good, such as being involved in essential activities (behaviour patterns that follows). It is one thing then to know about the concept of "educational ethics" which is *said to have a value* and another thing to imagine it *as* a *value*, the former is a matter for language analysis without any causative effect such as orientation, whereas the latter, only when accepted to be true, that is, in fact "a value" (for which I argued at one place), might have any effect on humans. However, I will still not remark on the likelihood of "orientation" because now I am not concerned about what it really amounts to. Hence, values taken as a matter effect, that implies patterns of behaviour, is a matter for careful logical scrutiny. Similarly, whether values can and should be used by us to orient character is a challenging question. Closely related to this is the challenge of "inculcation of values", to which we shall come later on.

Nevertheless, educational ethics have something to do with "facts", that is, facts constitute an important aspect in educational ethics, which we have said, is "a value" and not disvalue. A sweeping remark is needed first in order to correlate facts, values and educational ethics. We are not considering now "value" as concepts rather we are trying to correlate the ways in which both facts and values find a role in educational ethics after harping about great value of the same. First, let us take the case of education. In its wider sense, which I earlier called 'non-formal' or 'unofficial', almost everything around us might educate us. Here, the role of human reason and intuition are not enough because it is said that "nature" is a great educator. Many people have the idea that nature educates us only in an extremely qualified and not broad sense because it can really educate us in 'scientific' matters. The gross nature and its teeming changes are educative in the strict sense of 'science-education', the positive and the social science in the main. However, this is a misconception when we consider the importance of what goes around us in nature with regard to non-scientific education as well, where non-scientific is not unscientific rather, "other than the sciences, positive and social". We easily forget that education in logic, ethics and aesthetic along with many other things form the huge body of "philosophy", which is not unscientific but non-scientific. Further, we have the liberal arts, the different language education and axiological education of values. All these normative and liberal studies are not conceivable without deep relation with what things are around us or what happens around us because it is in nature that we thrive, experience, acquire knowledge, reason, think to generalize, abstract and so on. To be specific, let us take the case of moral education, value-education and education of educational ethics, which are believed to be education in its relatively "narrower" sense, not in the above broad sense in which John Dewey took education to be, but we shall return to it. Civilized people involved in the enterprise of education and in any of its branch, are involved in educating, teaching, training and so on. These enterprises are necessarily influenced by natural things, events, facts, and phenomena because human enterprises simply cannot be out of these things even if they strongly wish to do so. Let us consider value-education first but with a qualification that it does not include teaching any kind of scientific value and natural values like value of environment. Perhaps we are left with many other values like aesthetic, moral, logical to educate. Aesthetic values are for sure not beyond this world because the concept of "beauty" cannot be necessarily and sufficiently described entirely without a reference to the world or we may call nature. It is a matter of common sense that "beauty" is not the same as "abstract beauty", beauty and appreciation of beauty is not necessarily and sufficiently of abstract things, though "beauty" itself may be a non-natural and abstract concept not synonymous to natural beings and things. Beauty being a non-natural concept does not prevent us to analyse for its meaning on natural grounds. In this sense, we speak of not only beautiful ideas, beautiful thoughts but of beautiful painting, beautiful acting and so on. Interestingly, can ideas and thoughts be beautiful without ideas and thoughts of something in and around us? It can be because we may have beautiful ideas in a novel or a poem, which do not exist in nature or beautiful thought of living in the seventh heaven. But all ideas are not like that, many of them are grounded in reality, in this world. Hence, the very idea of some values may be rooted in us but without nature's existences, they are non-existent because for idea of such values we need among other things, idea of natural values, which consists among other thing the ideas of a valuable life and a life of values. Truly, ideas are not things or facts, but ideas of something have components related to our life and world most often than not. Hence, even if there are abstract ideas, which are unrelated to facts, that do not prove that, therefore, all ideas are unrelated to facts. When we come to the idea of values, it must be abstract in nature but values themselves need not necessarily and sufficiently be thought as merely abstract and unrelated to facts or nature. To be precise, aesthetic ideas may be abstract but many aesthetically relevant values unlike pure ideas or abstractions are related to facts, where 'facts' are 'natural facts'. Nevertheless, what we have argued does not prove that values like aesthetic values are nothing but facts. No one prevents us to say that such values are related to facts and thus become sensible to us.

Coming to the logical values which appears to be abstract in nature and thus unrelated to facts, we find that this may not necessarily and sufficiently be the case because logic is simply not a body of formal rules, it is something more, and its values are simply not those of formal values, truth value and so on rather consists of pragmatic value of being logical, thinking, judging, evaluating, and arguing logically. It involves logic of a discourse and heuristic understanding and informal logic, which are all supported by what things are around us. Logic cannot be conceived as completely divorced from our life and world, as mathematics is not. One should be careful here to notice that as I am not proving that facts justify aesthetic beauty or justifies logical rules or *vice versa*; hence, there is no logical fallacy such as the naturalistic fallacy.

When we come to moral values, the same may be the case because morality is closely related to active human life in the world. The moral value and moral virtue like being "dutiful" for instance, are directly related to our active intentions followed by decisions in autonomy to do what is to be done for the goodness of doing it. Hence, the universal *principle of duty* may be abstract in nature but the conception of duty is not. Even a proper *explanation* (not logical definition) of the concept "duty" cannot be without natural aids. For instance, to make us believe what is a duty, no great intuition is needed rather, simple natural description of telling a truth without any idea of what follows as a consequence, that is, as an intrinsic worth would be good enough. Real life instances, as we often cite also help us knowing what it amounts to. It is very difficult for me to imagine moral values, having nothing to do with either life in the world or facts. Again, this does not mean that moral values are to be logically defined in terms of facts rather; a proper explanation of any conceivable moral value or *a moral value* needs aid of facts. The conception of moral should or ought or desirable, are all *related* to facts. Something interesting is said when people argue that a moral value is essentially abstract because it is nothing but *metaphysical* or *spiritual* in nature. Inherent idea may be that such moral values are completely unrelated to facts. Simple logic states that when two things belong to categories essentially different from each other, one cannot be the same as the other though in some sense they may be related somehow. Hence, a 'relation' between religious or spiritual ideals and morality does not justify that the relation is either real or the things are equivalent. Morality as we have seen is not at all equivalent to spirituality and religion by any degree of imagination. Morally relevant education does not take up in its field of either discussions of nature, kinds and number of fundamental reality or discussion of such entities as the core of human life and/or world. It may be argued that normative ethics, as we know it, does discuss about highest ideal of human life as spiritual in nature, which is thus fundamental to moral life. It is not difficult to find this in the normative ethics of Plato, Bradley, Christian theists and many others. However, normative ethics is not a body of such ideals alone; it is something more. In fact, such ideals are *non-moral* in nature and we do argue that whether its justification as a moral ideal is at all logically sound. Why should morality beg a basis, which is beyond it? Hence, moral values cannot be equivalent to religious and/or spiritual values though in stray cases, there may be some 'relation' which is either fictitious or insufficient to justify the equivalence of these categories. To make a list of "moral values" for inculcation in the name of "moral education" or "value education" or "value based education" is too common a feature now, but I am sorry to say that these popular notions about moral and value education are completely unfounded. First of all, as we said, "moral values" are not the same as "metaethical or religious or spiritual values", and for that matter educating in moral values cannot be the same as dealing in "spiritual" values. "Value education" as we know it is educational enterprise dealing with what are worthwhile such as the moral, non-moral, material, biological, economic and other worthwhile things. Hence, "value education" is *not* the same as what we say "moral education". Without repeating what consists of "moral or ethical education" or simply ethics education, we assert that "value education" might include among other things, education of ethical values or moral values but it is not the same as ethics. It is clear that education of moral values is only a part of "value education". "Value-based education" is different from "value education" in so far as the former means and educational enterprise taking up "basing" values, mostly "human values" in humans as core programme. Or, it may mean an educational enterprise that takes up many subjects to be taught formally but always "basing" them in the broader context of "worth" or "values", that is, subjects in consideration take on issues keeping an eye on what questions of "worth" makes sense with regard to those issues. It also means an educational enterprise that focuses on the "inculcation" of many relevant values, human values being chief among them. In any sense, such education is not the same as either ethics education or value education or even religious or spiritual education. It is not ethics education because ethics education essentially need not aim at inculcation of ethical values to learners, though in the course of such education one might pick up some values. It is not value education because value-based education is just a part of value education or education of axiological values, not the whole of it. It is not spiritual education either because "value-based education" does not keep an eye only on spiritual value basing, though the latter may be a part of it. Hence, ethics education, value education, value-based education and spiritual education are essentially different but most of them may be related. To say, therefore, that "moral or ethical education" is what is "spiritual education, which is the same as value education or value-based education is not to understand these categories at all. I am still not coming to the point whether "value-based education" *can and should* try to base values in learners, though this point is important.

Let us ask, even if moral education is not the same as value-based education, is it not desirable that it should be like that? Is it not important that ethics education, if is it ethical, should be spiritual as well as value based? Well, moral education poses some problems for many among us because the term "moral" for its vagueness is taken necessarily as dealing with what is right and good for human beings according to some rules laid down by authorities such as religious, social, political and so on or as based on traditions and customs of particular societies. I have already said that "moral" should not be taken in this way because it is always important to evaluate whether authoritative and dogmatic moral opinions amounts to "moral". In the common ethical parlance, we have the habit of writing "morality" meaning thereby *philosophical study* of morality, knowing it fully well that in philosophy we need not study "morality" in the narrow sense in which it is often used. No one has given us the task of unphilosophical study of morality and no one can prevent us in criticising the same study on different grounds. Taking this to be true, we can sensibly interchange "ethical" for "moral". Now that we know what the 'tasks' of ethics (and now morality) are, we have seen that it is not the same as those taken up in the general study of value, value-based education, educational ethics, spiritual education and spiritual ethics. Taking some risk of repetition for clarity, ethics as such may be treated as a part of general study of value because here we deal in ethical (or moral) value, but they are not the same. Educational ethics on the other hand is an ethical study of particular nature, so ethics and educational ethics cannot be one and the same. Spiritual or metaphysical ethics is also a particular ethical study within ethics, and, therefore, they cannot be one and the same things. Value education is within education specially dealing with the study of relevant values, which we are expected to know for different purposes, and for that matter it includes knowledge of ethical values. We may also know about educational values or values of education, though knowing about values in education forms only a part of it. Understood in this sense, value-education is far from being similar to ethics or moral philosophy or loosely stated, a study of morality. Spiritual education is also within education dealing specially in different aspects of spirituality and its values, which is again by no extent of imagination same as ethics or morality. The ideas that 'morality is spirituality' or 'morality should be nothing but spirituality' or 'morality has no significance without spirituality' are to my mind all whims and not rational because two evidently different subject matters cannot be one and the same. To argue that after all morality teaches us to attain a spiritual *summum bonum* in life and/or to obey commands of spiritual authorities is to confuse "morality" as a study of uncritical dogmas of right and wrong, which begs something other than itself. Ethics or moral philosophy about which we are more interested here does not for the first place discuss only about *summum bonum* of human life, which is only spiritual, it does many other things which spiritual study does not. Most interesting is that an ethicist might remain *secular in the critical analysis* of relevance of spiritual ethics and spiritual education. Even if ethicists are devout religious persons, they remain non-religious in spirit when they take up a critical task, which is best for them to do. Metaethics, practical ethics, environmental ethics has least or nothing to do to lead us to the spiritual good or rather spiritualisation. In fact, education and spiritualisation are different goals; the former does not necessarily and sufficiently take up the latter. It is important, therefore, to note that though ethics *can* be easily equated to many other things, which it is not, we should not do what is needless. When education is not essentially spiritualisation or when ethics is not essentially the same, though a few ethical studies are spiritual, the whole of ethics *should* not be so. Hence, to understand and make people understand that when ethics in some sense, 'can' be close to spirituality, it should be so, and thus ethics is spirituality, is not only a poor argument, it is an unethically oriented argument for it does what it should not do. Finally, drawing some sense from what has been said, value-based education for the first place cannot be the same as ethics education or moral education when "moral" need not be taken in its old sense; moral education need not be taken as moral science as well, which is so popular among theists in particular, because it is spiritually oriented, which 'moral philosophy' or 'ethics' is not. Moral philosophy and ethics deem it useful and sensible that education should take care of values, among which are included 'moral values'. It hopes that education does not go in vain, it should among many good things to achieve, make educated people caring about moral values in real life situations. It does not have any apathy to devout spirituality and even spiritualisation by spiritual people of those who voluntary deem it good, though itself it does not and should not do such things because people of ethics are not spiritual saints, they should not take that role as when they deal in ethics. Ethics as a theoretical and practical enterprise in philosophy does not and should not include saintly people making people saints. Among many "tasks" of ethics, this is not its task. Nobody has really given ethical philosophers this typically difficult job of spiritualisation even if some self-claimed ethicists advocate such things under 'spiritual and/or religious ethics'. Hence, education as based on values need close scrutiny for its meaning because to take it loosely 'as based on spiritual and/or religious values', which is nothing but 'moral or ethical values' is a weird realm of study. We have just seen that the major part of this assertion, that is, equivalence of spiritual and/or religious values and ethical values is completely unfounded, and to say further that "value basing" is just this (that is, the unfounded idea), must itself be unsound. Establishing unfounded ideas as valid is unethical apart from being irrational because it is intellectual dishonesty and intellectually wrong persuasion. Can 'value basing' be the same as indoctrination and inculcation of several or all values relevant for human beings in education? Is value-based education educating and inculcating all or many values in learners? Or, is it for a change, a unique enterprise in education and educating (as well as training) in which different questions of worth or good or value or what are value-oriented or value-laden, considered thoroughly for analysis and resolution? It is this moot issue which further enable us to justify why ethics education which is ethical, needs value-based education or even value-based education needs ethical values and yet both are not one and the same. This debate needs more elaboration, and for that, we enter into models of value-based education because it is the question of wrong models that leads us to justify that value-based education is ethics education in the spiritual/metaphysical sense of the term. The clarification of the debate is all the more important in the context of the great Indian hullabaloo about "value-based education" (as spiritual education) in the recent times because many among us have suddenly discovered that one Mr. Macaulay made us unethical (unspiritual) through his ways of education in India, which was erstwhile very ethical (spiritual) and today new *avatārs* of very ethical (spiritual) education will give us glory through "value-based education". Several seminars, symposia, debates and workshops are held to give this issue desired importance. A number of books have come up, more are expected to come up and a full-fledged deemed university of "value-based (*sic.* spiritual) education" may be the only fertile imagination which noble people just did not have. However, things are not so funny for noble and serious people speak of *universal values* found in religions to inculcate them. Hence, for many of us, "value-based education" is inculcation of a number of worthwhile or valuable elements or virtues in our character, not because we are characterless (Mr. Macaulay did not succeed in that because completely characterless nation cannot suddenly jump to pump values in us), rather we are lacking in a wholly good character. In any case, we are in hand a debate about what such education amounts to so that we can further (as ethicists) critically examine such education. In the final run I hope to be successful in explaining what "value-based education" is according to me and what should be the model of such education. Apart from these, we may expect to find out intricacies in *human-value-basing-education* and ethically relevant issues involved therein. Finally, something specific with regard to *virtue-based education* and its ethical aspects might be unravelled. Let us first start with the general nature of value-based education and its models in the broader context of general, human and spiritual value basing in major educational institutions. However, readers need not take this as discussion of nature and models of education of ethical values in schools and colleges. I would like to take this issue in a later chapter.

We have seen that an axiological theory of value considers a number of values to be of great importance, some of them most important from *human perspective*, that is, the values which humans *qua* humans should possess and not that the values which humans think are beneficial to them or what they believe are of their interest. Truly speaking it does not merely mean the values, which humans have in them from birth. Biological values, which we have, along with many psychological values does not completely explain the worth of humans as humans because most values *qua* humans are *acquired*, which we often call *virtues qua humans*. These virtues are those which we *should* have or are expected of us on ethiçal grounds. Hence, to say that man possesses values by birth is too imaginative, rather, man acquires worth with growth. In fact, the term "value" as we have seen does not only mean "intrinsic worth", it includes "worth" of a varied proposition, some of which with respect to humans amounts to "acquire them" and "expected of them". In this sense, "having an erect posture" for a quadruped, omnivorous in appetite, adaptive, reproductive without seasonal inhibition and so on are intrinsic to us, which are countless *psycho-physical* "values of humans", most of the time we do not expect that we 'should' *have* them rather we better 'keep them up' by our judicious efforts. Hence, balanced diet and restrained sex for humans are values specific to them so that they maintain what they 'have' by birth. Keeping intrinsic 'psycho-physical values' intact by sincere efforts are unique "human values". We know that orang-utans have many psycho-physical intrinsic values which we have, but they fail to educate themselves, to make flying machines, to fight diseases and so on, though they are successful in many ways to live in harmony with nature without any formal education like ours, which are values unique to them. The range of acquired values further tells us that some of them are *desirable* for us or morally desirable of us to have. Hence, we can be equally apt at living in harmony with nature with or without formal education and we *should* do that because we can deliberate on the desirability of value of harmonious living, which orangutans cannot. In this sense, humans have acquired a value to 'deliberate' on ethical aspects of living and educating whereas orangutans did not acquire. This does not debar orangutans from being ethical animals by *our* imagination but what we find ethical about them are mostly 'natural' to them — humans are not naturally ethical, they have acquired the virtue of being ethical. With all respect to those who believe that we differ with orangutans on the count of spirituality and therefore, "man is a spiritual animal", I beg to say that man *is not* a spiritual animal, rather some of them *have become* spiritual, many others are in the process and others left the same in ignominy or have left for its ignominy. To argue that man *is* spiritual because only they have acquired the quality of being ethical is a near foolish argument because ethicality is not spirituality. The list of acquired virtues or values of humans are enormous, not all can be assured by thoughtful persons to inculcate so easily, particularly if they come under the purview of formal education but that is a different story. Without taking much pain to give a list of such human values, we can say that some of them are 'social' in nature, whereas many others are individual or simply "personal". Humans as such have thus acquired many personal values such as striving to know different things and unravel mysteries, acquire social values such as just distribution of wealth for an equitable social life. For themselves, humans acquired the value of fulfilling their desires and needs and the value of helping others to fulfil their desires and needs. We can go on in this way to find many human values. Finally, we come to the values human beings should have, that is, what is morally expected of them to have whether they are beneficial to them or they have them or have acquired them. There is a hidden claim that irrespective of whether we have through the ages acquired many values, some may not be desirable of us to continue with. This is not true because there is clear logical contradiction in having and acquiring things that are valuable and at the same time to say that some of them may not be so and only some may be valuable or worthwhile. However, it may well be that we have many properties or capacities or abilities and acquired many of them, which however, on proper evaluations or careful deliberations on *ethical grounds* turned out to be *disvalue* or completely undesirable. This may be an ongoing moral scrutiny for values expected of humans to *pick up*. It is important to 'pick up' morally worthwhile things for us because they are not in us and for that reason should be acquired. In this sense, "morally worthwhile things" are acquired properties, which should nevertheless be acquired after moral scrutiny on moral basis. Education and educational ethics deals with such human values because education does not want to be value neutral, which is also the case with ethics and educational ethics. However, "dealing" with such matter does not necessarily amount to inculcate or teach these values. Many people believe that if education is not value neutral then it must deal with the theoretical and the practical aspects of values expected of humans to have, that is, it must analyse which values are desirable and *how* young and grown people should have these things as part of their character. Yet, there are others who do not believe that education should aim anything impossible and undesirable to do. We shall come to this issue at a proper place but for now we must clarify that there is perhaps little room for debate about whether ethics and educational ethics should take up the task of inculcation of human values because ethics *per se* has a practical function of a different type, which is, resolution of value-questions in education. In this book on educational ethics, it makes sense to discuss 'why' ethical values should be inculcated at all and 'which' among them should be taken up. Or, 'why' the entire idea of value inculcation is misconceived.

Taking note of these important aspects of the nature of human values in the context of value-based education, we should find out which human values are most desirable for us to have while we are engaged in an educational enterprise. Most educationists (Indians inclusive) believe that spiritual values (which covers both religious and metaphysical), need inculcation for individuals. To this, some add the value of satisfaction, pleasure, happiness, bliss, joy, entertainment and others, to be put simply under *self-regarding affective values*. More than these values, other values needing care are *self-regarding cognitive values* like *knowing* what is knowable, known, unknown, the unknowable or the mysterious, and which ought to be known and not to be known. Further, we have *self-regarding conative values* like, *doing* what are doable, done, undone, the undoable or the impossible and what are said not to be done. In the social category, we are expected further to take care of those human values which are *other regarding affective values*, *other regarding cognitive values* and *other regarding conative values*. In most cases what are other regarding values are not averse to self-regarding values stated above but in some cases, they might conflict. In such cases, the basic human value to *deliberate in association* becomes most important. Hence, there are *dialectical values*, which need care on moral grounds when self and other regarding values need an overriding 'cover-up value'. Now we can go on filling the baskets of all the categories mentioned above by simple act of thinking which values fall where, and soon we will find that the sorting is unending. This gives us an idea that it is not at all wise to make an absolute list of human values needing inculcation because there can be truly no such list. No one really wants to have some such thing may be the reply but we try to be specific at times. This must be avoided, as relativism in such matters is better off than absolutism because in social dialectics more often than not the filled up baskets are overturned after analysis of worth. It was believed not too earlier in history that students should go to hermits at hermitages or Academies for education of body, mind and spirit because this was believed to be of great value, which has changed radically now though not completely trashing them for ever. The tension of 'having-which-values' cannot make us steadfast in value perceptions in education. Perhaps, it is due to this that in value-based education the idea of *new values of* humans and *for* humans becomes so important in the context of theoretical scrutiny and inculcation, though old or original or *basic values* remain knocking for their care. Similarly, "our" values always knock our heads when "their" values are given more care. Traditionality, modernity and modernism along with regionalism and internationalism always were in tension in value-based education, each of them almost pointlessly heading for head on collision with others for their absolute worth in inculcation. This is a stifling social phenomenon, unavoidable so to say but can be managed very well if relativism and wisdom, power to shun bigotry and orthodoxy, and social dialectics are not forgotten. Hence, *status quo* in human value education is dangerous. The clarion call for exclusive Indian human value-based education must be a palpable bigotry, therefore, if this "Indian value-based education" is spiritually camouflaged, it is anarchic because it is unconstitutional in a "socialist, secular, democratic republic". If it is exclusively Hindu or Muslim or Christian value-based, it is *fundamentalist* and Nazi so to say.

Then we ask, which "new values" are so important for humans to have through education, if that is required?' Mr. N.M. Bhagia reports in his essay "New Values and Education" (1986) that "Our National Policy, (1968), calls for an emphasis on the development of science and technology"[2]. He further states that "awareness of environmental unity... has come to us in view of the enormous interconnected environmental issues which have made us to create, develop and cherish new values"[3]. He further stresses on "value to be economical in using resources", "to limit human population growth", "to restore the natural environment", "non-pollution in nature" and "cultural and religious tolerance" among "new values" to be incorporated in value-based education, most of which fit in our "self and other regarding cognitive and conative values". It is very interesting to note that many people now recognize the value of sex and love as "new values" in value-based education, where "love" has mundane connotation percolating to the exclusive man-woman level. The values of recognizing safe sex and love in dignity become all the more important at the face of the AIDS threat. Swami Yuktānanda writes in *Values and Ourselves* that sex and love are significant value components that work within the complex form of value-attitude-behaviour. Though sex and love are personal and behavioural concepts, as values they significantly affect both individual and social life. They are indeed very important in the formation of social norms. However, the Swami thinks that both sex and love have deeper transcendental significance as values, which is not new to us. However, many people say that the stated "new values" are all very old; they may be at best, "renewed values". Whatever they may be, human values need to take care of them. Not only this, we also speak of values of democracy, socialism and secularism as emerging values for inculcation and the recognition of the value of work ethics and quality of work life in the deontic sense in a corporate or a public organization. Those with a broad view of religion in our times also speak of the renewed *universal values* thereby sidestepping the dogmas and hegemony in religions about "their" values. This is believed to be so important that they transcend the limits of absolute metaphysicality and embrace what may be valued as of much importance for humans whether they belong to a state or a culture. These universal values are often thought as "objectively" valuable that is, irrespective of cultural relativism they are taken to be worthwhile as such having little or no room for disagreement. Most humans, for instance, value fresh air, water, sunlight as valuable; however, they are material-values. Even in air scanty high mountainous areas, in and around the polar regions when sun is a distant dream and places of draught where food is not available sufficiently, people still believe that these things are valuable. No *yogi* can boast of disvalue of these things even if he does not need them. However, we are not concerned here with material-values rather, with human values and moral values. We are reminded here of an example given by James Rachels in his essay on cultural relativism. He says that throughout the world, at any epoch we must recognize the 'universal value' of telling plain and simple truth so far as human social existence is concerned because if human society has to exist in the way it should, we must have the basic virtue to tell such truth. He says, if someone asks us what time it is, and all of us replied that it is 6 PM, when it is 5 PM, the society cannot run in the way it should. Though there may still be need for some spoken untruth or spoken falsity in any civil society during war or civil unrest when intelligentsia and administrative bodies takes recourse to such extreme steps. Generally speaking, we need to have the value to be truthful. In an uncivil society, though difficult to find around us, perhaps in a remote tribal area where people do not have conceptions of GST or IST or whatever, no watches, no pendulums to tick, people still have their age-old ways to gauge time and communicate with each other when time becomes vital for running their life and societies. Honouring time, that is, having minimum regard for the importance of time in life is then valuable for us. The universal human goodness of keeping time in normal courses in social life shall always be respected, therefore, it is expected that humans throughout the world should have the value to acquire basic information about life and world, that is, what surrounds and what happens around us. This may be further associated to acquire some knowledge of reality. It is also expected of us to have the universal value of performing our allotted duties, personal or social, whether in the family or in the corporate or in the public sector. It is unimaginable even if in primary group relationships that one does not respect the value of performing one's duty. With this, we have for us an account of new and universal values required of us as moral agents to honour.

Let us now come to the question of *models or methods* of 'value basing' in education, which gives us further idea about what exactly value-based education is like. Most of the thinkers believe that value-based education should follow the *direct and indirect* or the *formal and informal* methods. Some of them speak of *formal*, *non-formal* and *informal* methods. Some others speak of the *critical inquiry*, the *total atmospheric considerations* and the *integrated concurrent methods*. These methods are taken something as inculcation of values (including human values) in very young to grown-up students in schools and colleges. As the youngest students are the best ones to be equipped with these values because they have the whole life ahead of them, the thinkers concentrate more on basing values in schools. It is also conceived as important, therefore, to discuss about the methods of basing values in teachers, particularly school teachers while they receive training. This is needed because if teachers do not care for values, the responsibility to inculcate the same cannot be given to them. Moreover, they come to know which values need care for inculcation and how the same has to be done when it comes to the young students. The discussion of 'value basing' methods thus have two aspects: the methods to be obtained for the students and for the teachers. As I have said before, how moral teaching and moral value teaching can be and should be done, will not find a place here. The methods of value-based education is perhaps underlined in report of the Education Commission in India in 1964-66, which is an instance of the way we should progress in this direction though other nations have their own programmes. The Commission stresses on the "direct, indirect and the integrated methods" of value-based teachings.

The 'direct' or the 'formal' method of value inculcation among students is based on the assumption that the numerous values to be taught, even the relatively limited human values, is difficult nay impossible by one or a few persons in the society. The family (whatever may be its size and stature), is not fully equipped to impart these numerous values to our students. Moreover, families have their own value perceptions, their own evaluations of moral values and their own ways to impart value related teachings by picking up values of their choice. If the same is left for our neighbourhood or community (if it is not too large as in small villages or a small township), the fate may be the same. Who among the village or the town should take up this responsibility and how is not clear. Hence, value-based education begs a fixed place, a group well defined to do the job in a well-defined environment. The place is our institutions, schools and colleges, having a well-defined environment and group of professional teachers who are bestowed with the tasks of enlisting or *selecting values* which need most for inculcation, fixing up the exact ways in which these values should be inculcated well-defined age-groups of students and the ways to monitor or judge the changes in value perceptions in the receivers of such education, which may be one way to evaluate the consequences of value-based education. This method is, therefore, highly controlled, dependent on well-defined curriculum and for its success; it depends on teachers, students and the entire institutional environment. The method has many problems, almost one at every point of its administration. Greatest problem is, which values need to be taught? It is clear that values are numerous and therefore, it is difficult to formulate an exhaustive list. NCERT has reportedly formulated eighty-three values to be taught. With all regard, it must have left many gaps. Hence, the values to be inculcated needs constant evaluation. Most interesting feature is that with the changes in time, and the nature of education, some changes are noticed in value perceptions. Political and economic changes in our societies often change our gradation of values for their relative importance in our institutions. Hence, there can be no absolute list of values for inculcation, but we cannot doubt that with very young to grown-up boys and girls, we should start somewhere. Even if we know that there are many values to be taught we cannot jump to enlist them for further inculcation without an eye to start exactly at the proper place. For instance, we know very well that sexuality education has its own value because apart from many other practical aspects, it is extremely important to remove unnecessary myths about sex-life of the male and the female population, and we try to know the value of our body, the way it works, the value of human progeny and reproduction. Nevertheless, we cannot discuss these things with our students at any point of their life. We ought to be judicious in judging 'when' to start education of such important value. The outcome of the issue is that it is very difficult in formal education to decide which values to teach to whom and when. Most important feature about selection of values is that without inviting a thorough *public scrutiny* or debate about whether some values at all needs to be taught and why some values should be taught by us, that is, why some value-inculcation in school is morally desirable we cannot decide on our whim to select such and such values for inculcation. It is not difficult in India to find instances of selection of values for teaching at the whims of groups of politicians or educationists influenced by political ideologies. Why at all, in India religious or spiritual values be inculcated at any stage in secular institutions still remains a stiff issue for us because by this time many *official* views of value education have belligerently fought each other for their justification. Is it desirable that wisdom tells us to move beyond such controversy and concentrate elsewhere? If this be the case, and with the complexity of the private and the public schools in India, there is perhaps a state of indecision in selection of values. The public schools, for instance, are directly under the guardianship of the Philosopher Kings in the educational world and therefore, there goes a tug of war for *imposing* some values as great and imperative for our students. This is good example of selecting values by the peer and the politically motivated groups or otherwise intoxicated groups to determine values pupils need when the pupil, their parents and the public are completely at mercy of the peers. Hence, in India, with changing history, the books on history have changed rapidly, the poor students and perhaps the teachers are mere onlookers. The private schools are perhaps in a more pitiable condition. There the Philosopher Kings are profiteers, the esoteric group either influenced by what a central body has outlined as core course of values, which they must follow or else they simply fix things all by themselves because that is in their view the most desirable. In such cases, values are often passed on to our poor students through our poor, confused and grudging but voiceless teachers. This is the way value-based education faces stiff challenges at the first instance. Let us come to the next one, that is, formal techniques obtained by value-basers (or value-educators).

Hopefully, this is not another sub-profession under the broader profession of teaching, even if it is so they must be paid people to do a good job with great difficulty. If there is no such people, all teachers must be value educators, who have decided or have been asked to go through 'eighty-three worthwhile ideas' (or more) fixed by people in charge, understand and then start indoctrination in a controlled environment of schools and colleges. There is fixity in this technique as we leave our teachers under peer-pressure, though at the ground level when it comes to 'teaching' it is the teachers who should have liberty to adopt methods in and outside the classroom to impart the knowledge of values. Let us imagine that the students need to know the value of animate and inanimate beings and things, which is not simply a matter of plain talk, it needs supportive aids, demonstrations, examples at the real level. Next imagine that the same students need to value cooperation, which is again not a matter of plain talk, it needs some thinking on the part of the teachers at the real level to convey the message, perhaps aided by an example, say, a game of football. Now the poor value-educators must know and do a number of things for value-education that the wise gatekeepers of Nalanda would envy. Hence, the job is complex, demanding and of gigantic propositions which is possible in the association of students 'without a holiday'. Clearly, therefore, value basing is a shared business of several teachers in schools and colleges. The selection of techniques in formal education is not wide open for the teachers, because mostly they exhaust their energy "quota" of duties or to complete the syllabus. Hence, the teachers first "finish" the allotted theoretical plain-talking job, mostly in an artificial atmosphere among pupils who love to listen to real life or imaginary stories that convey a message. Well, performing this task does not prepare a student, who is, value-based, ready for a go in the social life. A lot more has to be done. A 'game situation' in a classroom is so unreal and hackneyed that it hardly passes the required value-message, though the pupils often have fun in the game. At the real level, message are of great value but most of the students do not have them in the way things go most of the time in the supervision of a teacher. The most trifling part of the formal method, particularly when it comes to "techniques" to be obtained by the teachers is an implicit *artificiality* in the entire project followed by *indirect persuasion* at its worst. *Chauvinism* or a one-way traffic obtained by the peer group to convey messages about values does not succeed, therefore. Though you cannot hope very young people to have a dialogue with you on value matters, they nevertheless, go on asking interesting questions and doing marvellous things that have some link with conveying the message of desirable values. After all, one has to keep in mind that given the sacred list of values in the curriculum something has to be done, like enforcing them as religious commands. The whole approach becomes "text-bookish", for example, the way in which even today we are trying to convey the value of environmental protection artificially. Planting a sapling to celebrate *Van Mahotsava* much like the *mahotsava* of Hindi week or Hindi month in our government offices, hardly passes any value, though they appear not to be text-bookish. A fanfare is a valueless way to convey the message of a value most of the time — values come in other ways, flowing as they are like unstoppable stream completely taking us in their fold because we are already dipped in the stream of values. Various subjects, which are receptacles of values, need teachers who incite us to see values for ourselves when they teach a subject. But this instantaneous free flow of values through teaching takes us to a different model to which I shall settle finally. Now let us further realise that the text-bookish artificiality is also persuasive and chauvinistic because teachers tend to press on students what the artificial method demands most. They will ask questions, take oral and written texts, urge to follow what is required by hook or by crook because they *have to do* all that. The compulsion of a course on values and its need for persuasion robs off the gem out of it—it is dull and hackneyed. Every time the idea of a value-based education crops up involving "ethics" or "moral science" or "ethico-religious philosophies" or "realms of values", I am filled with ominous dreams a boy has while sitting in a class to whom a teacher of good character tells him how to build a good character because the boy is characterless. I think of running out of the school campus where such things are done. But I am still not trashing value-based education because for me it is an entirely refreshing idea sans teaching of that weird subject to students. Hence, though value basing has been predominantly formal, it should not remain so because it encourages chauvinist teachers who *find values for us*, mentally cripples us and turns us to characterless creatures. Let us remain free in the stream of life, school life is just a part of it and let us find values, see them and just not pick them as skills of mathematics is picked up but soak them while several information and experiences are gathered to see further what consequences follows in real life as we go on in a long journey of man-making while we leave out many values and hold on to others never to be left out. Ms. Sushma Bhagia in her paper quotes from Raths (1966): "Persons have experience; they grow and learn. Out of experiences may come certain general guides in behaviour. These guides tend to give directions to life and may be called value"[4]. But where does school and teachers come in this journey? This is what has to be answered by value-based education; I will come to it in a short time.

A quick look at the *indirect* or the *non-formal* and the *informal* methods would be sufficient now as many things in terms of the unworthiness of the formal method have been discussed. The obvious shortcomings of the formal method has led people to advocate about the 'non-formal' method meaning thereby imparting different values which are deemed to be necessary and desirable for persons of different age groups in an unbound or uncontrolled environment, that is, not in the confinement of school classrooms by teachers in text-bookish way. Naturally, the role of the *impersonal agencies* such as the *mass media* and different *activities* and *programmes* are thought to be vehicles of values. Here, 'impersonal' does *not* mean lack of person or persons rather not present in person. It is said that television, newspaper, radio and films are important value careers or value-inculcators, mostly in an unbiased and secular way. Among the activities and programmes are included mass activities and programmes in schools and colleges like assemblies, meetings, festivals, meditations, celebrating internationally important days and events, watching films and documentaries. The group activities like music, drama, sports, social work, club activities and so on. There are individual activities, writing for school/college magazines. I have carefully avoided among these prayers, religious festivals and group-specific cultural events, that is, events focusing values of preferred groups on caste, class and advantage bases. "Informal method, says Mr. V.R. Taneja, is "incidental" or "residual". In this realm, everything that a child does under the sun is included. From the influences of home environment to the community fairs and festivals, there is vast array of behaviour patterns learned by the children. From the interactions with the peers and conversation with the elders stem habits, interests, attitudes, social adjustments and values"[5]. Let us have a look at these methods. If we go by this explanation of informal education, as compared to both the formal and the non-formal education of values is beyond the bounds of institutionalization of the said education. We have seen that if education is taken in its wider connotation, that is, an enterprise in which humans are initiated towards many worthwhile things as they grow up and thus build their identity as moral beings, which is possible not only in our institutions either in a formal way or non-formal way rather informally. Education itself testifies much informal participation such as the family, the neighbourhood, the market, the crowd, the groups, the religious organizations and so on. Similarly, these are the sources of educating us in values, not in the sense of someone teaching us a course or involving us in activities or programmes as a matter of allotted tasks or roles we need to play but in the course of our simple participation in the wide range of life forms and activities that we come to know what things are worthwhile, what are worthwhile for us and what things are of unworthy. Subsequently, we come to pick up certain ways of living and doing which are valuable in essence, and valuable for our well-being. Non-formal value basing requires teachers and administrators fix up activities and programmes for children supporting that they will pick up some values needed for humans among which are moral values. Informal value basing come to us from various sources most of the time not-programmed or in indeterminate ways while we live in this teeming ecological community. In any case, both have their own problems. The non-formal method should first reply the basic question: which values should be fixed by whom for value basing? Though the method does not always give stress to individuals, rather mass media run by people have great value; we cannot overlook the importance of institutions making some rules or codes to get involved in extra-curricular and other essential activities needed for value basing. Radio, television, newspapers do impart values in us, one is the motivation towards knowing what things are happening around us and why. Other things are indirect suggestions and persuasions that such and such values should be picked up. The informative, educative and the entertaining programmes are key to mass medias' ethos; they unknowingly become more like our official institutions where value-pedagogy gives ways to another set of things. The mass media no doubt have their own scheme of things to do, very close to institutionalized value-pedagogy, they too have fixed ideas about what are valuable for us, particularly our students and then arrange dialogues, dramas, songs and so on, which we often press our students to watch or read at home or in school because we too believe that such things were and are valuable for our children. This is not complete chauvinism, there are options but most of the time in secular set-up they hardly remain disinterested towards peer pressures for selecting values. Still there is some time for our children to select as well to reject some values and criticise others as they grow up. Hence, institutionalization and chauvinism in value basing go hand in hand not completely eradicating the vice of pressure and persuasion in the non-formal ways of value basing. The activities in our schools, have the same fate because most of the time those involved in these activities have no choice, they are determined by peers. The school clubs are testimony to this fact. The cultural functions are not free from it either. However, we cannot completely trash these activities even if the activities are determined by the peer groups to some extent we cannot disregard that they do provide us with useful values in a non-formal way. This is an important truth, which enable us to realise that formal value basing apart from its defects is hindered for a thorough value basing, needing support from the non-formal value basing. In the schools, for instance, formal value basing must give major way to non-formal basing provided value basing itself has been sanctioned after undesirable intentions giving it desired meaning. As I said before, this basic issue of worth of value basing in education is due for careful scrutiny.

Informal value basing on the other hand is natural, so much so that it is perhaps difficult to imagine who bases values and when it really happens. Most of the parents think, speak and do many things which reflect their value systems but they will hardly say that they were *intended* to pass on the same values to their children. It is one thing to say that teachers and parents should behave as they should because what they think, say and do are receptacles of value and almost sure to influence their wards, which is certainly the case, but the point is that what they should, does not necessarily include what they must. Peers are receptacles of values do not mean to say that they must *artificially* try to teach us values. This is basic to teaching to be value-based as different from becoming value-based. This is the crux of the basing values and having them. Keeping all these things in mind, we have some models of value-based education, which Ms. Sushma Bhagia in her paper "Approaches to Value-Oriented Education" (1986) calls, *Critical Inquiry*, the *Total Atmospheric* and the *Integrated Concurrent* approach. The 'total atmospheric' approach sounds much like putting the formal, the informal and the non-formal value-based education at one place, but this is not the case because the crucial point in this respect is to consider the whole condition in which value is imparted to the students. The 'whole' must consist of the school wherein formal and non-formal value basing goes on as ever but with a difference that the 'artificiality' of curriculum and teaching followed by fixity of values is replaced by the natural desirable processes that goes on in our school. The point "natural and desirable" is most important because what things "naturally" or "obviously" go on in education should be kept in mind. When we speak of school education, we expect apart from classroom pedagogy, many activities and programmes about which we have already discussed, but to this we add, what is "desirable" of education. This is more important because we have found that many activities and programmes are not desirable at all. Hence, they should not be considered under value-based education. In the recent times, therefore, we hesitate in incorporating spiritual and theistically oriented education in our secular institutions. More important now is to remember that the desirable way to pass on different values in students should not be chauvinistic. It is rather important to encourage students in different good activities, allowing them to "catch" values and not "indoctrinate" or "teach" them. A great degree of freedom is given to the students as they grow up in the whole atmosphere of learning through doing to "catch" the worthwhile things for them leaving out many when no one in particular has told them about do's and don'ts. However, it is extremely important for the school administrators to arrange for an atmosphere of "catching" values but not indoctrinating or prophesying them.

The insight of non-indoctrination and no-chauvinism in value education is drawn from what Bhagia says, 'critical inquiry' approach advocated strongly by John Dewey in *Democracy and Education* (1916) and R.M. Hare in "Adolescents into Adults" (1964). They hold that values particularly moral values should be "discovered" rather than taught or indoctrinated. In an open and secular atmosphere of learning, it is the students who have the liberty to discover what is right, good and just. It is they who come to know through a critical acumen that such and such things are worthwhile and should be inculcated in us for proper growth. Teachers are not persuaders or the brainwashers rather, they allow us to see what is good, they motivate us to participate in several worthwhile activities to find out what really needs care. The students should be better helped to develop their reasoning skills with regard to values than developing the art of valuable actions, which is nothing but sophistry. Further, taking a cue from both insights the author herself tries to support an *integrated concurrent* approach in which keeping freedom or autonomy of moral agents in the focus, the range of desirable school activities in mind, and the role of the teachers to see worthwhile things without imposing their values are most important. It is important that the teachers should be motivated enough to take up any topic or issue in any subject in a classroom situation or outside it in a manner that the experiences of the students are considered as important when they rationally analyse and thus discover needed values.

All these things are good for us because it tries to remove the most objectionable things—chauvinism and fixity in value-based education and therefore, tries to remove a basic misconception that 'value basing' begs a division of labour that is, one party prophesying values and another party picking them up as it is. Hence, value-based education as we now get it does not amount to teach only ethical values or spiritual values or theistic values or many values rather values which should be rationally and judiciously taken up as they come to us in the course of our physical, mental and moral development. To this, I would like to add that when we are speaking about school education in particular, the role of teachers in classroom teaching and subsequent discovery of values by students without chauvinistic peer pressures has to be kept in mind. The teachers should remember that not necessarily, they are epitomes of value. They should not pretend to be so but it is equally unethical to imagine that they become ignorant about what they know and what they think is extremely important for the students to know. So the question is how in schools and outside it, we the sane, grown-up and responsible people *participate* in terms of "discovery" of values for inculcation. Let us accept that values should not be taught artificially though we can do so. We should have some responsible role to play while teaching certain things as part of curriculum in and out the classrooms. In my mind, value-based education is that academic enterprise in schools and colleges in which any subject and issues and problems therein are informed, analysed, appreciated and if needed justified in a lively *participatory way*, a part of which is *discursive analysis* among students and teachers taking an example (imaginary or real), anchored to the solid grounds of evaluation or appreciation for any element of value or worth implicit in the subject in consideration. It is extremely unwise in my opinion to forget or conceal the 'element of worth' which makes a good case for study even in the classroom to be surfaced clearly by the teacher but further incite students to 'participate' in *discourses* and *agreements* if needed to 'discover' whether the said 'element of worth' needs 'absorption' or to be left out after further scrutiny or to be modified to some extent. Subjects we come to learn are full of value related matters, they need thorough rational analysis. Value-based education should take them up. Let me proceed a little farther with value-based education in schools where teachers are *moderators* and *corroborators*. Take any subject, as I have said, they have their 'own value' in the capacity of the tasks they undertake and the aims they fix, which is perhaps the basic value our teacher often teaches us. In the broad field of these subjects are topics or issues, some of them are problematic, some raise stiff dilemmatic questions and so on, which are also "value-laden", that is, raise questions of "worth", for instance, pragmatic worth, utilitarian worth, deontic worth, emotive worth, moral worth and so on. It is the task of the teachers to know properly the 'value-laden' aspects of issues and raise some of them, which needs to be raised among students, depending on the appropriateness of the age groups and mental maturity of the pupils. This is needed because teaching different subjects does not mean informing, explaining, describing several issues rather making implicit the value aspects, which are otherwise implicit, or hidden to immature learners. This is simply, "keeping an eye on value-laden features of subjects to be taught" so that analysing, answering and resolving them students orient themselves towards the subjects learnt differently, not in the hackneyed way to be aware of them and learn them for an examination but soak them in the heart, so that education itself becomes value-oriented and teachers and students become parties to value-based education. Keeping an eye on values inherent in what we are informed and trying to face the trifles if any about values is what is to me, basic to "value-based education". Anything from philosophy to computer science, philosophy to robotics have value issues, raise these value questions and ask students to resolve them for a 'quality of life' to be lived in this world. When teaching takes this fresh set of task, it *adds* some value to it. In this case, teachers by virtue of their experience and maturity raises issues of value, which are implicit and further moderates and corroborates dialogues about values in and outside the classrooms if that is deemed to be necessary. This gives both the teachers and the students a great boost to see education and its value in our life differently. Our perception of subjects, teaching and learning changes dramatically. Taken in this sense, several activities and programmes in schools forming important parts of non-formal education might raise serious questions of value. Let us take the case of yogic practices and meditation as part of non-formal value education. If the instructors do not tell us the value of such practices in life, it leaves out a major thing, then we have the value questions *about* the said value of such practices. For instance, if we are told by virtue of our hackneyed traditional teaching that these practices are valuable because they lead us to spiritual realization we are immediately leaving a greater task to find out with our children whether they really followed what we mean and then throw it open for a dialogue whether such practices have practical value, the biological one and not the spiritual one or whether such practices need a boost in life because they keep us fit and alert, or they have both the biological and the spiritual values. Hiding anything is unethical in education if subject are basically value-laden. We need not ask such difficult questions at an early age because that is not fitting to age, but equally unethical is to profess that they lead us to God or heaven or whatever when that may be a palpable untruth or a mere belief or completely meaningless to a student at that age. It is perhaps due to this that many among us have reacted very sharply to the so-called *moral science* education in schools of theistic parentage in secular societies because starting a book on moral science by saying that "God has made everything, the world and us", is hiding many value questions in the name of spreading a value. What value does it really have to press some weird ideas in young minds regarding the physical surroundings they have in the name of value-based education? Value-based education opens the can of worms if it goes in the wrong direction. We should challenge it because that is a disvalue. When slowly and surely we start inquiring seriously about many value questions, which we came across at some time, open the can of worms which we should face without fear. Socialist, secular and democratic educational institutions should base or orient values among pupils in a most challenging way even in a 'plain-talking' class or in a formal educational atmosphere. There is no official value-based education because such education is essentially iconoclastic, it hits on the head of official philosophies put sophistically on our heads. The greatest value of value-based education is that it enables us to a great extent our rationality, and moral and practical wisdom to live a qualitative social life by virtue of being agents actively engaged in the enterprise called "education" and "educating".

Aided with this conception of value-based education, we are doubly sure that it does not only amount to spiritual and moral education, but it covers both in its field. However, I have serious doubts about the worth of spiritual education in other than spiritual institutions. For me, it has little or no worth in secular institutions; hence, as I remarked earlier, many activities and programmes such as divine prayers, *bhajans*, religious indoctrinations and celebrating religious festivals in schools raise serious value-related questions, and not to be blindly taken as valuable. It may be a matter of great interest how best we can flush out systematically from our text books any references to different religious activities and festivals in the name of 'harmony' which is believed (wrongly) to be crucial in a secular state. Why secular institutions need to accommodate each and every religious activity in schools is a matter of good value related exercise. Keeping these things in mind let us now find out what "value basing" amounts to teachers training, that is, which values are important for our teachers in the real life encounter with the process of educating. For this, I would like to turn to the essays by Dr. S.P. Ruhela and Professor Kireet Joshi[6]. The essays are useful particularly in the context of their content, which raises many important and interesting value related questions, which we need to answer.

From the foregoing discussion, it is clear that value-oriented education is meant for both students and teachers because a person bereft of values cannot be a teacher of values. Even if value-based education means keeping an eye on aspects of worth in different topics of subjects, which needs communication as well as evaluation, we cannot overlook the importance of participation of students and teachers in the formal and the non-formal methods of value basing. Dr. Ruhela cites the NCTE paper *Teacher Education Curriculum: A Framework* (1978) wherein after much brainstorming the following were decided: "To develop Gandhian value, to perceive Gandhi's role as an agent of change in the community; to perceive Gandhi's role as guide to the community; to integrate community life and resources with school work; to have warm and positive attitude towards growing children and their academic socio-emotional and personal problems with skills to guide and counsel them; to use and preserve environmental resources and historical monuments and other cultural heritage; to develop awareness of the school in achieving the goals of building up a democratic, secular and socialist society; to develop understanding, interests, attitudes and skills for all-round growth and development of children; to develop competence to teach on the basis of the accepted principles of teaching and learning; to develop communication and psychomotor skills and abilities to promote learning in and out of the classrooms; to keep abreast of the latest knowledge of subjects and to undertake action, research and investigatory projects"[7]. Dr. Ruhela adds that a teacher should be a "mediator between the individual and mass information; to be able to be conscientious enough to become aware of the realities of the social situation and to develop a social climate in which hero-worship, sycophancy, irrationality, sensuousness and exploitation do not find a place"[8]. Without commenting on any aspect of what Dr. Ruhela has said, let us immediately move to what Professor Kireet Joshi says in this regard. For him, value-oriented education should be the core of the teachers' training programme, which should cover twelve broad aspects of value education. He classifies them as "Philosophy, Education and Values, Psychology, Science and Values, Philosophy and Values, Religion, Spirituality and Values, Art and Values, Psychological exercise of aspiration, Will and Introspection as aids to the pursuit of values, Environment and Values, Works of Community Service, Courage and Heroism, Physical culture and its values, Selected Stories, Play and Passages of literature that improves the pursuit of Truth, Beauty and Goodness"[9]. Professor Joshi further enlists thirteen ways in which value-concerned teachers should guide and help children in achieving the aim of value basing. To be precise, these are: to recognize and encourage wisely the inner *psychic and spiritual being* (my italics) in children as distinct while they often turn to truth, beauty and good; to develop sincerity among children; several values to be inculcated by examples than speeches; to be careful in punishing students; to encourage frank and spontaneous *confession* (my italics) by students at fault, which should be forgiven; to encourage scientific thinking about wrong impulses and to encourage to overcome sins and falsehoods; to encourage pupils to see that unformed virtues are not rejected as faults; to assure growth of practical knowledge to create bonds of trust; to encourage curiosity; to stimulate the will to discover and realize; to encourage conversations among students for the growth of values and to give opportunities for growth of noble virtues"[10]. In a few pages to follow Professor Joshi thinks that the teachers should be enough value-oriented to encourage systematic ways of mental, vital and physical education as chief contributors in the value-oriented education; to encourage community service among students; to encourage a life of peace, international understanding and artistic endeavours; and to find out several fitting techniques in value education such as developing the sense of inquiry, "inter-disciplinary study" to widen and heighten consciousness and so on.

Most of the things that Dr. Ruhela and Professor Joshi has noted with regard to value-based teacher's education is worth appreciating because among other things, they have realized the truth that values cannot be taught simply by lecturing or professing, nor can they be inculcated if we wish to do so all by whim. They have also recognized the truth that not one or two values, human or moral or spiritual needs to be inculcated, values are many and most of them need some care, not for teaching but for motivating the teachers from within to see what things are valuable for them and the students in life. However, a few remarks are needed when I find value basing to be free from chauvinism and hegemony. First, why should Prof. Ruhela think that all teachers should (or rather must) develop Gandhian values in them and hopefully among students? Because Gandhi is father of nation? Or, he has strong ethico-spiritual philosophy? Why at all should *all* Gandhian values be absolute means to value-orientation? These are unanswered questions. If Gandhian values are so important for inculcation, what I have said should be kept in mind because doors should be open for us to evaluate the case and if we are not sycophants (because Ruhela says that is a disvalue); some or many Indians do not support many Gandhian values on strong grounds. There must be some ordinary people whose arguments should be given value. Among other possible objection in the inculcation of spiritual values which Gandhi advocated so strongly, we add that secular institutions need not inculcate spiritual values at all. Even the case on inculcation of values of *satya* and *ahimsâ* in their spiritual overtone need careful scrutiny as well. The spirit of catholicity among teachers who are expected to base values as motivators and corroborators deprives us from being so orthodox, clinging to values preached by great people, though trashing many of them which are well acceptable is not good either. Almost on similar grounds we ask Dr. Joshi what exactly is the value of religious and spiritual values with respect to teachers and students? If we argue that the participants in the enterprise of education at any level has nothing to do with religious and spiritual values, what great harm will be done? This does not mean that a religious person cannot or should not think in this way; but it is again perfectly possible because there is no logical relation between being religious and inculcating religious values in teachers and/or students. A religious person can argue on non-religious grounds that education being a non-religious matter, does not beg religious teachings or spiritual teachings. It may be argued that there are many values common to religions and spiritual philosophies, which need inculcation. Most of these so-called 'universal values' on careful scrutiny either turns out to be equally regarded as valuable by non-spiritual persons on grounds available to them or they disagree on strong reasons that such values are not universal. In any case, inculcation of spiritual values is not necessary and sufficient, they are not commonly agreed upon in education. Hence, we must leave room for our teachers for logical disagreement on several matters on value. An esoteric coterie of thinkers cannot decree on such delicate matters in the national policy of education. Why should Professor Joshi presume that a child is inherently spiritual being which is reflected in his or her actions more often than not and teachers should have the worth to "turn" them to 'what they really are'? It appears that the conception is much like Butler's conception of human nature, which has been refuted thoroughly for its inherent fallacies. A child's turning to truth, beauty and good may be empirically verifiable with some difficulties though, but the point is truth, beauty and good are not spiritual concepts, and a child's turning to such things has no logical relation with their inherent spirituality. I personally have no regrets to say that humans are not spiritual beings inherently, some of them become so because the virtue is 'acquired' and not 'inherent'. Despite these aspects in Ruhela's and Prof. Joshi's conception of value-based education, many things said by them are of great merit. What is commendable that teacher's training should take care of value basing in so far as it considers a large range of worthwhile things in a number of fields of study provided teachers take care of discourses about matters of value in different branches of study.

With this, we come to the end of the discussion about value basing for a while but some things were left out in this regard, as we thought to take them at a proper place. It is now proper to consider what is believed to be most important in value basing, the *moral value basing*. We have seen that there is some difference between value-based education and spiritual value basing in education, value-based education and moral value basing in education and moral value basing and spiritual value basing in education, though both moral and spiritual value basing may be treated as parts of value basing understood in a wider sense. However, we are always free to ask whether any part of the whole does justify to the larger whole, that is, 'education'. Value basing itself is a part of the 'educational enterprise', spiritual value basing is a sub-part, about which we are free to ask whether it does any justice to education taken in the general sense, which is essentially *secular* enterprise. However, there is no doubt that religious and spiritual value basing does full justice to 'spiritual education' because here we are not concerned with a secular enterprise rather, a specific one that demands us to be spiritual and/or religious. We should notice here that the word "secular" in the context of general education has a special significance, it does *not* mean "what is to be equanimous in religious and/or spiritual ideologies", or alternately "what is a neutral position with regard to religious and/or spiritual ideologies" rather, "what in essence does not include religious and/or spiritual aims and ideologies". Secular education is the one academic enterprise that does not include religious and/or spiritual man-making or basing such values in participants of that enterprise as its major aim. Understood in this sense, it is clear why the educational enterprise of philosophy (and branches therein) need not necessarily aim at any other than *philosophical* non-secular goals. Hence, spiritual and religious education is not philosophical education, though its secular critique is a part of such education. Taken in this sense, ethics as a branch of philosophy is a "philosophical study or critique of morality" and not "study of religious and spiritual morality", though it may be a secular critique of the same. Therefore, ethics has nothing to do with making us religious or spiritual or orients us or base in us these values for "man-making" (as if without that we are non-human animals). It is a hopeless argument that since a long time religious ethics have tried to orient us in the desired direction. In fact, ethics has not tried to do that though religious/spiritual ethics did try to do the same, which ethics always tried to study secularly by virtue of its own principles. The point is whether educational ethics should be understood as aiming towards religious/spiritual ends? If educational ethics within ethics is a secular inquiry or critique of whatever is ethically relevant in the educational enterprise, it need not and should not have such aims. Yet within it, we can and we do sensibly analyse whether having such non-secular ends in educational ethics, for instance, ways to orient participants in education to achieve religious etc. goals is at all ethically valid. We may sensibly ask whether moral value basing is itself ethically valid if at all it is taken either as religious value basing or a non-spiritual value basing enterprise? To answer these questions we have to delve deeper into the ethics education in schools or ethics education as means to moral value basing in children. Here the basic questions are: what is exactly moral value basing? What are its aims and what are its models? Answer to these together is finds out whether moral value basing in education can really lead children to be morally good. The problem about the role of ethics in moral value basing is a problem of relevant model of moral value basing as well. It is asked how teaching ethics can make us morally good or morally worthwhile? Simply asked, can ethics be a means to make us good? In fact, both the issues of moral value basing and ethics teaching are mixed up by thinkers of such issues so that it becomes very difficult at times to treat them separately, but I will try to be as clear as possible in this regard. However, it is extremely important for us to recall that a discussion about "moral values" should not be confused with that of "non-moral values". Hence, we are here poised to inquire about the 'deontic moral values' and the 'aretaic moral values', that is, for instance, we are here asking the need for value basing such as promise-keeping, truth-telling, benevolence, forgiveness, so on, and the ways in which we should do it in education. Whether ethics or moral philosophy in particular has something or nothing to do with such things and whether it is at all sensible to take up the programme of moral value orientation to make some people good is the moot issue. First, a few words about moral values, which has to be based or inculcated. As we know that it is most important to distinguish moral from non-moral values, any programme in education that loses sight of this basic truth, is completely misguided. We have to keep in mind that those worthwhile properties or traits needs to be inculcated which are either expected or desirable of a moral agent like, "keeping promises". "Keeping promises" is thus a deontic moral value or virtue which should be or ought to be inculcated in us in so far as they are good themselves. However, there are moral virtues like 'benevolence' called aretaic moral virtue which do not tell us about those human traits by virtue of which intrinsically worthwhile actions needs to be done rather, those human traits by virtue of which we judged moral agents' motive, intentions and character as good or virtuous or saintly and so on. Thus, deontic virtues are related to what we do as our obligation, duty and so on, whereas the latter is related to what we intend to do or what reflects our character. It is believed that a range of such virtues needs to be "cultivated" because moral virtues are not hereditary or by birth rather, they are acquired. There are different ways and sources to acquire these virtues as we grow up, and taking "education" in its wider connotation, there are a number of channels through which we acquire these virtues as if we were being educated in moral virtues or were oriented that way. Our experiences are key to the adoption of these moral virtues, and even without a formal institutional education, we may still be morally oriented or be morally virtuous. This is important to note as there is no logical relation of necessity between school education and moral virtue inculcation or adoption to become morally charged person. I have argued in the *Primer* (vol. 1) that moral virtues do not beg chauvinism on the part of teachers and/or ethicists. Yet, there is no point in trashing the whole idea of school education in which the inculcation of moral virtues are kept in mind, but there is a difference between a mechanical approach to make man moral by teaching a fixed set of virtues or showing them by example and a participatory approach which is so natural as we grow up in an atmosphere of education. Virtues in fact, comes to us uninhibitedly, whether we wish or not, vices too follow the same suit, but it is we who receive, nurture, reject, refuse, change and modify them as we grow up in society. In this flux of things, *intervention* is a serious matter if that is well planned, that is, if it is mechanical or artificial. What amount of preaching will make us benevolent? Which acts in classroom exemplify benevolence to be picked up? Which teaching makes us dutiful? These are tough questions to answer. More serious is, why 'benevolence and dutifulness' is good? Who told us that these things are good and should be thus inculcated? Or, does it really beg being 'told' by someone? If not, how can we at all know that these things are good, and therefore, needs to be cultivated? Can a child really 'know' the good of truth-telling if no one 'tells' that to him or her? Then, how can we at all avoid indoctrination? The mechanical model of moral virtue inculcation appears to be our fate! Educational ethics, when it takes the responsibility to answer these tough questions, enters into its virtue related task. Interesting things happen when our teachers in the course of indoctrination starts telling us on which grounds 'benevolence' is good. They in fact, give us doses of principles while teaching about the basis of moral virtue. Hopefully, they call this a *principle of welfare or the principle of Self Realization* or any other, but it is difficult to convey to our young students what these principles are and why they are good.

Before coming to the delicate issue of models of moral teaching as source to virtue basing in schools in particular, we need to clarify next, what are the aims of teaching moral virtues to our students, and what if any are the value of such education in schools. As we have seen before, we may conceive of two important 'aims' of such teaching.

One is to contribute to "man-making" and the other is to contribute to the filed of ethics and educational ethics or what is to contribute to the "growth of knowledge". The first aim includes many things such as making persons of good character, citizens of value concerns, persons having good intentions, persons who realize ultimate good and so on. The other is different, it does not directly want to see moral agents in a particular way rather, it wants to see a field of study in a particular way, that is, it wants to guarantee that what is expected of ethics and educational ethics as fields of knowledge flourish to their full. By participating in such knowledge-process we may become virtuous or persons of good character but that is coincidental, not intended. Moral virtue basing or teaching, for man-making, is thus an alien affair in 'pure academics'. Hence, philosophers as philosophers contributing to academics have nothing to do with the touted man-making, but nobody prevents a philosopher to be good or to play the moral saints in personal life to orient others. The problem is, philosophers do not in principle learn and teach common morality, they learn and teach moral philosophy. Hence, the moot issue is whether they contribute in any way in man-making in teaching moral philosophy, a part of which is educational ethics. So far as I am concerned, I have never thought of doing such things because as I got mature I realised that a bundle of good and bad that I am, after being a student and teacher of ethics for quite some time, I fail to teach others to be morally good while teaching ethics or ethical values and virtues. I simply teach them as demanded in our professional duty to do so as a matter of teaching a course of ethics for different teleological reasons, which surely reflects some of my virtues but ethical teachings did not grow those virtues in me. Some of my friends in ethnology or ecology are as virtuous when they take on their professional duty to complete their course in teleological sense. In fact, we were taught as first lesson in ethics that it has nothing to do with *making* us ethical, no one in reality should do so for we are already ethical and unethical in the course of our development as men and women. Even practical or applied ethics cannot *make* us ethical because it does not intend to do so. Equally true is philosophy does not intend to *make* us philosophical. Hence, the aim of teaching moral virtue in moral science or in the name of ethics or 'man-making' is extremely different from teaching the same for 'growth of knowledge'. However, is it not possible that if we compulsorily teach adequate courses of ethics or even moral science at *all* levels of education (formal ones), we are sure to 'make man'. People armed with ethics does become very good people, must be true. Thus moral value teaching widely in institutions, even if unintended would make a few people very good people. This is a terrific idea for me. I do not foolishly argue that as I have become bad, all ethics education intended in my case has failed and shall fail in all cases. Rather, I want to assert that ethics taken in its parts or whole, in all institutions will soon be thrown to dust if people feel that it has been imposed on them as they were very bad people or lackadaisical in morality. People will do the same if they smell that their children have been made scapegoats of another foolish experiment. We need to understand that there is a palpable difference between a "moralist" and a "moral philosopher" — a moralist aims at moral virtue teaching in schools to make us moral. However, as I have said before value-based or value-oriented ethics teaching should be never aloof in raising questions of value in the subject and find ways to resolve them. But to be sure, this may not necessarily make us moral and should not try to do so.

Let us continue with the analysis of *value* of ethics and moral virtue teaching a little farther. One touted value of teaching ethical values or virtues in the subject called "ethics" by expert teachers is that young learners come to know the *necessary rules or codes of conduct* so that civilized way of living in our societies is possible. Not only teaching common codes of conduct such as 'spitting and pissing in public places is bad', rather teaching overreaching principles of moral life, such as 'to lead social life in the spirit of cooperation' or which is "contractual" virtue. It is very important for children to have some basic moral virtues like these because without them they will be anti-socials in the long-run. No one denies the role of such principles when they are needed at very young stages in life. Hence, one has to be oriented as: "All beings and things around us are valuable, they need some concern on our part", which further grows in them the moral virtue of "other regardingness". The inquisitive children are also provided by moral teachings the needed rational justifications of why "cooperation" or "contractuality" and "other regardingness" are so important moral principles for us. Teachers and parents do often face the many sensible 'why' questions regarding moral matters and rightly so. It is moral teachings that enable teachers and parents to further justify at later stages of maturity 'why' the rules and principles as *starters* need modifications as well as complete rejection if needed, but that is a different matter. What we come to know is that the value of moral or ethical teachings provides us with "starters" of moral ways of living. However, not everything is well with these explanations because the major task of ethics as we found finally is not to supply a set of moral codes or rules of them and do's and don'ts of moral life rather to analyse and appreciate and reject them if needed. What often parents and teachers in schools pass on to us as moral 'starters' are highly questionable and even objectionable because more often than not what they profess are not about spitting and pissing but about serious moral matters, the meaning of which is not clear when they are passed on, justifications are being more problematic. Of course, with age we learn many things, but why should we assume that without being specifically concerned about such teachings in and out of the schools, there is no moral growth among children? Informal education need not be so planned or routined particularly when we speak of non-professional educators. Teaching of moral matters just happen in civil and relatively uncivil societies in the so-called educated and the so-called illiterate societies, they are not necessarily "taken up" by concerned groups in societies and in institutions like family and schools and colleges. When such things 'just happen' in even an illiterate family or in a well-educated family, they need not be taken as ethics education by any extension of the term. Hence, we need not confuse "moral education" with "morality education". The former is formed, which does beg teaching rules etc. in closed situations by specific groups which still raises questions for methods because many people believe that these are putting children to another intellectual hegemony which is decorative than pragmatic. The latter is, however, not moral teaching at all because it teaches us codes of moral behaviour, do's and don'ts reflecting the peer pressure obsessed with certain principles, these moralists are not needed in moral teaching either.

It is said that the value of moral education lies in the empowerment of learners to take independent moral decisions in tough situations of moral conflict. Such empowerment is not through teaching of courses in schools rather, depends mainly on exemplary behaviour of teachers and parents who are seen facing dilemma, making their own minds and solving them. All these are possible as paradigms of moral behaviour. Our parents and teachers (most of the time), appear to be epitomes of truths and values, and they are seen determined to resolve tough moral issues. The value of moral education through exemplary behaviour is that it grows with the moral virtue of individuals to resolve value questions not at wish rather in accordance with other persons who are concerned about such questions. Interesting features emerge here in moral value education as it is now clear that such education does not amount to teaching a course of morality or moral philosophy, rather following 'exemplary acts' of exemplary personalities. But this is not 'ethics education' rather, *experiencing* moral features of life we live in this world, which nevertheless, grows some virtues in us. Hence, getting education of virtues informally is not education of ethics by any extension of the term.

Nevertheless, we have found that teaching morality to young people is not pointless because since ages we as parents and teachers were teaching moral behaviour, moral codes, commands, rules, common sense moral dictums and so on for a greater satisfaction. However, it is unethical not to be critically appreciative of our habitual ways of life, our customary moral codes and common sense moral ways. Ethics provides us the necessary acumen and zeal for this, which is a great idea, but not everything taught by 'moralists' needs to be trashed because morality-education needs thorough scrutiny for ethicality, which is under the 'virtue related task' of educational ethics. Nevertheless, if education covers information and subsequent empowerment of children to question morality, we move closer to what is truly 'desirable' for us, and this is possible in 'ethics education', which has a value. Therefore, moral education needs to be denuded of its camouflaged morality-education because that is wholly confusing in educational enterprise. Yet, if moral education as morality-education enables students to motivate towards facing moral dilemmas in life, initiates them to go for moral dialogues, and most importantly takes on common people as of great value for their moral opinions, it surely succeeds as a social enterprise.

I have said at the beginning of the discussion that there is a lot of confusion about the nature, value and methodology of virtue based education, which is, nevertheless, a part of value based education. Much confusion is between morality education and education of ethics or moral philosophy, which I have tried to focus here. Any careless or loose use of "moral education" does more harm than good to the non-philosophers who take academic interest in such matters. Often in the schools, we are worried about pressing group morality or moral dogmas of the age, which often becomes *mantra* for modern age moral crises. Moral crises were acute in older days perhaps acute than what we see now — orthodoxy, hegemony, serfdom, exploitation, wars all were there. Do not curse ourselves for losing values and virtues because we have lost nothing, we are continuing a heritage of disvalues. If we find that we do not have "values" and "virtues" as our predecessors had long back, have faith in secular education which grows many values in us when we study many things not losing sight of the questions of good, right, desirable and just that keeps on emerging as the subjects grow while they are taught and learnt, and we are in a flux of moral issues to resolve them together, not alone.

This finally puts us to consider seriously, what are the nature, value and methodology of "ethics education" as contributory to value and virtue based education, the sense in which I find such education to be, but we should not come to this point immediately. This, and the question of possibility of teaching to be moral or ethical, shall be considered in the last chapter when we will discussed at length the nature, value and methods of ethics education as well as educational ethics education. It is important now to come to the *practical task* of educational ethics, which gives us an idea of the way moral discourses about moral trifles brings educational ethics closer to life.

NOTES

1. For detailed discussion about kinds of values, readers may go through W.K. Frankena's *Ethics*, Prentice-Hall, New Delhi, 1989, pp. 9-10, 81-83.
2. Bhagia, N.M., "New Values and Education", in S.P. Ruhela (ed) *Human Values and Education*, Sterling Publishers Pvt. Ltd., New Delhi, 1986, p. 133.
3. *Ibid*, p. 134.
4. Bhagia, Sushma, "Approaches to Value-Oriented Education" in S.P. Ruhela (ed) *Human Values and Education, Ibid*, p. 148.
5. Taneja, V.R., "Inculcation of Human Values: Educational Approaches and Strategies" in S.P. Ruhela (ed), *Ibid*, p. 165.
6. Essays by Dr. S.P. Ruhela, "Value Orientation of Teacher Education Curricula in India" and Professor Kireet Joshi, "An Outline Program of Value-Oriented Education" in Dr. S.P. Ruhela (ed.) *Human Values and Education, Ibid*, pp. 214-225 and 226-240.
7. Ruhela, S.P., "Value Orientation of Teacher Education Curricula in India", *Ibid*, p. 221.
8. *Ibid*, pp. 221-22.
9. Joshi, Kireet Prof., "An Outline Program of Value-Oriented Education", *Ibid*, pp. 228-230.
10. *Ibid*, pp. 232-34.

4

The Practical Task of Educational Ethics

Educational ethics as we now understand is a branch of ethics, which intercepts a number of problems emerging in the broad field of education, which are *ethically relevant*. What things are "ethically relevant" in the field of education? We have seen that to intercept the problems of 'normativism', mainly the problem of standards of value-judgements in education is important. It is important to find out which standard or standards are valuable in this regard or, is there no need of standards. Another 'ethically relevant' issue is of meaning and truth of value-judgements in education. It is important to find out which theory of theories of meaning counts most in this regard or, none of these theories makes sense. We have found that ethically relevant discussion in education is to consider the questions of worth or value, which includes human and ethical values in the main as well as human and ethical virtues. This also includes the question of teaching to be virtuous and teaching about values to become value oriented. The value of value-based education and its model comes within this purview. Now we are at hand another ethically relevant discussion, the importance of practical or applied aspect of *value resolution*, that is, the nature, importance and models or resolving *value-laden practical problems* emerging in education and educating, particularly when we consider formal education. This is in accordance with the applied task of ethics (for details see vol. 1), which considers the various practical problems of ethical importance for resolution. A number of such problems are faced by students, teachers, parents, administrators, planners and the common people in our societies which asks for urgent "resolution" because it is an ethical expectation on the part of the members of civil societies to resolve issues of great ethical ramifications than live with them in either agony or utter callousness.

The practical problems in education becomes all the more demanding for value-resolution when they raise serious questions of ethical desirability, justice, rights, obligations, duties and so on. The reason being that not all practical problems are to be taken 'as they are', rather 'as they should be'. It is due to this that the problem of "reservation of seats in elite professional institutions on caste basis" is not the one which we consider as what is the case rather, what *should* be the case. It may well be that reservations as it is now, is a practice under legal approval, and, therefore, natural for us to abide by the law. Still, there are questions of 'should' or the ethically just, right, good and so on about this practice. Hence, in the name of legality and common practice, the matter cannot be deemed to be resolved or believed to raise no more questions. On the one hand, it still raises practical questions such as the validity of *widening the net* of reservation on the basis of recognition of more deprived castes, classes and income groups, and on the other hand, it incites us to consider why at all 'should' there be on ethical grounds any further 'widening of the net' as well as any reservation in educational institutions as such. Hence, a number of practically troubling issues in education are worse still when we find them laden with questions of ethical value or ethical goodness or simply, when they are "value-laden". We simply cannot and should not be callous towards these questions because facing them boldly we come to know that many things around us just do not happen rather happening things involve us for questions of "worth". We come to know that since a long time we have been mechanically deciding and acting on legal basis because legality becomes a social dogma, but we suddenly feel that dogmas need a shake up. Thus, we raise to ask: why should it happen like this? Or, why should it not happen like that? If we find after collective ethical scrutiny that what happens needs to continue on ethical grounds, the legality-patronized dogmas change their garb to become relatively "humane" — it has a new face so to say because now it cares for whether, what is legally just, is ethically worthwhile. Or, if we find after social rumblings that something is extremely unworthy on ethical grounds though the same be legal, we start thinking about the ways in which our legal obsessions may be ethically or humanely overhauled. History of legally justifiable acts is testimony to the fact that at different epochs, the ethic of acts as churned by the public has pressurised the sacred system for quantum shifts. The justifiable act of class-based education under the British rule could not stand not because of shaky law rather the shady law the British carved out at whim. In fact, many such laws were configured by the rulers of societies to govern because emotions and ethics do not form a basis to the legal system, but ethical sense of people overwhelms the so-called rock-solid laws of pragmatics and prudence when it is most needed. Ethical issues in education thus needs care, they need not be left out as what goes on should go on as backed by legal approval. Educational ethics, if it is itself ethical should come up with this task of value resolution.

The greatest problems are about the ways to the "resolution" of these problems, to which we shall come now, but before that let me put in a nutshell what amounts to the "practical task" of educational ethics, which is not to be treated as "purely theoretical" in nature. First, educational ethics needs to start with a pure part, that is, to discuss the reasons for either having or not having a practical task. This is "pure part" because an inquiry into the 'justification' of a practical task of educational ethics is itself metaethical in nature, and therefore, purely theoretical. However, we must come to see that the matter of justification is not being practically-oriented in educational ethics. Second, educational ethics has a 'pure part' while justifying that such and such model or models of practical involvement in educational ethics is best suited. Hence, the first pure part of educational ethics leads us to the second one because the justification of the practical task of educational ethics calls for the justification of the method or methods in which practicability holds well. There is no doubt that justifying practical part of educational ethics calls for an explanation of why it is to be practical and this in turn calls for an explanation of 'what' and 'how' of practical educational ethics. Clearly, therefore, we have to find out what exactly do we mean by the 'practical' task, which I believe has been roughly explained in the first few pages of this chapter. Next, we have to come to the ways in which we can practically resolve many things needed for resolution in educational ethics.

The *practical part* of educational ethics should be understood as a part of *doing* something in the social milieu to encounter ethical imbroglios in the field of education. The 'doable' aspect reminds us of the fact that education and educating as unique social enterprises amounts to functions or doing something, which in their part calls for a thorough scrutiny for good or desirable, just, right, and so on. However, we need to remember that "doing" is a sweeping expression that includes thinking, planning, deciding and intending apart from courses of actions or patterns of functions related to the field of education. Hence, the practical aspect of educational ethics is to do something in order to resolve ethical issues emerging out of something that has been done in the field of education. In this sense, a practical educational ethical enterprise is the one within the field of educational ethics and not education because not everything 'done' in education raises ethical issues for resolution, and subsequently, does not call us for doing something in order to settle these issues. This is to say that only those thinking, planning, deciding, intending and functioning in education and educating that raises ethical issues of desirability for urgent resolution, awaits adequate back-up actions that come in the purview of practical educational ethics. This begs on our part a sound knowledge of distinction between those 'doing' in education, which raises non-moral questions of 'should' or 'desirability' as opposed to moral questions of 'should' or 'desirability'. For instance, we need to differentiate between the questions of whether we should reserve seats on *caste basis* in institutions of higher studies and whether we should reserve some seats for the Eskimos who live under great challenges in institutions of higher studies in India. The first question raises issue of moral desirability or ought whereas the second question raises issue of non-moral desirability or ought because in the first case a well thought out and planned action of 'reservation' as based on 'caste' inquires whether such things are good or desirable on any sound *moral or ethical ground or reason*, not necessarily on any moral principle, whereas in the second case a well thought-out and planned action of 'reservation' as based on 'geographical inaccessibility' inquires whether such a thing is good or desirable on any sound *pragmatic or prudential ground or reason.* Before I clarify what are moral and pragmatic grounds of judging goodness, some clarifications in order to avert confusions about moral and non-moral "should" is needed here. In this context, both the cases of 'reservation' fall in the category of factual matter or what we call, "matters of fact", which are essentially "non-moral" in nature, that is, matters beyond the realm of morality. The problem is how we say that reservation in the first case deals with 'moral should', whereas the second case does not deal with it. We have to realise that though both cases of 'reservation' are factual in nature, both does not transcend the realm of morality because in one case, moral basis for factual decision-making, that is, 'reservation' is necessary though not sufficient, whereas in another case, such basis is neither needed nor sufficient. Without referring to people's moral sense, opinions, arguments, reasons as well as principles of morality, the matter of reservation for the geographically challenged people and not those of a caste or creed may be resolved, which, however, takes a complete U-turn if the *limit of reservation is exceeded or imbalanced* and if new definitions of such challenged people is pressed into practice. In such cases, the matter of reservation for these challenged people comes within the realm of moral inquiry and does not remain out of it. Hence, we have to take care of distinctive moral reasons available to us which comes to counter the question of desirability of reservation. Clearly, 'moral should' in case of factual affairs in to inquire about desirability of the same on clear *moral grounds* available to us, whereas non-moral should in case of factual affairs is not to inquire about desirability on the same grounds. The non-moral grounds available to us are extremely important when it comes to resolution of purely practical matters.

With this it is clear that in educational ethics, we take up the task of resolution of ethically relevant issues or issues raising questions of moral should, that is, issues which incites our moral reasons to flow for resolution of these issues. Now we come to the problem of models of resolving ethical issues. This is to ask, following which 'method' should we resolve value-laden practical issues in education? To be clearer now, "value-laden" in this context should *not* be taken as: (a) ethicists or others trained in ethics or experts in axiology *discover and/or impute* 'value' (ethical) to a practical problem in education, which thus turns the problem to 'value-laden practical problem' and (b) ethicists or others trained in ethics or experts in axiology by virtue of *knowledge of ethical principles* come to *know* that some practical problems are 'value-laden'. To add, 'value-laden' does *not* mean the *discovery of the public* that some practical problems in education are either in accordance with or in contrary to the *conventional morality*. Let us consider why 'value-laden educational problems' should not be understood in these ways. First, whether we imagine an expert in the field of academic ethics or value studies or a common man having no such expertise, 'value-laden' issues are not so by virtue of a person or a group of persons applying their theoretical knowledge of ethics or their conventional conception of morality because people having no knowledge of academic ethics or values as well as not obsessed with conventional moral dogmas are perfectly placed to realise that some problems in education are not merely practical in nature rather laden with "value", that is, they raise questions of good, right, duty, justice, obligation, virtues and so on. However, we need to clarify here that "value" in "value-laden" should not be understood as widely as both "moral and non-moral value-laden", rather narrowly in this context as 'moral value-laden' or 'ethical value-laden' or simply, 'value-laden'. In this sense then, knowing the intricacies of normative ethics, the different normative theories and their justification, which leads to good knowledge of normative and metaethics, does not in any way lead us to assert that, therefore, we know what issues are 'value-laden'. In fact, in many cases, normative knowledge in particular does more harm than good in knowing which issues are 'value-laden'. Our commitment to Kantianism or Epicureanism as normative thesis might lead us to 'see' a partial truth most of the time because obsessed by these theories we tend to see or believe (wrongly) that such and such problems are 'value-laden', whereas others are not so. However, the truth is that a problem may be realised as 'value-laden' by ethicists having knowledge of a moral theory or many moral theories or none. The reason for this realisation is fairly simple, which I shall repeat with some welcome risk here (for details, see vol. 1). As academic knowledge of ethics does not keep us in discovering or imputing values to a problem, both the conceptions of "discovery" and "imputation" need a few words for clarity. Here, 'to discover' is to find out a truth about 'value' in a problem aided with theoretical expertise, which is, therefore, too technical for laymen to do. "Imputation" is far more technical on the part of the moral experts as it is not finding out "a truth" rather to impose a truth on the basis of moral expertise. In the first case, experts are satisfied with using ethical theories as means to find a value, whereas in the second case, they are more satisfied when they use theoretical knowledge as means to justify that such and such ethical value accompanies a problem. In any case 'discovery' and 'imputation' of values by experts to enable them to project some problems as 'value-laden' is both practically and ethically unacceptable because on the one hand in doing so our experts artificially and whimsically apply their theoretical ethical knowledge to declare something 'value-laden', and therefore, impractical and on the other hand in doing so our experts become ethical chauvinists, power assuming exponents of a division of labour in which ethicists or axiologists find value-laden issues for resolution and others become spectators. This may be true of any non-ethicist who have the tendency to track power on matters of value because much like the experts, these assumed or pseudo-experts of morality either impose conventional moral knowledge or the morality of a group or class or clan to say that such and such are value-laden issues, or else, they take their belief to be true in such matters. In any case, dogmatic people or self assumed moral *gurus* cannot be discoverers or imputers of 'value'. It would be equally difficult for us to imagine that some problems are value-laden because they are inherently so, that is, they exist as a separate category of phenomena in our societies. The changes in human society enable us see that a closed set of issues which are value-laden, does not exist since eternity or shall remain so. In the field of education, for instance, the emergence of privatization of education or reservation of seats in higher education as value-laden issues are not eternally existing issues, they were more or less non-existent in Indian society at some past epoch but now they are the most hotly debated ones for resolution. It may well be that at a future epoch the issues will no more haunt us for value resolution. Equally true is that resolution of these issues at this point of history may not quash it forever. Value-laden issues in education emerge, grow, fizzle out and remerge in time, the set of such issues is 'open ended', not closed. There is thus no closed set of value-laden issues in education which were found by experts or pseudo-experts. This last assertion takes deeper into the 'model' of ethical resolution in education. We have for us a message: 'no division of labour created by moral experts is needed when it comes to identify which practical educational issues are value-laden and some issues are not value-laden absolutely and eternally and thus exist as an independent category.'

The problem is, 'how do ordinary people as well as experts come to identify 'value-laden' educational issues'? To be precise, it comes naturally to us. This is not to say that it is all in our nature rather, it is our participation in the community life that enable us to identify these problems, though the community life varies greatly according to the nature and extent of the communities. Hence, there is a likelihood of having varied moral experiences and knowledge, which includes the knowledge of value-laden issues, like educational value-laden issues. There may be differences in the perception of any practical problem being value-laden largely owing to the nature of our participation in the communities and the different theoretical dogmas we nurture in society owing to our intellectual capacities to think, reason, imagine, assume, hypothesize and conjecture as helped by the nature and extent of education we have, which does not necessarily and sufficiently include ethics education. In fact, being completely illiterate does not prevent us from being able to identify value-laden practical problems; people do identify them and contribute to some extent to resolve them if needed, but remaining illiterate or uneducated or even maleducated is not a great advantage. It is poor to argue that as uneducated people are able to identify values and resolve them, it is better to be uneducated. The flip-side of the coin is that the illiterate, uneducated and maleducated people have more often than not myopic value perceptions including human and moral value perceptions, which end up in the myopic identification of value problems and their equally bad resolution. It may well be that proper education of these people might have encouraged them to have brighter value experiences and knowledge. We ought to remember that our life of community participation grows more and more varied with age. We begin with a family having a wide environment to interact that includes natural beings and things and gradually start other interactions with fellow pupils in schools, colleges and offices, each having unique environment, each educating us in virtues and values though there may not be any intended classroom education of the same. Hence, all people, low or high, young or old have community life, a life of interactions with humans and non-humans, which combined with processes of formal and non-formal education gives us the power to recognise that some problems are starkly practical whereas others are value-laden or ethical in nature, that is, some demand pragmatics for resolution whereas others demand our latent moral experiences and knowledge to wake up for resolution. In both cases, the literate and the educated people have an edge over others as they have wider and qualitative life of community participation. Truly, education gives us many moral dogmas, illiteracy and pseudo-education, but the power to counter them, to eradicate them and to form better moral opinion and moral acumen comes from education. Education does not merely enable us to identify value-laden issues better or with ease rather enable us to face them with greater boldness as dogmas are put to critical inquiry by virtue of spirit of freedom in us to know the ethical truth over the dogmatic ones. Illiteracy and pseudo-education are failures in the face of challenges to dogmas that curb the spirit of ethical inquiry. Hence, participation in community life should now be seen as qualified with a "qualitative" participation by virtue of education, which is the basis of *our* moral experiences and knowledge or simply, 'our' value experiences, though this does not necessarily need moral education or normative — metaethical education. In other words, being illiterate about normativism and metaethics does not harm us least with regard to recognition of value-issues and resolving them, but being illiterate in life or remaining uneducated does harm us with regard to the recognition of value issues and their resolution. In any case being illiterate in normative and metaethics does harm those to a great degree who wants to participate in the process of value resolution in the capacity of a *moderator* or a *corroborator* of moral debates as well as *analyst* of moral debates. We shall come to this point at a later stage.

Our discussion thus far has revealed that those 'models' of value resolution which starts with the conceptions of a 'division of labour' as made by expert ethicists who also champions expert knowledge in matters of morality, is unacceptable. Hence, we must be careful about those models of ethical resolution of educational matters, which relies on the misconceptions that some people identify ethical issues in education whereas others acknowledge them and some people resolve these issues and others obey them, and this is due to the theoretical advantage some people have over others by being ethics educated. Clearly we criticise those models of value resolution in education which are artificial and chauvinist, that is, which begins with the idea that ethics education is needed for all people to become experts to sort out value issues in education. Nevertheless, such education may be of great help when it comes to the moderation of the process of ethical resolution.

Moving further towards unravelling the models of ethical application with regard to resolution of value-laden educational problems, we find that those influenced by ethical expertise and artificiality believes that all value-laden educational issues needs to be resolved either by an expert or group of experts in isolation or association. The idea is that expert ethicists have complete knowledge of theoretical ethics, particularly the knowledge of norms and their justifications as well as the fittingness of these norms in value cases in education for their resolution. Hence, theoreticism followed by fitting theories in value-dilemmatic situations like solution of jigsaw puzzles by expert puzzle masters is the key to educational ethical resolution. This may be done by a power-tracking expert ethicist who thinks his or her normative conception, which is most of the time absolutist or monolithic is overpowering in *all* cases of resolution of educational ethical dilemmas. Or, at best, they find more than one theories to be applied in some cases as a mechanical conception of resolution. Or, this may give way to some experts brainstorming together to find a consensus in resolution following the same line of 'theories-fitting-cases' in a mechanical manner. Or, still better, these experts include able administrators, educationists and policy makers who join esoteric coteries of ethical thinkers because they have great knowledge of many things to find out which issue needs which theories for solution. Most interestingly, what these people thrash out after meticulous thinking needs to be accepted by the public who, however, were directly related to value-crises. We have to believe, therefore, that privatization in education is a value-laden issue which needs ethicists, well-read thinkers, administrators and policy makers of esteem for a sound resolution. However, the brunt of privatization may be faced by several poor Indians or not well to do Indians and their children, who are neglected even if they are well educated or if they are illiterate. This conception of theoreticism followed by action by a group of elites in education is based on an extremely poor idea that all value issues in education belongs to the *campus* or are *in-house*, whereas the public, have enough ethical experience and ethical knowledge though not the knowledge of theories to resolve. Interesting is to know whether all the 'in-house' people are well read in ethics? No, they are not. Then why should they be so important in value resolution? Their level of education, intellect, brilliance, position, post, responsibilities cannot be the determinants of their inclusion in the 'in-house' party for resolution. More often than not, these responsible people have no idea and care for the commoners who face a problem of value. Intellectualism need not be overplayed when it comes to value resolution in education. Ethical expertise is thus uncalled for in value resolution because in isolation or in association of select groups, intellectualism and power relegates public to a non-entity in moral matters. The public were similarly neglected when it comes to identification of problems of value in education. All this is distasteful to us. A model of resolution of value-charged issues in education needs to be public-oriented and thus ethical. An ethical model of ethical resolution should be careful about the value of the public participation in terms of interactions or debates in which their moral experiences are put to test along with the educationists, expert ethicists, administrators, planners, law-makers and so on. Education touches every strata of the public in our societies, at least it is expected to do so. We cannot, therefore, neglect the power of the people in value resolution. We need to remember that in India, children of illiterate and uneducated people come to school and college education, and almost many value-laden issues involve them as well. However, as I have said before, due to the lack of education, a large chunk of the population are bereft of qualitative participation in social life, which causes irreparable damage to their ability to participate with vigour and flair in moral dialogues for moral resolution. However, in a democracy like India, which is also largely infested with poor people or very ordinary income people, we have to find out ways to involve these people to some extent at least to know what their moral opinions are though they may be aghast at wonder if you talk about morality with them. Knowing moral opinions for a moral resolution does not beg academic 'moral talk' with the public. In what ways can we involve these people takes us to another model of value resolution, to which we shall come shortly.

We have gathered that we are critical about those models of value resolution in education which are anti-people and pro-clan, that is, in favour of a clan of intellectuals and educated moral experts who manoeuvre morality by virtue of academic ethics and/or ethical experiences they have which is largely 'in-house' affair, where 'in-house' amounts to 'in the academic institutions', 'in the administrative institutions' and both of them. Next, we come to the criticism of models encouraging value-resolutions in education where experts in ethics act as 'moral guardians' much like Plato's noble people who have the 'moral authority' to decide finally what things are ethically desirable in education though many other intellectuals give their moral opinions. This is so because it is these noble people, who by virtue of their moral training and education enjoy authority of deciding courses of action after other people have discussed about what may be morally acceptable in the face of a moral dilemma. This model is highly chauvinistic as it tends to downplay the role of formulating the moral courses of action of the non-philosophers, who are 'in-house' people directly concerned with the educational activities. Hence, we have to believe that moral experts shall not only have the 'official responsibility' to arrange for moral dialogues to resolve an issue with 'in-house' people rather, at the end of the dialogue when the experts believe they had enough of arguments to come to a conclusion, other parties leave the 'official job' of formulation of morally oriented decision-making rules to these moral experts. This is easily understood by us when we imagine a micro-level example. Much like what happens in our schools when ethics teacher assumes the power of value-resolver and after talking to concerned students and teachers about a moral dilemma, they further take the charge of the situation to formulate moral behavioural codes or rules of thumb for teachers and students. Imagine at the macro-level that an ethicist has been empowered to resolve the issue of religious education in our schools along with concerned 'in-house' people and after some brainstorming does the final homework to frame do's and don'ts for the in-house people in our society. It is acting much like a breadwinner of the community of deprived philosophers who otherwise find no positive role in social life. Hence, the idea is that the ethicists shall save us from our impractical ignominy in society by having some authority over others. We thus come to the end of our criticism of moral chauvinism in all forms. Our suggested model needs to be pro-people, as I have said. We shall come to it now. We shall also come to the unique role of ethicists in this regard though the official status they now enjoy is not the one, which were given to them as authorities. How can an unauthoritative ethicist come to life and action in the field of education?

An ethicist should come to life and action first at the point of "value identification", that is, to lead way with many other concerned civil people to see that the society at large is fraught with such and such value crises. Next, the ethicist (along with other concerned parties), arranges moral dialogues to come to a consensus about value maters. However, by virtue of orientation in ethics, ethicists and others trained in ethics such as teachers of any subject or students or other professionals of ethical interest should further take the pain to structure adequate questions for moral debates about value crises so that the participation of laymen is made possible. This is extremely important for a moral debate because it cannot proceed like any debate. It has to be based on replies to questions, which are intended to bring out our *moral opinions*. There is *no* structuralism here as ethicist are not given exclusive official status to structure questions by virtue of theoretical manipulations or to arrange dialogues. Then we come to the selection of the in-house and other people related to the value-laden issues, whose opinions be taken by ethicists and others oriented in ethics so that they come to know after *initial* introductory talks with a number of people, whom to choose for the dialogue. We cannot simply go to any person without any context to invite him or her for a dialogue, it needs some vision, planning and explanation before people are selected for debates. Moving further ethicists and others oriented in ethics act as "moderators" and "corroborators". (Readers must be aware of this point mentioned by me early on). This is to say that people taking pain for moral resolution on voluntary basis (which is not an official task), should guide moral debates by putting questions, initiating agreements through a number of disagreements to the desired moral consensus regarding a value-issue in education. Hence, these people act only as 'moderators' and 'corroborators' of debates *not* experts imposing theoretical views on moral matters as well as framing decision-making rules after debates are all over. In reality, the ethics moderators not only act in association for consensus, they formulate decision-making rules in association as well. And do not foolishly apply them in society because the task of application is better done when appropriate administrative wing takes up the tasks of formulation and enforcement of rules. Finally, there is a task for the *trained ethicists*, which is unique to them because it is technical, and in no way contributing to the real life public debate. We call this *analysis of moral debates* to find out on theoretical grounds the viability of norms of ethics in real life debates. The analysis reveals the real dynamics of academic ethical thesis, which is of some *academic interest* to persons interested in academic ethics. I must assert that non-chauvinism in ethical application in education does not mean that ethicists or persons interested in ethical application has no role to play and common public needs to do everything. Non-chauvinism, as found in, *intersubjective corroboration* gives importance to the ethicists in moral debates and resolution with a difference that other persons interested in ethical matters having ethics-background may have moral authority to initiate moral dialogues and later on analyse the points of debates for a normative study. The discovery of moral value is thus a collective task of the public in which ethicists and others trained in ethics are moral guides. We need to remember that moral debates are highly technical in nature; it needs declassed ethicists to take enough leadership to come up front because it should be initiated somewhere by someone at least. Hence, public participation in ethics is not an 'in-house' affair; it is very broad and risky because we need to involve the public irrespective of caste, class, creed, status, role, post, position and degree of education.

As we turn to the micro-level, the 'in-house' moral dilemmas in schools, need not be resolved only by ethics teachers. The participation of the teachers and students are needed with the administrative bodies if needed, but well planned and moderated by persons who have good orientation in ethics. Value resolution in our educational institutions needs to be democratic and decentralized. In fact, this may form a part of our school life and not curriculum where teachers oriented in ethics take the pain of value resolution, which might be gradually transmitted to students as a way of life so that such practical orientation in values helps them in their professional and social life when they come across crises in values for urgent resolution. Education in this way may be both value-oriented and social-oriented. It is good to have a crop of teachers who care for values and value crises in the spirit of being a moderator and a guide so that others come together to discover what could be the humane way to resolve a dilemma. Interested teachers might analyse the outcome for academic interest to find real dynamics of ethical theories, which is however, not a matter to be taught to the students. In any case, all interested teachers in this regard should have good ethics orientation because moderation of dialogues preceded by framing questions and succeeded by analysis, demand such training on their part. Hence, ethics teaching may be an optional part of teachers' training lest anyone takes such interest, though such teaching should not be either compulsory or optional for our students in school because it is over demanding, unpragmatic and wayward because we can socialize students as well as value orient them in our institutions without formal ethics education, the ways have been already discussed by me in the previous chapter. However, ethics teaching is needed for those students who in life, apart from other things would love to lead the moral way of moderation and analysis, which I think, is a matter to be taken up only after the high school education.

I would like to remind the readers about Mr. Adrian M. Dupuis who remarks that "the major objective of education, at all levels should be social efficiency, i.e., school experiences should develop in students the skills and abilities necessary to interact with other individuals and groups in order to achieve social consensus. Realization of this objective implies the necessity for training in group problem solving which becomes the very heart of the educational process."[1] He further adds to mention, "These conclusions arising from consensus are not considered right and better for all groups at all times but are at the best means to intelligent actions for the solution of the problem in hand.... The implication is that there are no right and wrong answers, especially to normative problems, no right or wrong ways of doing things either in the classroom or in administrative affairs."[2] Dupuis is right in thinking that intersubjective corroboration or models like these for value resolution in-house or in-society does not give us fixed set of decision-making moral rules. We do not claim to find sacred answers from the public at a point of time. Hence, the process must go on until fresh set of moral churnings do not give us preferable set of rules. I must add that in countries like India, one must not stop the process of combining the ideas emerged at different parts of the huge nation of different cultures, races, languages and faiths. Nevertheless, the method has its own problems because it is difficult to see such things in our schools at this stage and more difficult to find them in our country as led by ethicists or others. Yet, ideals are there to be followed whether they are still followed or not is a different matter. However, people like Karl H. Popper (in *The Poverty of Historicism*, 1961) and G.H. Bantock is of the opinion that in-house group consensus is not necessarily superior to that of an individual in value issues, particularly when the group consists of children. To this, we need to say that the democratic vision of value resolution as we have said does not consist of immature pupils coming to consensus all alone. At the macro level, the same does not happen. The democratic methodology asserts the need of the people participating in moral ways of life to come together to form a consensus which is certainly ethical than what an individual says. Individuals of great intellectual power have said many wise things about values but these things emerge and change with time, which an intellectual need not necessarily resolve in a manner acceptable to all of us for all times to come. A historical belief it is to say that rather than people together, individuals by virtue of intellectual power play have decided the moral fortunes of nation. If that has really happened, should not happen any further because intellectual power-tracking is most unethical in ethical matters.

With this, we come to the end of discussion of models of ethical resolution in education, which is an important task of educational ethics to take up. It is now important to find out some value-laden educational issues of our times in India needing urgent resolution. I will then provide a list of questions which were used by me along with many participants to resolve these issues so that readers themselves have an idea of intersubjective corroboration, and if needed they may change or modify the questions to independently move for value resolution. Hence, I shall refrain from providing the details of ethical dialogues I have moderated, consensus reached thereby, decision-making ruled framed subsequently and the outcome of the analysis of moral opinions. However, at the end of the chapter, I shall take up the value-laden case of privatization in education in India in more details to show how application of ethics in education is possible. Indian education as I have discovered after talking to a number of concerned people, faces the following major value crises:

(a) Teaching spiritual and religious values in the name of value-based education in schools and colleges.
(b) Adopting English as the major medium of instruction in schools and colleges.
(c) Making corporeal punishment in schools an act of offence.
(d) Compulsory sex education in schools.
(e) Privatization in Education *vis-à-vis* government responsibilities in education. There are other problems of concern among which two needs special mention:
(f) Using animals for education, particularly in the bio-sciences.
(g) Reservation of seats in higher and technical institutions on caste basis.

Many, other value-laden issues may be discussed. For all practical purposes, I will take up first the issues (a) to (d) briefly avoiding details of dialogues and consensus.

To take up the value-laden issue of *spiritual education* first we need to note that it has raked the Indian educational circle in the past six years, though traces of this controversy were visible when religious and spiritual education in the name of teaching moral science was in practice in many Indian schools and colleges. To add some fuel in it, a number of educational institutions, some enjoying the status of deemed university were openly advocating the need of spiritual education. Some religious institutions backed up the idea in the cover of universal education. Hence, the Hindu, the Christian, the Islamic and the Sikh educational bodies came up with the ideology of ethico-spiritual education as value-based education. Not to be left behind, the secular government of India now and then felt the need of such education, which was at every instance vehemently opposed by educationists and common men. The role of the educational bodies fathered by the central and the state governments were in fact, in the eye of the storm because non-secular institutions had to go by ceretain ideologies. So much so was the government pleased with the conception of value-based education that the Union Ministry of Human Resource Development allocated Rs. 200 crores headed by Mr. D. Swaminathan to Ramakrishna Mission, Mysore, Gujarat Vidyapith,

Jaina Viswa Bharti in Rajasthan, Avinashalingam Deemed University, Coimbatore and others to conduct sessions on "values". Interestingly the ministry was very balanced in allocation, mostly fine-tuning important religiously tinged institutions as well as the Regional College in Bhuvaneshwar, which is non-religious in essence in the name of "value-based" education. The honchos in the sacred University Grants Commission backed up by great ideologies pressed value-based education on poor learners not forgetting the great ideal of a nation's spiritual facelift. The NCERT was not left behind as they set up National Resource Centre on Value Education (NRCVE) to deal with the issue of value-based education, and in doing so they called up a mess of religious people in the year 2000 representing flag bearers of value education. The ministry was then upbeat at the introduction of jam-of-values in our secular institutions in another set of textbook. Allegedly, the entire exercise of value-education in connivance with the religious mess, which ultimately tries to find some undisputed values for teachers and students to inculcate, is a peculiar effort on the part of the government to secularize education under the veil of non-secular ideologies. Hence, in and out the government voices were raised against religious and spiritual education in the name of value-based education. And this entire hullabaloo was due to one Mr. Macaulay who was supposed to destroy our value-system by imposing domineering English education, which now needed an overhaul by ushering Indian values among our students. Our students need to know the treasures of values hidden in the Vedas, Upaniṣads, Buddhism, Jainism, Sikhism and in many theses of the neo-Vedāntins of India. There was no zealous argument to cover value education with religion or spirituality because the cover was not needed at all. Protagonists felt that religions impart great spiritual values that make us humans in the true sense of the term if we inculcate these values in the learners. It is not the championing Hinduism or Hindu values but "universal values" picked from the great religions. The ground of moral controversy was thus made ripe when spiritual education went too far.

What was happening in India from 1998 to 2004 was not shameful in terms of morality. Take this: Professor Suprakash Ray of Bose Institute in Kolkata in his essay "Volatile Mixture" reports that "the Kansas State Board of Education has banned the teaching of the theory of evolution in schools, including Darwin's theory of biological evolution, the geological theory of plate tectonics and the cosmological Big Bang theory. These religious fundamentalists known as Creationists believe in the "young earth", that the entire universe was created only a few thousand years ago.... Such is the influence of the Creationists that since the Kansas Board approved of their stand, other states in the Bible belt have not hesitated to follow suit"[3]. We can close our eyes to imagine what would have happened in India if the Hindus advocated such things. The euphoria in the great democracy, which boasts to have highly educated population, nevertheless, has a state religion, which overpowers education if needed, but all universities did not follow suit. In any case, nothing close to this happened in India. Yet, people were up against a hidden agenda of Hindu spirituality being pushed in educational curriculum in India. Why was it immoral if the Indian secular democracy pushed any spiritual thesis in school curriculum be it Hindu, a non-Hindu, or a *kitchery* of religions? We are at hand a good debate about the moral value of a value-education which includes spiritual education because it raises questions of moral desirability which may be faced with many pro and con moral arguments. Interestingly, something must have happened by late 2002 in India, which compelled the Supreme Court in India to warn that government should refrain from any step to indoctrinate school children with particular religion and referred in its place to encourage "religious pluralism". Why was this warning? Was there really a hidden Hindu indoctrinating agenda or was it misconceived? More interesting is, should the hidden agenda be corrected by plural religious indoctrination? Was it proper to do? If you believe people like Professor Amlan Dutta and many other educationists one way to value education is to encourage the idea of celebrating different festivals of religions in schools because they unite us. Maybe they make us secular. Why should religious ways make us secular? Is secular education having respect to religious ways of life and nothing more? What if education carefully sides all references to religions, their celebrations, rituals, faiths and indoctrination? Will it make us less united? What if our schools simply ban any religious activities in our schools? Well, I believe that our readers are getting the taste of a moral controversy. I am just adding some fuel to fire to show why certain issues in education are not practically problematic; they are doubly troublesome as they raise stiff questions of moral right, just and so on. Going farther, the issue becomes all the more important as one finds learned judges Mr. M.B. Shah, Mr. H.K. Sema and Mr. D.M. Dharmadhikari stating that though religious indoctrinations and instructions cannot be state funded in the secular state, a "study" of religions is a matter of right to understand own and other religions, which cannot be stopped because without it the possibilities of the religious growth of man will be frustrated. This gives rise to a number of moral questions. One is, why should all citizens of secular India have religious growth as supreme ideal? What if one did not have such idea though he or she ardently studies many religions? Still one has to "study" religion to be free from being religious, but does that beg an institution where the taxpayer's money goes, many among whom have strong reservations about study of religions in our institutions? Is it not possible unofficially or at the personal level if that is so needed? Where did many great Indian spiritualists study religions for their moral growth? If studies can make us non-believers as well, why should it be linked to the moral growth? What if government institutions switch off any studies like these and leave them to *religious institutions* or any private institution that has religious agenda? The crux of the moral debate gradually shifts to the role of the state in spiritual indoctrination and/or studies in the name of moral or value-based education. The responsible persons representing the state argued differently. Mr. J.S. Rajput argued in an essay "Equity in Education" that the people opposing value-based education on the ground that religion is one of the sources of such education were myopic in so far as they could not see the lurking threat of rampant value degradation, corruption and anarchy in our society, and secularism or pseudo-secularism should not stop values to be derived from religions to be inculcated to our pupils. Mr. Rajput then reminds that in value-based education we are also speaking about secular, cultural, plural, democratic, environmental, human rights and other values. Again, he goes back to his basics to say that "Religions are a reality in India. The Indian state is secular but society is religious. There is no contradiction between the two. The Religious texts like the Koran, the Gitā, Upaniṣads, Bible and Zend Avesta constitute a huge ocean of universal values. If children learn about these in different classes, they will develop respect for religions other than their own"[4]. This was in accordance with Professor Kireet Joshi, the director of the Indian Council of Philosophical Research in his interview published in *The Times of India* on 18.01.2002 where he said: "The late Indira Gandhi was the first to moot the idea in the early 1980s. She drew a distinction between religion, which cannot be propagated in a secular state, and spiritual values… we (the ICPR) shall debate the values that we should inculcate in modern times"[5]. Keeping the questions emerging out of the apex courts' observations and what Mr. Rajput and Professor Joshi says, more debatable moral questions crop up. Is India a state intoxicated in religions? It may be a partial truth because in the same society huge population of *anti* and *non*-religious people live happily, and they are our people contributing tremendously to the uplift of the nation. Why should they and their wards be hurt by forcing so-called values taken from all religions? Is it not true that being compassionate, loving, helping, altruist, truthful are values well recognized by anti and non-religious people? Is there a logical relation between the discovered universal values and religions? Perhaps it may be a confused perception about 'universal' values because what are truly 'universal values' cannot be the same as 'universal religious values', they are categorically different. Universal values need to take care of cultural relativism in mind and thus relativism in value perceptions and then find out what is *objectively* true. Certainly in Indian milieu, we have tribes completely unaware of the religions of cultured people or rather, accultured people, they are non-religious people having regard for several values we imagine as religious. Among us are people who do not prefer to have for them values from religions ushered on them or their children. Similarly, the anti-religious people may have some regard for universal religious values but they disregard many of them. Did we take care of these values? Strangely, if some people are intoxicated by the idea that the *summum bonum* of human life is religious or spiritual, it is a value of accultured people or rather people who have been *made cultured* by religions. Whereas acculturation is possible without such things. Hence, what is "objectively valuable" in Indian society or any human society, which is truly "universal", does not beg picking values from religions. Both Mr. Rajput and Prof. Joshi realises that value education needs to spread its wings to cover non-religious values, which may be the value of "environmental protection", "regard for the life", "ways and thoughts of non-religious persons" and so on, which no one will contest. But the theory that "religious values are the basis of universal values" will be definitely contested for its hegemony because that is a fallacy of implying something from another thing not belonging to that class. We have a bad habit to imagine that non-religious and anti-religious people are not virtuous people in any society. This imagination is hawkish and thus unethical. It is, therefore, unethical to let our children know that they have such and such religion, which are different from others, though every religion has good things. Nevertheless, one should have a different way of respecting others because that is secularism and they ought to imagine that this is the Indian way of life. This is truly a non-secular teaching most intolerant towards the common man who has no religion or any faith or contests faiths. It may well be that carried to an optimum limit such education amounts to what Kansas has done, banning secular scientific outlook. It may be that Mr. Macaulay is replaced one day by Mr. Hawks in Indian education if they nurture the extremely poor idea that values from religions combined with other objective values constitutes value-based education. We leave here one question unanswered, that is, even if we have a set of values cut out for us in education, what does teaching or inculcating them aim at? Does it aim at a preparing a lot of good people by a few years? We shall leave it now as the ground of moral controversy leads us to frame a questionnaire for moral debate. The debate is necessary with proper representation of non-religious people, as we now understand. We should not be scared or apathetic towards them. Let me provide a questionnaire, which I used along with some concerned people to find an answer to this value-laden educational problem. Looking at the ethical dimensions of the issue which I came to know after reading newspapers, articles, essays, opinions, debates, talking to some concerned educationists and lay persons, and a number of ethical essays on religious and spiritual indoctrination, I thought that the following persons will constitute a good panel for debate:

1. Dr. K.K. Nag, Former Vice-Chancellor of Ranchi University and Vinoba Bhave University, Hazaribagh, an eminent Botanist, who has now retired.
2. Sri Tej Bahadur Sinha, Advocate by profession in Ranchi, who is concerned with value issues in education.
3. Fr. Johnckheere, S.J., Rector of St. Xavier's School, Ranchi and now Dean at St. Albert's Theological College, Ranchi.
4. Dr. Malancha Ghosh, Former Professor of Zoology in Ranchi Women's College participating actively in the feminist movement and most expected to have a non-spiritual outlook.
5. Dr. K.C. Prasad, Head of the University Department of Mathematics and now Director of the Academic Staff College, Ranchi.
6. Dr. Hasan Raza, Professor of Urdu in the S.S. Memorial College, Ranchi and now in the University department of Urdu.

7. Dr. Icchapurak, Professor of Botany in the Ranchi Women's College, Ranchi.

The panel was constituted keeping in mind a good balance of people having different faiths, having no faith in spirituality and those, who are not directly related to the field of education but are concerned about it. It also consists of educational administrators. Moreover, in the audience we had a number of students and teachers of different disciplines who asked questions to the panellists and gave their own opinion. They were asked only four questions which took the fierce moral debate to three and half hours before there emerged a consensus after students and others asked searching questions and ended up in shaping and decision-making rules.

QUESTIONNAIRE

1. What are your views about morality, spirituality and religion *vis-à-vis* education, and value of religious and spiritual teaching in educational curriculum? Please justify your position.
2. If religious and spiritual teaching be valuable, which set of religious and spiritual philosophy should be promoted in educational institutions on priority basis and why?
3. If religious and spiritual teaching be valuable, what should be the manner and method to impart the same in educational institutions?
4. If such teachings are not valuable, suggest a humane and acceptable manner to discard all such teachings from the educational curriculum.

Readers now get an idea how they will themselves like to face these questions. They come to know that the questions are not drab theoretical ones related to a practical problem rather they incite our moral experiences to apply them in resolving these questions without fear. Interestingly, none of the panellists were philosophers or trained ethicists because they are *theory co-opted* people and try to do some sort of theoretical or normative chauvinism. Yet, a number of them present in the audience participated in the discourse in a different way. The questions stated above are trying to make explicit what was implicit in the mind of the participants. My experience is, none was able to hide their moral view about the value-laden issue of religious education. In the capacity of an ethicist, I was simply trying to guide a discourse through very rough waters till it reached the shore of consensus. I believe I had not uttered a word of wisdom, though at times I read a few provocative passages from newspapers or journals or books regarding this issue particularly when one panellist ended his course of arguments and we switched over to another panellist. In fact, these passages incited the moral views of the participants and ignited moral disagreements as well, which, however, gradually moved towards agreement. In the meanwhile I was also recording the whole discourse and noting which *normative thesis* was emerging in the moral debate. These were subsequently *analysed* for their normative ethical structure. I have no intention to encourage here the details of these things because here my intention is to initiate some interested persons (ethicists inclusive) to read literature about this issue, think about the supplied questionnaire for further modifications, construct panels with more care, go for dialogues and see how non-philosophers come to ethical consensus after raging ethical arguments to which philosophers always have a chance to agree and differ. Yet, it will be sufficient to say that most strangely, the debate reached a consensus that (a) value-based education is not the same as religious/spiritual education; hence, religious/spiritual education cannot be sufficient in value-based education; (b) such education should have no absolutist religious agenda, that is, to propagate values of a religion or religions; (c) such education should be careful about the introduction of any bigotry, orthodoxy, hegemony and anti-people ideologies through religions; (d) such education should be humane, scientific, secular, and encourage camaraderie; (e) If religious/spiritual education amounts to what has been visualised as above, it may be incorporated in our institutions but that finally amounts to a value-based education, which is humane, secular and scientific, and certainly not the same as a *purely* "religious/spiritual" education. I can see the readers excited to disagree but for that, they have to take the pain to enter into what is called practical task of educational ethics through intersubjective corroboration.

Exactly in the same manner, we can now proceed to discuss about the value-laden features of English instruction, corporeal punishment and sexuality education. Let me give some idea about these issues and provide questionnaires before I take on the details of private education and the government obligations. To start with, the issue in a multi-cultural and multi-lingual country like India, education faces a stiff challenge with regard to the medium of instruction, that is, which language or languages would be most appropriate while informing, communicating and sharing ideas with a large number of students. The nation has its own aspirations, so have regions of the nations and the units of society, our families. The greatest aspiration is to grow and develop in all respects so that a dignified living as independent civil citizens is possible. Given the great aspiration, education comes as a huge contributor because without it, there is no growth and development, physical, mental, economic, social and ethical. The problem is, how do we cope up with the people of different regions having their great aspirations at personal, family and national levels, which they need to fulfil through education? Having education, as a right or necessity is not the bone of contention, question is how to have it? In which language? Certainly, every family in regions in India have their 'own' mother language, which is hopefully their breast-milk, but do they need supplementary food? If they do, which food is needed in schools, colleges, technical institutions? The truth is, we do not have one language, which works uniformly in all levels of education. It is also a truism that in a large number of schools, colleges and technical institutions English is the *lingua franca* though it is a mere additional food, not breast-milk for majority of Indians. There is a rage over Hindi as the *lingua franca* at all levels of education, though many people simply do not digest the idea of education in that medium at all levels. However, equally true is that by 1981, 42.88 per cent population had Hindi as mother language, which outwits the nearest rival Bengali by a huge margin (8.32% against 42.88%), and if we put Kannada, Malayalam, Tamil and Telugu together, it comes to approximately 23 per cent of the population. Yet, many people say that the figure 42.88 per cent is camouflaged by many sub-Hindi dialects, which cannot be used as medium of mass instruction even in the Hindi belt. Most tragically, *Khadi Hindi* is still used by tramps in Bollywood movies when they have to make us laugh. So in the Hindi belt we have to speak or instruct in distorted versions of Hindi or localized Hindi for good or at least workable education. Many people do not buy the argument that India can be like Japan, France, Germany, Russia and China, who have their official uniform language of instruction. Chinese had its own problems but people stuck to develop it, and succeeded. In fact, long before the independence, we were multi-lingual, Hindi being a language having additional benefit to be understood by more people but that does not make it a good case for 'one' language status in education in particular. In fact, long before we had Hindi, people spoke, read, communicated, taught and studied in Sanskrit, which would have been good case for 'one' language but not Hindi. Still worse, raising the case of Sanskrit as the language in education has created great flurry because people see it as a hidden hawkish agenda. In the midst of all this, English remained undisturbed, rather it has grown tremendously in our educational institutions though many regions still fight against imposing it as the language of instruction and against its status as official national language because that is a sign of genetic disorder caused by Mr. Macaulay and his forefathers of East India Company. In any case, careful of being called traitors, we have switched English off and on in our institutions. We have since independence grown a habit (bad perhaps) to experiment with one, two and three language formulas in education because none was ready to accept that Hindi could be the language. The more the experiments we had the more the English language grew because after years of experiments with breast milk and *kitchery*, tinned food got stronger. Take this case of sub-divisions of West Bengal, which contributes importantly in the next-to-Hindi status of Bengali language in terms of percentage of population we have just seen. (Incidentally, it boasts of Tagore preaching high for mother language as the language of primary education at least). *The Statesman* on 11.05.98 reported: "A study by State Council of Educational Research and Training, West Bengal, reveals that a section of students are shifting from Bengali medium schools in many areas of the state"[6]. This is in wake of the 'switch on policy' of English at the 'primary level', which was cashed quickly by the private schools and non-governmental ones. Why were Bengalis leaving their mother language in primary education? Was it forced by external agencies? Or, a shift in the perception of education? Or, an insecurity that at higher levels Bengali won't be of much help and thus hepless in life? Is it ethically good to lull our children into false security for the sake of mother language? Is the present world so static to cater our emotive needs? By the times there was a switch on policy in West Bengal by virtue of the report tabled the Pabitra Sarkar Commission, right from class III something peculiar cropped up which may be true in many cases in India, that is, it had little impact on mass education or grassroots education in the small or big villages and tribal lands because for education (in any medium), we first need basic infrastructure in our government schools which caters the need of the poor. Most rural schools have only one classroom, somewhere one teacher and at places none visible regularly. At places, there is only one room to teach. So medium of instruction or introduction of English as a subject does not make any desired impact. Most frightening is that as compared to 19.9 per cent budgetary allocation for education in Japan, 3.5 per cent in Sri Lanka and 2.1 per cent in Bangladesh, India's allocation is meagre 3.6 per cent during the period in which switch-on-off were going on. The issue is, why should we not quit government schools to go to private ones even at the cost of selling a piece of land if needed? What would be the use of teaching all subjects in Hindi if teaching does not start at all? What is morally just for the government then to introduce English or Hindi or whatever, rather than to allocate more funds? At the time the Pabitra Sarkar Commission tabled the report, Manipur, Tamil Nadu and Tripura had English as a subject from class III whereas Sikkim started it from class I. So there was no uniformity in language policy at the primary level in India, and most states had their own ethic and emotive issues looming large over a uniform policy. Is there any moral obligation on the part of state governments to come together to have a national agenda? Why should there be lack of national policy for uniformity? Who should take the burden? We find that a petty practical issue is now growing in a Frankenstein stature when moral problems creep in. Added to our woes, till date most of the branded items our poor villagers purchase have labels mostly in English and we suddenly feel in the market, in bus stands, in public places all around that India needed English so much! This is just a tip of the iceberg as below it lies freezing truth, 'the job-market' is replete with English phobia. What *should* this nation do, which is not a precocious youth of fifty-eight plus?

Now take this. Our honourable Union Human Resource Development Minister Mr. M.M. Joshi during the time of turmoil had a solution. He favoured the *vernacular* medium rather than English as medium of instruction at the primary level. Reportedly, he refrained from commenting on Pabitra Sarkar's decision to reintroduce English in class III in West Bengal because it was a 'state matter'. But what should be the matter for the state of India? We believe that vernacular must be mandatory for *science students* in India because that will help us fight the bitter patent related imbroglios we face in world arena. Our ancient texts need to be deciphered for their scientific value because this will strengthen our "cultural nationalism". Why *should* we, therefore, not go back to the mother of languages in Indian education? Mr. R.K. Dasgupta, the former Director of the National

Library of India was also emphatic in this regard. He enthusiastically traces the non-Indians, the European *sahibs* in particular to justify that even they were so wise about the value of Sanskrit but we were not, which people included one Mr. Raja Rammohun Roy who for his love for English and English education forgot the value of Sanskrit as a mass-language, though in 1825 he established the Vedānta College in Calcutta. Yet, Rammohun could not save ignominy because Mr. Macaulay in connivance with Bentick and then Derozio with his western fervour doomed Sanskrit as mass language. Dasgupta reveals that Vidyasagar and Bankim Chandra Chattopadhyaya frustrated Sanskrit in comparison to English literature but all this came up nearly 40-50 years after Macaulay did the damage but to our tragedy, Rammohun preceded Mr. Macaulay. After this, others did their bit to further damage the vernacular as a uniformly understandable and communicable language or at least the one, which had all qualities of such a language. Now the point is if all this happened in history, and much more, was it ethically just for us *now* to harp the time of Macaulay and others who favoured English language over Sanskrit? Was it good on our part as Indians to shelve the important issue at the stroke of independence or after it? Dasgupta asks: "But how to turn to Sanskrit to make it the foundation of our culture? What is the place of Sanskrit in our education? The Radhakrishnan Commission *Report on Education* (1949) made a plea for more attention to Sanskrit"[7]. So we did not forget to shed tears for Sanskrit which was further proved by the 'Indian Government on 1-10-1956 by appointing a Sanskrit Commission under Mr. Suniti Kumar Chatterjee, says Dasgupta. Reports came in 1957; requests were made to incorporate it general education in schools and to raise public expenditure on the subject's growth. So is it not ethically obligatory on our part as Indians to act accordingly? Was it not evil on our part to forget something, which would have united us? Well, no one really believes seriously that Bengali or Tamil should replace Sanskrit as mass-language of instruction, but strangely, English tends to take the place gradually though Hindi has been forced with all might but failed in relative terms. Why is it like that? Are we genetically unethical people? Or, something is there in English instructions and English as a subject? Is it the global pressure, which we could not withstand, the market that pressed English on us which was so bad for us to succumb to, as we became so greedy market honchos? Is it not the same unethical timidness we showed when the British for ruling the country destroyed our culture and language? Was it moral then and now? Moreover, was it not unethical to be so myopic to understand the truth that most poor illiterates who find some courage to educate their children at some pain would be harried at the extra threat of an un-understandable language which also has the reputation to make children disrespectful towards parents when they start learning it?

Many among us do not buy the argument that the market and the *videshi* mentality had pressed English on us and that Sanskrit would have done better because English in India became indisputable for a greater interaction with the world community and even among people of different regions. The argument goes as this: "West Bengal is part of a global village. A village is held together by a common language and that language is English"[8]. Mr. Sunanda Sanyal argues that though we do not dispute the truth that in the international scenario, English is now not internationally the most fit interactive language than Spanish or Chinese but "the crucial choice is between developing our society and economy through the linguistic medium already in use, and postponing it till we prepare our own language for it"[9]. The problem is for how much more time should we postpone and which among "our" language? The greater issue is why we, the poor should and the middle class worry about a golden day when we have "our" language in India, whereas well-off people have "their" English language while they find "our" language? Why is it not ethical for all of us to have English when the stark truth is that it has become the only medium of instruction in higher education? Why then shield the worst-off from receiving English education? Hence, it has no ethical value to pretend to be pro-people by harping on vernacular or Hindi as the language of instruction in India (or Bengali in West Bengal). There is in fact, no ethical point in relegating English to a language of the class, vernacular as the language of the mass and Bengali as the language of the proletariat. Or, Sanskrit as "*Rām-language*", Bengali as "*Bām*-language" and English as "Sam-language".

So our ethical juggernaut does not stop until we stage a debate now to find some resolution. This was tried at a small level. Take the questionnaire for a trial of your own, the cues for preparing one is already before us.

QUESTIONNAIRE

1. What according to you ought to be aim of teaching languages? What should be moral basis for choice of one language over others in education?

2. Though a child grows up mostly in a climate of mother language, he or she comes across other languages as well. Should the growing child be not free to choose their own language for communication and learning?
3. Why should or should not a nation like India have English as a common language for instruction at all levels?
4. Should the government at the centre and the state be morally obliged and dutiful to cater to the need of Hindi as a compulsory language for instruction at all levels?

Without explaining in details the debate that was arranged by me and the resolutions found subsequently, I have the opportunity to mention the panel because that gives a hint for constituting a debate like this one. The panel includes:

1. Some parents and students of different age groups.
2. Teachers and students of philosophy and other subjects.
3. Dr. R. Badrinarayan, Professor of Physics and Former Pro-Vice Chancellor of Ranchi University.
4. Dr. Dineshwar Prasad, Former Head of Hindi and Dean of Humanities in Ranchi University.
5. Dr. D.K. Chakraborty, Former Head of English and Dean of Humanities in Ranchi University.
6. Mr. R.Y. Thornton, Principal, Bishop Westcott Boy's School, Ranchi.
7. Mr. R.B. Prasad, Principal, Central School, Doranda, Ranchi.
8. Dr. Suresh Jha, Director, NIFFT, Ranchi.

Apart from many suggestions given, the *ethical thought* of the esteemed participants was: "No more play with English, it has become our basic need in instruction, but at the primary level of education, regional languages and Hindi should be encouraged. The chief ethical reasons being the desire-satisfaction of the learners and the welfare of the masses on the whole."

Let us leave many things for our readers who want to be ethical corroborators and analysts to move to the issue of "*corporeal punishment* as an ethically justifiable necessity" in educational institutions. The related issue is whether it is ethically just to *ban* corporeal punishment in the educational institution and extend stringent measures to the families and the homes for children. The problem has gained some importance in the recent times in India as a number of cases of punishments in the government and private schools and families came into the limelight. The punishments meted to the students were so harsh that it raged the concerned citizens to ask whether in educating the children their mentors should be valueless or inhuman. Hence, it raised questions of a complete ban on punishments of corporeal nature in particular by an intervention of law, and thereby enable appropriate agencies to retort adequately on legal basis to punish (not corporeally), the mentors. Reportedly, a class VI student in a government school in Delhi, Mr. Rakesh Kumar was paraded naked in his class and beaten up by the vice-principal for taking a bath in water tank in the campus as a teacher was absent in the class. The student subsequently filed a case with the Chief Metropolitan Magistrate, who summoned the principal of the school. The complaint was initiated at the leadership of the Parents Forum for Meaningful Education in Delhi for many reasons amounting to gross unethicality on the part of the vice-principal. First, the vice-principal tortured an immature boy physically and mentally by parading him naked before his classmates. Second, he forced the boy to write that no one is responsible in punishing him, which is an act of coercion. Finally, the boy was threatened to face further beating if he narrated anything, which is an act of intentional threat. The counsel of the Forum argued that children of our nation are totally unprotected against crimes of such magnitude, and criminal jurisprudence should be wiser and active to safeguard assets of nation, as good as what we do in case of cruelty to animals if not better than that. In fact, the ethic of cruelty cannot be less important when it comes to our students. In another case, about twenty students of a prominent school in New Delhi were fined Rs. 500 each for loitering in the corridors as a matter of exemplary punishment to teach them to behave. This may be one way to avoid corporeal punishment but there are questions, which may be equally important because it deals with "extortion of money". In any case, the matter of physical punishment in schools in India remains a good passion among teachers of government schools in particular. Reports constantly crop up in this field. A student of Shyamnagar Kanti Chandra High School in Kolkata Mr. Subrata Saha of class XII was beaten so mercilessly that he became deaf in one ear for his so-called grave mistake. Tragedy is that his father could not gather courage to file a case due to his poverty and for retaliatory act on the part of the teachers. In the same school, Mr. Deepankar

Chattopaddhyaya of class VII was served with a beating amounting to shoulder bone fracture, though his father complained the police.

In the face of the rampant practice of corporeal punishment in schools, one must remember that this is nothing new. It is as old as the philosophy of "spare the rod and spoil the child" which has been carefully nurtured by teachers of old generation as most of us who are in their 50s, 60s or older remember one or the other teacher who was famous for beating and was scared as demons, but not at all loved. However, we have the habit to forget these things and now find that absence of one such teacher in our growingly indisciplined students in schools causes great harm than good. Why do we suddenly find that the new generation students are more indisciplined? Maybe, it is one way to forget the past we lived in indiscipline as bad as now or even worse. In any case, the story as it now goes with corporeal punishment is that the students and the parents are more organized and morally and legally conscious of such punishments, which has resulted into a call for "ban". The State Government of Bihar in April 2006 has come up with the idea that a rule is needed to be framed to ban the corporeal punishment in the government schools of Bihar. Why the government schools alone? Why not the private schools? Is it not possible for state governments to interfere in the disciplinary matters of private schools when these schools run their business from their territory and get students enrolled within that territory? These problems boils down to the main issue: is it not an ethical responsibility on the part of the state governments to protect students from physical and mental agonies? When it comes to the malevolent treatment of children, irrespective of private or public enrolment status, they need to be protected from malevolence. But the point is, whether or not there is at all any "malevolence" in an act of punishment. The supporters of physical punishment argue that ethically speaking, the intentional act of punishment is "benevolent" and not malevolent, and that the act of retribution is necessary, pragmatic and serves the greater good of greater number of students. Hence, ethical justification of physical punishment to school children is grounded on their good or their well-being, for the sake of their future disciplined life by not repeating some such acts in campus life or cooperative living in society, which is ethically undesirable or causes harm to civil society. Physical punishment is thus an example of retribution and not revenge or deliberate infliction of pain rather, to *reform* a child by teaching a lesson, which has to be learnt for reform. Such 'low degree' retribution is "officially" necessary, that is, must be provided by professional teachers as part of duty in the campus for the good of the campus as a whole and on the whole. Arguments follow that only a teacher encircled by a gang of notorious and unruly pupils in schools know what it means to speak of morality in a cool hour than facing hot situations. There has always been, there is and there will be such gangs of notorious pupils in our schools who ruin the campus life by shattering basic discipline which very young to young pupils tend to imitate as indiscipline spreads like bush-fire. If it is not controlled the whole atmosphere of education is ruined. However, this is much against the wishes or desires of the students but all desires are not desirable. Therefore, teachers are bound by their duty to punish and discipline. Moreover, physical punishment does not amount to third degree treatments given to criminals because teachers know it very well that a child is not a confirmed criminal even if wanton mischief tend to create a lot of problems because at this stage of life the child may be cured of unethical ways of life which helps in not becoming a criminal in the long run. Often a rogue in college or high schools who gradually turns to be a criminal is mainly owing to lack of retribution at a *desirable limit*. If the 'limit' is known to mentors, it does a lot of good for individual child, and therefore, ethically good. Strengthening the moral argument retributors argue that given the social conditions in a country and in a state, we need to decide the courses of punishment to be given to the children. In the present day, with the growth of mixed schools and sex related notoriety of some students there is more and more need for the mentors to be strict. The conditions are serious in the government schools because there is no limit to mal-administration in these schools. The result is that the classes are mess of mischief, mostly targeted at the girls. In such stages, the teachers cannot be good preachers or counsellors because they have to face harsh and grim unholy conditions. If they flee, they are unethical for not doing duties, and if they stand timid, they are mocked and tortured. Hence, nothing is unethical if teachers take the rod to keep things straight. In the private schools, the situation may be vastly different as there is initial control on students at the point of entry or admission. They are checked for number and quality. Moreover, money is a big factor as the parents put some energy to keep their children on track. It is not that all government school children have parents of lackadaisical attitude, where people do not care much for discipline, but there is least or no threat in these schools in terms of expulsion. No government school teacher thus wants to be 'tactless' in punishing students and more often than not treat palpable notorious stuff as privileged persons.

The readers are aware by this time that an apparently simply issue has dragged us to a debate of the good and the bad, the desirable and the undesirable. More is in store, when we peruse further about the decision taken in Bihar about punishing students. The point is not that teachers should not spank the students at fault rather, spanking should be "banned", that is, should be *legally prohibited* in schools. Hence, the morality of punishment has entered into debate about the legal aspect, particularly when legal punishments may be given to the teachers. In Bihar, it is still not clear how the rule will be enacted and who will ensure booking of the errant teachers. Nevertheless, it has been urged that competent people should book the errant teachers as per rules. Moral debate opens here. Why are teachers "errant" if they punish students for necessary discipline? Expectedly, they are "errant" on the basis of law or rule or set of rules. Hence, if and only if the basic laws or rules are not morally erratic, they become necessary and sufficient grounds for declaring who are 'erratic' and how should they be treated. This question of morality might take us as far as the ethic of retributive punishment *vis-à-vis* deterrent and reformative punishment, which many ethicists happily enter into with the risk that no one really contests reformation of a child as good but does not trash deterrence and retribution as good *means* to reformation either. Only if deterrence and retribution are ends themselves, many questions will arise because it is difficult to justify ethically that physical punishment of students aims either to teach potential offenders a lesson or to treat them on equal footing and nothing else. Hence, physical punishment may be ethically glorified as *means* to a glorious end, which is, "reformation" of the child. Yes, it may be ethically glorious to give errant children to recover, to come to the mainstream but why should deterrence and retribution as evil themselves be good means? The point is, on what grounds are they themselves evils and not good? Hence, the debate that the means must be ethically desirable if the end is so, takes us to the question whether deterring and retribution are at all ethically viable means if not ends in punishing students. This further takes us to consider banning rules and their ethical status because the rules *per se*, aims at declaring some such acts illegal or unlawful which are essentially *means* to a good end, that is, "reforming a child". How can physical punishment as means to reformation be itself ethically bad and/or unlawful? They may be unethical only if they are not at all means to the said good end. The moot point is: whether retribution in the form of corporeal punishment in schools is at all a means to reform a child? Well, we cannot overlook the reality that retribution is more often than not taken as "means" but ethics is certainly not about what is, but what *should* be the case. The supporters of banning retributive punishment to children argue that the ban is ethically just on the ground that the so-called good means is not a means at all. In fact, it is completely misconceived to imagine that physical punishment can in reality reform an errant child. Hence, it should be taken as an act of malevolence whether threat or thrash in the name of reformation, and therefore, ethically bad as well as legally punishable. One cannot buy the argument that it does well to the errant child in the long run. Then for the supporters of ban the most trifling task is to pronounce clearly which means are ethically and legally just to achieve the end of reformation of errant children in schools, particularly in hard cases of sexual assaults on fellow students or physical assault on them or targeting the school property as well as the teachers for harm. Most hard cases will be those in which the above acts are repeated often by a child or group of children. Timidity, tolerance and tactfulness all pay to some extent in school discipline, but what if these are put to their limit? Is it not ethically just to protect other children, the girl child, the school property and ourselves? The debate may go on. If we believe Plato and many others, physical punishment is an evil as it destroys the inherent goodness of human self or human excellence. The horse is turned to a donkey by flogging but not the other way is true. Hence, physical punishment is reflection of an *untrained* teacher who is helpless in the classroom, an utter failure, may be a poor staff who does not make teaching enjoying. Or, a rash man, temperamentally a rogue. Is it not proper to put them to task because their beating causes irrepairable damage to the reputation of schools in particular and education in general? These are all sensible ethically oriented questions, but the moot question remains: What is the humane way to punish when punishment is so needed?

If you believe the Montessori sisters, who swear by their peer, there is no sense in "punishment". Hence, why worry about humane ways of punishment? This question may be the ultimate one to put us to the dock because it questions the ethical status of "punishment" itself. For them, this word in the field of school education is repugnant. Others say that this is flying your imagination too high, too Platonic to say because ground reality is that school education is not the same as

Montessori education most popular at very young age in the preparatory schools or even for the students of seven or eight years of age. Beyond that, we enter complex psycho-physical development of children and their intricate interactions with environment, wherein deliberate acts of criminal intentions cannot be either overlooked or over hyped. In such complex states, it would be too Platonic to say that for the sake of unblemished love for the child, punishment has to be banished altogether. However, the proponents of banning spanking in schools are championing banishing "punishment" because they prefer a memorable deal for errant teachers. How can they be partisan in love? We have to remember, says the proponents of punishment in some form at least that age counts most as does psychological and moral development of a child to determine whether punishment is needed in any form, and if it is needed the problem is not of physical or mental punishment, the problem is one of *degree* because any form of punishment ultimately shatters us from within and degree of punishment is crucial in that matter. Surely, we should be shattered from within at times because it is the inner realm of children, which has a malady, needing correction. The ethical disagreements and agreements with regard to corporeal punishment in schools are thus rife in India. On the basis of the report: *Teachers may no longer spank school students* (*Sunday Times of India*, Patna/Ranchi edition, 23-04-2006) I quote the following before I place a questionnaire for our readers to go for an intersubjective corroboration dialogue.

Bihar government official: "Severe physical punishment such as caning is definitely a major punishment. But we also plan to being public humiliation of a student by a teacher under the ambit."[10]

Shailendra Kumar Sharma (Science Teacher in Gramin Uchha Vidyalaya, Chakberia): "Parents request us to punish their children occasionally if they do not study hard. In fact, we feel only teacher dedicated to the cause of students would take pains to teach and also punish children who do not study."[11]

Now consider the following questions:

QUESTIONNAIRE

1. What according to you should be the aim of punishing students? Do you think that punishment is a valuable means towards attaining a valuable goal in education?

2. Do you think that in educating children, they should be seen as "objects" of experimentation? If in the process of such experimentation, there is a demand for punishment, is it good to do so?
3. What kind of a relation do you think is desirable between the teacher and the taught? Does punishment come in way of that relation and should be thus abolished?
4. Do you think that punishing children amounts to (a) take someone as my own for reform; (b) take someone as another who may be useful for society and thus reform; (c) take someone as alien to us as a potential criminal and reform?
5. Does punishing children amount to cruelty at the physical, mental and spiritual levels? Is there any humane way to punish children, which is not cruelty at any level?
6. Kindly suggest some rules for punishments in schools for students and teachers who are errant in someway.

Those contributed in the dialogue arranged by me are:

1. Sr. S. Rosita, Principal, Holy Cross Montessori Bal Niketan, Ranchi.
2. Dr. N. Datkeolyar, Former Principal, Government Teacher's Training College, Ranchi.
3. Dr. S. Basu, Child Psychiatrist, Central Institute of Psychiatry, Ranchi.
4. Mr. C.P. Sharma, Principal & Dean, Government Teacher's Training College, Ranchi.
5. Mrs. S. Sinha, Principal, Surendranath Centenary School, Dipatoli, Ranchi.
6. Mr. C.J. Jacob, Principal, Army School, Ranchi.

The upshot of the dialogue: *Abolish physical punishment in any form* but not punishment as such. Train teachers for counselling, self-analysis and motivation.

The interplay of ethical theories: *The ethic of empathy and love*, and *the ethic of self realization.*

Let us now come to the value-laden issue of *Sex Education*, which has gained some importance in the recent times in Indian education though much has been said in this regard in the European and American institutions since a long time. In India, the AIDS bomb is ticking too fast and the sex related unwanted acts, particularly those involving school and college students are growing at a rapid rate, which must have caused some concern among the people to talk about sex and sex education. Talks about teen sex have become extremely important, and to break the psychological jinx of teachers and students at school level to talk about sexuality raises ethical questions. Let us first come to the state of the matter in India. In 1999, the Madhya Pradesh State Council of Educational Research and Training conducted a survey about sex education in schools under the sponsorship of the U.N. Fund for Population Assistance Programmes. The survey was based on fair samples of parents, teachers and students from the rural and the urban areas of the state. It covered students of the secondary and higher secondary level students. The findings of the survey writes Md. Shahid Pervez of the Statesman News Service, "may startle those who think that sex education can induce "promiscuity" among students and lead to "degeneration of collective morality", and therefore, should not be imparted at schools"[12]. Before going through the findings of the survey we have for our interest important moral thesis that traditionalists in education put through the ages, namely, sex education in school is morally undesirable as it induces promiscuity among students, which is an evil because it destroys collective morality and thereby evolves a nation of sexually pervert people. One thing has been taken for granted; destruction of public morality is injurious to the health of a nation because moral evolution of the public is desirable as against the growth of sexual perversions of the public. An evolved public morality speaks of the general well-being of the people of a nation, which is destroyed if we teach sexuality in our schools. In the common parlance, the age-old wisdom hold the adults particularly those holding the responsible office of teaching young people should not talk sex with their pupils or their own children because that is an area of adults, it needs some maturity to understand and assimilate. Rather, our ancient wisdom teaches us that teaching young people the art and value of self-control, temperance and abstinence are more important. A teacher should not tread into a path, which is most unsuitable for young people rather, find out ways in which we should control our passions, urges and cravings in life that may save us from psychopathic situations injurious to individuals and the collective. It is unimaginable, therefore, that a teacher talks sex with students. In a mixed schooling, the problem is more acute because the inquisitive boys and girls might be dragged to unholy thinking when teachers initiate to know something which they know was private to them, and thus do not bother to unravel the hidden mysteries. We are all aware with this way of arguing against sex education in schools. No one can refute the idea that talking sex and sex education is of no use before the age of ten because most of the information and message directed to the students do not reach them properly because in most of the cases psycho-physical development of the children and their mental maturity stands as a barrier. Sex education thus needs a level of maturity, as it is a scientific education, which can be taken up gradually at a stage when important biological and emotive changes are distinct in boys and girls. But this does not amount to prohibit the scientific education after a particular age in the schools on fictitious moral grounds, says the proponents of sex education. The basic moral counter argument is that the collective well-being depends on social behaviour of humans among which is their sexual behaviour in society. Hence, an individual should know what is desirable and undesirable when it comes to his or her sexual urges and its fulfilment, which has deep physical and psychological impacts on the individual. By nature we are not in a position to suppress some basic human urges, it needs some extra effort to do so to become perfect ascetics. No one can argue that a society of ascetics is morally good because in that society the unethicality to not to procreate would lead to its disastrous end. It would be an unethical life of self-abnegation that slowly shatters the collective life. We have sex urges, we need them and sex behaviour should be safe and judicious, is the crux of the argument. Hence, an education in school that does not unravel some of the mysteries of sexual life and the sexual myths that often do more harm than good to the students is unethical because mysteries and myths give rise to obsessions, orthodoxy, ignorance and distorted behaviours. It is extremely important to notice that the ethical ground of the well-being or good of the collective life becomes the basis for evaluation of its moral worth or unworth. However, for the antagonist, such education results into distorted sexual behaviour of students and thus does harm to the collective life, which is bad, and for the protagonists lack of such education distorts human behaviour and, therefore, harms public life, which is an evil. Hence, leaving aside the basis of morality, the moral debate boils down to the issue whether sex education should be at all seen a *means* to public good or should it not be a *means* to public good.

First, the protagonists say that the world has not remained the same as it did two decades ago. We have to face and live in the world in which we live and which will be infested by our future progeny for whom we should be concerned as well. The world we now live in has given us a number of sexually transmitted diseases, some are fatal. It has given us sexual perverts and criminals. We cannot ignore these harsh truths because to do is to be antisocial, which is ethically bad. We cannot live a life of seclusion, perfectly safe and unperturbed as people say we lived in a remote past. Hence, to harp on the good of *Satyayug* or an ideal epoch when there were no sexual perversions and diseases and to argue that the same will dawn when all of us practice self-control, yoga and so on is a palpable untruth and absurd imagination. Now onwards in India, for instance, countrywide training of self-control by several ways can do a little to safeguard us from sexual perversions and diseases which have spread menacingly because a training in self-control demands that the trainers tell students about basics of sex life, sex urges, sex satisfactions, sex perversions and so on and then the value of self-restraint and temperance. We should not have least doubt in our minds that self-control and temperance have their ethical value in the context of a wide range of corporeal or physical gratifications, which includes sex. Those who have read Aristotle's *Nicomechean Ethics* would agree that temperance as a cardinal virtue makes great sense in our life when we come to know that it stands as a worthwhile human behaviour in the face of satisfaction of sexual urges. The ascetic training of highest degree should thus refer to sex as a plain truth in life, and the abnormalities pertaining to it before these urges are balanced nicely in our life. The gist of moral argument of the protagonists is that most stringent ascetic training cannot and should not be based on sexual untruths; they should face a truth and then proceed to take care of behavioural abnormalities related to it. As we stand now, the most strenuous yogic postures and practices of ascetics cannot prevent AIDS and STDs, but they can help our students to realise that it is important to have some control over sexual urges, to channel sex behaviour properly in society and to do so, one may wish to go through physical and mental trainings. In fact, the physical and mental trainings derive their value from the overall good of human beings, which is possible through the contribution of several things, among which is "balance in sex behaviour". Nevertheless, the antagonists are suspicious that Western education in India is responsible in diverting our minds from the basic moral thesis that the goal of human life being self-realisation or the realisation of the spiritual Reality, proper education should teach us what it amounts to, what are its values and the paths through which one is able to realise the spiritual end of life. Given this objective of education, the education of sex is mere diversion of the focus, it is glorification of the flesh than self, and to do so is to run in the slippery slope of immorality because the students are suddenly attracted to what was unnecessary for their higher objective of education and thus inquire about the unwanted. In the name of scientific education, Western pattern of sex related education deviates us from the higher goal in life, which is unethical. Moreover, the *śāstric* education of self-control and self-abnegation takes care of the broad conception of total behavioural control and not part of it, and therefore, there is no need for a special reference to sexual behaviour or its abnormalities. If the general corporeal urges and craving are controlled it covers the urge of sex. Hence, sex-talk is not basic to the talk about self-control and temperance. Yet, going to the roots of the *śāstras,* protagonists argue that it is in them that the talk of sex under *kāma as puruṣārtha* is candid as is the talk of the value of healthy sexual life and its teachings. The rationality of the *gṛhi* stage of life, that is, the life of the family-man as bestowed with essential duties includes that of procreation and a balanced sexual life as an end of life (*purṣārtha*), which in turn needs some education at the preceding stage of life, which is *brahmacarya* or studenthood. There is a healthy debate in this regard in the *śāstras* whether in the studenthood a person should have the knowledge of all the four ends of life or the *puruṣārthas*. Hence, the *śāstras* since eternity were wise enough to tell us the value of discussing matters pertaining to sex. Why curse western education?

Let us turn to facts because they are stranger than theories. Take the following truth. Recent studies in the UK has revealed that eighty per cent teenager girls have their indomitable sex urge fulfilled without any precaution and loose virginity because they get drunk. Hence, drinking leading to unsafe sex is a testimony to the utter failure of sex education in the West, though STD and AIDS have their own dangers threatening heavily the public. Now, should we argue that sex education is a mere talk; it has nothing to do with controlling the young people in the West? If that be true, India should refrain from the burden of another education in school because that is hardly the remedy. Protagonists say that it is still the ignorance about the evil aspects of drinking and unsafe sex that results into such bizarre behaviour. Intensive sex education supported by counselling and alternative therapies and practices might get things correct. Moreover, it is not sex education which has failed rather, the social structure has grown follies from within those lead girls to such dangerous behaviour, which, however, may be corrected by other scientific ways of education and counselling. The antagonists may be dissatisfied about all this because they find many loopholes in the western education and ways of life which invites people to have undignified sex. They argue that drinking and sex are unnecessarily hyped in the public causing damage to the students. It is one thing to say that sex is important, it has its own value and yet another thing to justify that a lot of freedom in sexual behaviour is good. On the one hand, they feel need of sex education and on the other hand they ratify gay rights and the right to live together.

In the midst of the stiff moral controversy about sex education in India, something interesting has cropped up in the past 7-8 years. In an overwhelming response to the debate: "Is sex education necessary?" in the children's section called "Voices" in *The Statesman* (Kolkata edition, 1999) the following observations are worth noting:

Mohan Das Seal: "I am not a student, but I am for it (sex education). In India, sex has always been a taboo. This has only increased ignorance and this is not always for the better. If education means all round development of the child, it must include education in this. Neglect of sex education only encourages promiscuity and irresponsible casual sex. Most of the sex crimes can be traced back to this idea of our educational system which has been left deliberately dark."[13]

K.P. Roy: "I emphatically state that there is no need for revival of the sex education... simply because students want it. Sex education is partly imparted in schools through the Life Science course. Immature students in the affluent section of our society demand many things that are not essential for their development. Ambitious parents who create a void in the home atmosphere fulfil the unreasonable demands of their wards only to suppress their own guilt. The breakdown in the joint family together with the cultural aloofness of the apartment houses in towns and cities has considerably loosed the social fabric to admit various types of "sadistic pursuits". The situation is further aggravated by widespread misuse of electronic media like TV, cinema and the chat sites of the internet. No further deterioration is desirable. The need of the hour is moral education with emphasis on universalization of elementary education. An awareness campaign for adults for protection against Sexually Transmitted Diseases will be more helpful."[14]

Keeping the protagonist and the antagonist views for the perusal of our readers let me further quote what the parents in Madhya Pradesh said to the survey mentioned before.

Parents

1. 86 per cent of parents think that parents as well as teachers should give sex education to adolescents without hesitation.
2. 89 per cent believe that sex education can create awareness about AIDS and STD among teenagers.
3. 69 per cent feel that sex education should be made a separate subject in the school curriculum.

Teachers

1. 86 per cent of teachers favour sex education in schools.
2. 58 per cent do not subscribe to the view that sex education can be injurious to morality of students.
3. 71 per cent said that they feel hesitant to take classes on sex education.
4. 65 per cent felt that sex education should be given separately to boys and girls.

Students

1. About 82 per cent feel sex education should be made a part of school curriculum.
2. 60 per cent think that teachers should impart sex education.[15]

Finally, I want to provide the questionnaire, which I used for intersubjective corroboration with regard to the problem of moral desirability of sex education in India. The following people participated in the dialogue with a large number of students and teachers:

1. Dr. Indu Dhan, Former Principal, Ranchi Women's College, Ranchi.
2. Mrs. Mridula Sinha, Principal Government Teacher's Training College for Women, Ranchi.
3. Dr. R.K. Rai, Former Principal, Government Teacher's Training College, Ranchi.

4. Fr. James Toppo, Principal, St. John's School, Ranchi.
5. Dr. Sashi Shekhar, Male Surgeon, Family Planning, RMCH, Ranchi.

QUESTIONNAIRE

1. Do you conceive of something like "holistic education"? Should sex education be a necessary part of holistic education?
2. What according to you is the basis for calling sex education as either a social evil or a social good?
3. How would you evaluate the ethical values of sex education *vis-à-vis* ethico-spiritual education?
4. Is sex education another name for self-abnegation, asceticism and sex inhibition, and thus against human autonomy and freedom?
5. Is sex education in India desirable in mixed schools, particularly in the context of the taboos we nurture about women as mother or *śākti*?
6. What should be the ethical basis for participation of parents in sex education?
7. Kindly suggest some decision-making rules in this regard.

The upshot of the debate: "Sex education is desirable in the present age in India and elsewhere for its *pragmatic value* in the maintenance of a healthy social life, which is essential for humans on earth."

Theories in play: Ethical Pragmatism and Ethical Welfarism

Now I shall come to consider at length the value-laden problem of *Privatization in Education* in India. Here my approach will not be scrappy as our readers interested to find out what exactly are the processes in intersubjective corroboration, and the *post-corroboration* analysis of ethical opinions for an idea of dynamics of ethical theories, should be now given an opportunity to know all details. As usual, we will begin with the "analysis of the nature of the problem" in the Indian context and the value dilemmas that crop up for resolution. The analysis of the problem of private education is very complex, particularly when we analyse it for the revelation of the implicit value-laden aspects, which is however, my main task.

I perceive the issue of privatization in education as a value-laden issue when we consider its following aspects:

(a) The right to education and privatization;
(b) Privatization and the role of the Central and the State governments with regard to mass (not class) education which includes the problems of allocation in education; and
(c) The role of the teachers and the administrators in education in the public and the private schools.

To start with, we have the issue of right to education because any talk about the role of the private and the public institutions in education presupposes that there is at least one person in a civil state who enjoys the right to be educated, that is, enjoys the *claim right* because bereft of the right we conceive of a state full of people desiring to be educated, strive well to do so but stands no legal ground when they are either deprived of the due or deprived of the legitimate due. Let us close our eyes to imagine that we live in a socialist, secular, democratic, republic where we desire to be educated but fail to fulfil our desires because no agency was to champion what was due to us and thus have no status to complain in any case, will the state be liveable? Certainly not because a state without the conception of a constitutional guarantee to claim right to education will call for the serious evaluation of the state in terms of civility. However, any guarantee to claim right empowers the people of the state to sue the state on legal grounds. The point is, who takes the burden to face the music of giving such claim rights, the central government or the state governments or both? One reply is, none needs to face it because being a citizen of a state does not guarantee that somebody other than the citizens is responsible for *private privileges* like, being educated. Moreover, whether or not the citizens were educated or failed to be educated depends on many factors, most of them personal in nature, some are circumstantial and some others are environmental. There is no point, therefore, to imagine that for all things which are beyond the powers of the state, only the state should be held responsible and for that matter even if there are provisions for education, that does not assure a claim right to the public in general. This may be extended to the case of employment as well. The bone of contention in education is, therefore, whether all sections of the Indian population enjoys natural claim rights to education, not merely literacy and non-institutional participation of people and organizations to educate us.

The proponents of the thesis that the *duty* and *primary responsibility* of the state is to enforce the claim right to universal education, nevertheless, in their extreme stance propagate the idea that such education should be *free and compulsory*. Hence, it would be the 'duty' of the state to ensure universal, free and compulsory education up to the age of fourteen. In one sense, the extreme stance as backed by the constitutional provision of Article 45 (successfully implemented in the state of Kerala), holds that "right to education" is in fact, "fundamental and human right". However, those agreeing with the value of 'universal education' in a relatively *moderate* way holds that not necessarily should that be seen as "fundamental and human right" and for that matter there may be debate about the imperative of "free and compulsory education" up to the age of fourteen, failing which the public might move for appropriate legal justice, which will be taken with élan irrespective of powers of states. Avoiding education as a claim right lies in nitty-gritty of economics and not only politics because nothing in truth is "free" in today's world if it be compulsory—there is no free lunch in education. However, this thesis may be happily extended and supported by paranoid governance to encourage private education, holds the extreme view. Why on earth in democratic governance we need to be so sacred by the Holy Grail called, constitutional provisions and the rights, duties and obligations laid therein? Does economic truth swallow human rights? The moderates think that the constitution does not enlist education as fundamental right for obvious reasons (may be beyond economic pragmatics), to refrain from any legal claim on our part. However, history is testimony to the truth that the sub-committee on Fundamental Rights of the Constitutional Assembly initially proposed education as a social welfare programme in our welfare state and proposed *basic education* to be included as fundamental right, but the constitution makers rejected the idea subsequently, and as the story goes, one important ground being, "suppose the government runs out of funds, what then?" And the story ended up in transferring this clause to the Directive Principles of State Policy. So nothing is "free lunch", if we believe in the building blocks of our welfare state. However, many things can be *subsidised* goes the camouflaged welfarist agenda, which subsequently became the holy *avatār* of the planners in independent India until renewed debate was caused owing to bad economy of subsidies in education. Hence, can there be greater morality to save us from the ignominy of donor becoming pauper when it comes to subsidised education not to speak of free education? Didn't our constitutional makers have the foresight to reject the idea of a foolish welfare? But for the extremists, no welfare in terms of freeship or subsidy is possible without the basic morality that after all for the crores of poor people in India, let us think and do the needful to the optimum to somehow remove the blockade of poverty of resources in free and compulsory education than expending on fun and frolic. Can it not be a greater push or compelling agenda to bring the right back to the "fundamental" status to awake from the deep slumber of several decades?

By this time, we are already in the realm of moral debate, which is gradually shifting towards private education versus public education and the economics of welfare, subsidy, freeship and so on. We like it or not, trumpeting at full throttle, that education is not to be linked to money matters does not take the truth out of the fact that it is an economic activity; it needs to be placed alongside money matters particularly when it comes to free education to a huge population. However, there are two moral opinions about the economic aspect of free and compulsory basic education. A group of educationists and economists feel that the moral strength of free and compulsory basic education lies in the economic well-being of the overall population of a country, not that of a class therein. Hence, on the basis of "welfare on the whole" it is justifiable that basic education should be a human right, fundamental so to say which needs to be fulfilled at some cost by the government as a matter of claim. The theory of optimization of economic benefits has been championed by many including Amartya Sen, who has spoken uprightly about the myopism of the Indian governments to not to see the obvious social benefits by empowering the mass than a class. However, others have argued that far from truth, mass education at government burden only spreads education but does no good to the economy of the country or to those who are educated. Hence, morality urges us to evaluate right to education according to the maximization principle of economic welfare in a radically different way, that is, economic growth empowers people to be educated, which is thus basic or primary but not the other way round. Well, can there be economic growth in a fool's paradise? Or, does that growth depend on a class of people who have both intellectual and economic capital? The famous economists retort to say that not in a fool's paradise but in paradise of sensible people, financial and other aspects of education should be left to the parties other than the government who does collectively make us wiser and not uneducated. Thus, the lines are drawn in the moral debate of private and public education.

Nevertheless, the economists propagating the idea of economic empowerment as basic to education realises the simple truth that in reality the government of India was not silent through the years because educational *allocation* was one exercise to be taken by any government. Hence, the point is to shut all allocation towards public education or to move in some direction at least, whether it was meagre or plenty. In fact, governments of our times, which boast to be pro-public, needs to show their public face sparingly but surely. One way to show the public face (the welfarist one so to speak), and to do something about education of the mass some government allocation is essential. This can be done in the different plan periods and in the annual budgets, which becomes official as a matter of fact and not a play of imagination or high talk. As soon as we delve deeper into the aspect of government allocation, interesting value issues emerge. One important aspect of educational allocation is that governments of any ideology and welfarist conceptions do not have magic wands by rotation of which funds come to them, which they allocate. Whatever comes from the government, should come from the taxpayers. Hence, a country full of beggars or semi-beggars cannot provide government with paltry amount for education. Educational allocation handsomely happens in an economically able state and not a lingering poor one. In fact, it is shameful to remain poor and be thus poor in allocation at all sectors including education. Moreover, when it comes to a relatively not-so-well economy, what can the government do than first allocate for *roti, kapda, makaan, bijli and suraksha*? Bonded and unsheltered beggars living in dark do not need basic education first, this must be argument. Morally speaking, welfare has its own definition; none believes that imparting education is all about welfare or that it is primary because well-being or welfare is primarily a *quantitative* concept when it comes to the masses, that is, it is predominantly a "physical" not qualitative or non-material concept. However, the other side of the moral thesis is that well-being cannot be merely material because without the qualitative aspects of well-being, it is not well-being at all rather, "being well-off" whereas being well-off does not guarantee being well. The relegation of education to the secondary status only helps a nation to be worse off because a huge chunk of uneducated does not contribute to the national well-off status nor does the nation on the whole attains any welfare. Anyway, the fault-finding people are accused of criticising educational allocation in India for nothing, though it has increased pretty well through the decades after independence. Nevertheless, unfazed critics argue that their criticism holds ground on two counts of immorality. First, in comparison to allocation in other fields that saw revolutions such as the green, the white and so on, education saw committees and commissions. Perhaps educational commissions in India have outwitted global records of forming commissions for uplift but without much result. As late as 2001, we huffed and puffed to justify that 50 per cent of our population is literate but not educated (formally speaking) though many commissions and committees write pages about the betterment of education. It is difficult to assess whether literacy is sufficient ground for being proud, certainly, it is not sufficient for being well-off and well-being. In addition to it, education has been the most happy field for experiments and happy ground to justify an ideology to be great. All this is immoral because any government decision-making and allocation that does not hit the target and is thus wayward, does no good to the field. Everything done becomes fruitless, which is unnecessary expenditure of public money, squeezing the public (already at pain) unnecessarily is to encourage malpractice in spending, which is unethical. However, for defence it is argued that commissions are not always unnecessary because it was the Kothari Commission (1964-66), that suggested six per cent of GDP to be spent on education, which should have been in view within thirty years because three decades are good enough time to reach the target. However, in 1996 Amartya Sen and Jean Dreze found India at the 82nd position in the global list of spending in education, which was too painful for many who thought educational spending was ethically more worth than blasting a super-bomb. No one really doubts that self-defence, territorial integrity and independence are most needed for a country to exist in pride and we should be wise to spend sizeable amount on it, but the ethic of a super-bomb in the backdrop of military strategic deterrence than safeguard for independence needs some questioning particularly after the second blast. Did we not have enough? Was it not proper to spend a little more in educating for the hundreds and thousands of poor people? Are we in pride in world arena when hand to mouth people with rickety educational structure glorify being blasters of two super-bombs? These are different moral questions as they appear to us, but there are replies as well. We shall come to them but let us face bitterness a little farther. The plan expenditure on basic education was 56 per cent in the First Plan, which was very good to start with. This dipped to 24 per cent in the Fourth Plan and rose to 47 per cent in the Eighth Plan. The major share of expenditure in education is that of the Central and the State governments, which justifies that both feel obliged to educate the masses up to a level at least but the shift of education to the state list saw nearly 20 per cent of their budgetary allocation on education as compared to 2.2 per cent by the Central Government. Why should the Centre be not more spending? Is it not ethically desirable for the Central Government to allocate more so that welfare measures at the grassroots level turns out to be more decent and adequate? In any case in 1997 elementary education saw phenomenal budget allocation though huge amount left unspent in 1996, which focuses the additional callousness of the administration to use whatever meagre amount is due to them. Is this the ethical way to carry on our duties and obligations? Why educational allotment does not appear lucrative to administrators? We cannot buy the argument in this welfare state that illiteracy and mal-education are the tools at the hands of the government machinery to exploit people. Or, is that true? Replies to these awkward moral queries are simple. First, comparison of allocation on education with that of defence or infrastructure are pointless and needless because the nature of certain fields in which budget allocation are more is different from education. Certain fields necessarily involve greater spending than others, there should be no ethical crises in this matter. Second, quality education for all needs some time, it is not a process comparable to building a big dam which often takes shape more swiftly even due to dilly-dallying because educating the masses are faced with several counter pressures in the society including official callousness and malpractices. Poverty stricken people are always at the crossroads to earn or to study because for most people both cannot go together. Hence, morality demands us to be more pragmatic in social welfare through qualitative measures like education, and to add, we are speaking of education in India, which is not a tiny nation, there are problems but we have to bear. Can private education be a helping hand?

Let us now come to the role of teachers and administrators in public education, which raises questions of ethical value. The role of the teachers and administrators should be evaluated in the context of infrastructural facilities provided to them as guaranteed by budget allocation and efficient disbursement when we speak of organized formal education because education as we discuss it here is not amateurism. Interesting information came up about education in West Bengal in the daily *The Statesman*. One is 'Two teachers for two students' and another one 'One teacher for 200 students', and recently in the *The Times of India*, 'One teacher for one student'. Most amusing is that government schools hold the distinction to be forerunners in such records. This may be true of any other state in India, which many people say is mainly due to the bad shape of the school infrastructure, poor administration and lack of commitment on the part of the teachers, all of them grossly unethical given the earnestness of drawing salaries and other benefits. But there is another story to be found in *The Statesman*: 'The Calcutta Municipal Corporation with the help of UNICEF reaches the children not reached', which is just not like well-dressed goody boys and girls of the *hi-fi* English schools doing a one-day good Samaritan act on footpaths or slums. The government effort is not gimmickry; it is daring to go the dark by-lanes to educate. This may be true of any other state. More in store: 'Initiated by the Central Government, in West Bengal, the integrated schools run by the government that accommodate physically and mentally unchallenged and challenged boys and girls for education. However, seriously challenged boys and girls are not accommodated in these schools'. This must be unthinkable by the private players as a whooping Rs. 18,42,000 has been sanctioned for this project, though some private institutions try to do something like this, which is commendable. These cases place us to consider the role of the teachers and administrators in the public schools *vis-à-vis* private schools. On the one hand we have no lack of funds in principle but severe lack of the same in practice in the government schools which run in bizarre ways we have just seen, and on the other hand, hard earned fund raised for education is used most peculiarly, that is, give away something by taking away something else. We shall turn to this aspect shortly. The greatest moral issue in the free-fall of public schools. In the government run institutions, there is an eternal blame-game if you dare speak their free-fall. Certainly, it is not a mean achievement to educate the mass at the cost of reaching dingy and risky environments by the government schools, but the point is whether it is ethical to boast of greatness with the truth that the students not reached are treated shabbily, not anyway near dignified studenthood with legitimate facilities provided to them. What can be so great in providing something, which is nothing by the standards of decency? Morality may be better visited when good Samaritans can afford to do what they were expected to do. In fact, if government institutions reach all sections of population, it is their obligation and their duty because the same is part of a covenant that exists between those who serve and the employer. Is there any moral point in being boastful about all this, particularly, when what is done is not up to the mark? There is no point in hyping the fact that mass education is highly moral. False vanity and dignity is thus certainly not moral. The private schools, which do not have any pretension to be non-profiteering, do not take any risk to reach all sections of the society at any cost because that is not part of their duty. Rather, their contribution to the society must be well recognised. The moral status of private tuition in private institutions stems from non-hypocritical profit oriented work that expectedly helps society to a great extent. Naturally, the teachers in private institutions are equally unmasked, they educate as a matter of duty but the covenant is bargained in nature, that is, for profit maximization. However, these teachers feel that government teachers are perennially in all win situation (most unethically though) because they make a piggy ride on government cushion. Still, for the government teachers, in the midst of hyped quality teaching at some cost lies the truth of total exploitation of the most ignorant people. In fact, private institutions immorally thrive on the desire for quality education by the ignorant mass because ability and affluence have made some of these people the idiots that they are. A simple fact of private tuitions taken by most of the students of private schools is glaring hypocrisy in quality education. However, nothing is better in the government schools as they too allow tuitions to flourish. It is an old ball game, in which only students are tossed across the field of knowledge, only they are losers monetarily or otherwise.

The moral debate goes on. A close look at the value dimensions of privatisation with regard to the role of teachers in particular boils down to the ethic of private tuitions. Taking the public schools, colleges and university teachers first, we may classify them under the following types: (a) those committed to their allotted duties; (b) those performing their duties and take on some supererogatory acts; (c) those serious in their duties and find time to give tuitions to their own students who come willingly either for their weakness or for sharpening their skills or for cracking difficult competitive tests; (d) those serious in their duties and give tuitions to students of any high schools, colleges and universities who willingly come to them for competitive exams;

(e) those uncommitted teachers who do everything other than their allotted duties like business or tuitions (which is a form of business activity) to tone the skills of their own students or others who come to them for various purposes as mentioned above, and (f) those uncommitted teachers who do not perform their allotted duties very well, for instance, do not complete their allotted course but devote much time in research, writing and presenting papers in seminars and symposia in and outside their work place and abroad, they are "satellite" teachers twinkling up in the sky smiling at other teachers who are bound to their course but either do not move at all in seminars or move sparingly, once or twice in a year. These "satellite" teachers become members and high rank people in most of the universities, commissions and so on; some become Vice Chancellors. They are highly connected people, members of editorial boards, selectors in services and so on. However, not all serious researchers and speakers find plenty of time to devote in extra-academic activities, and therefore, not always big people, they are in fact, bound to their basic duties. In any case, teachers falling under the last category are not private tutors but a few of them do consultancy jobs for private parties secretly during their service period, mostly the scientists or those in the fine arts. A few of them openly take up consultancy job because that is legal within their institutional ethics and duties, something like this is found in management institutes. Nevertheless, it is not always that these 'consultants' as we may call them neglect their basic teaching job, but in some cases the same may not be ruled out. There are a number of ethical dilemmas faced by the teachers, students, parents and administrators when we consider the cases of teachers of public institutions who take private jobs like tuitions for profit making. Let us raise some ethical dilemmas. To start with, we have the category of 'committed teachers' or the duty bound teachers who know very well what their allotted tasks are and how to do them best. One argument is, what is so great about these stereotype teachers, who through the years read good books, prepare notes, mug them up, lecture and finish their course? Is it at all desirable on the part of a professional teacher to be restricted to fixed set of duties? What is ethical in not letting a number of students who do not have the privilege to listen to some of these teachers who have earned great skill and fame in teaching particular subject? Is it not for the greater good that these skilled teachers should apart from teaching their students, go to the challenging arena of competitive exams and tone the skills of a number of students?

And if they really contribute in thát way, they fully deserve to earn from the precious time they have devoted curtailing their personal work, studies, research etc.? There is no ethicality in being walking an extra-mile, doing supererogatory actions for a handful of students because the weaker students and the unprivileged ones should be given time in the institutions and not out of it. When teachers come to their private life, the time left for them should be used by either giving tuitions or simply doing nothing. But doing something is better than nothing and in that case, we can do research work, guide research works, write papers, books and so on. Looking deeper at the private motive, the extreme is to suggest that during private time any work done such as research and writing should be profit oriented because (a) precious time and energy is devoted at the cost of fun and leisure, which should pay the teachers and (b) teachers as skilled professionals are not well-off in India, whereas they deserve to earn as per their merit, they do not have enough perks and facilities. The crux of private tuitions is that skilled people in our institutions should not be narrow egoists; they should be broad-minded contributing best to the society. However, in doing so, the extra money they earn is not to justify that they are egoists or egoistic hedonists but balanced people who deserve extra money for the extreme pain they take by sacrificing their pleasure. This must encourage our poor government teachers, who are, however, not liked by many adversaries in India because in the name of performing their institutional duties for five to six hours or even less than that, they are supposed to earn proportionately higher than they deserved and therefore, tuitions as additive to benefits place them as hedonists than altruists. The work ethic in an institution is laid in the covenant that exists among appointed teachers and employers, which also binds them to be honest and dutiful primarily to the stakeholders—the students and their parents, though in the government institutions fee paid may be meagre. However, subsidies do not deprive stakeholders of quality and quantum. If it does, subsidies are aims with freedom to maltreatment, which right is enjoyed by the government any way. Nor do the teachers and administrators enjoy any right to be a party to malfunctioning, malpractice and indirect sabotage to the welfare measure of nation. Is it not being anti-national and anti-people and thus unethical on the part of the covenanted government teachers who have never agreed upon swearing by any university or school statute to earn as much as they can by giving tuition at home or in "parallel institutions"? Who on earth has given very skilled and intelligent teachers to be so kind to teach those who appear for competitions or who lack quality guidance as belonging to different schools and colleges? Is it not grossly unethical to not to use the time left for oneself for further study, research, writing and so on so that in the long run that helps a number of students in and outside one's own institution? We thus find that stiff argument flow from both sides because many ethical questions come up in private teaching, but this should not be equated to private education because the latter as an institutional process is something more than private tuitions. To continue with the case of government teachers a little farther, the quality-of-work-life of these teachers demands that mere 'seriousness' will not be enough, total 'commitment' is needed on their part, which may include supererogatory tasks to be undertaken because teaching as a profession has high *service based ideal* to educate the masses. Hence, mere completion of allotted course will not be sufficient, teachers have to devote maximum time and energy in studies, research, writing and arguably, counselling and consultancy. It may be that some of their efforts pay them handsomely, which the institution do not mind as they contribute to the growth of knowledge and education through the ages for generations to come. Hence, earning by publishing works should be treated differently from earning from tuitions, counselling and consultancy. However, all will not agree to this ethic of work-life of teachers because they might argue that any form of extra earning, amounts to profiteering. There is thus a tension in terms of morality when it comes to the ways in which government teachers take up non-supererogatory jobs which though beneficial for the society are nevertheless, like "business". Often the arguments of the protagonists of private education go back to the *gurukula* system of education. The idea is that saintly teachers should live in their peaceful abodes, the Academies, which are not like private schools either because nothing is for profit here. The whole work ethic is altruistic, charged with spiritualism, and supererogation is at its pinnacle, where students come, live and learn free of cost or paying paltry amounts for basic needs and the society is helped to the utmost. Many others believe that the whole idea is unacceptable now because organized institutional education even if it is run by the government for welfare and not profit cannot expect hermit-teachers doing the horrific altruistic job because self-satisfaction and self-needs cannot be ruled out for the teachers who do not commit themselves to the life of a hermit. In fact, best hermits will not be appointed in these institutions because they do not fulfil the criteria of *professional* teachers, who serve to pay or serve for adequate payment. It is hopeless, therefore, to imagine of a state, which never exists now. Let us now come to the case of 'satellite' teachers for our ethical consideration.

Many administrators and teachers in public institutions believe that we had enough of power tracking than mass contribution by our grand satellite teachers. Time has come that our schools and colleges need educators, the best performers in the classrooms and in the institutions' co-curricular activities because it is for these that they are paid, and which they know are their basic duties. Hence, work-ethic demands from these teachers that after performing well in these areas, for which they have to obviously study, write, do research work and so on, they need to take up other tasks such as presenting their ideas in different seminars, conferences and symposia because new ideas and opinions spread in that way, which are shared and evaluated by many others, which indirectly help develop the professional life of the teacher and the educational level of the society at large. Hence, no one really contests the idea that "roaming" is secondary to educating. Even a lot of writing and speaking at various platforms are secondary to basic teaching. It is thus unethical as negligence of basic duties to do more than what was expected in the institution. Nevertheless, the idea is not at all liked by our "satellite" teachers who argue that the primary duty of an appointed government teacher is to contribute to the optimum growth of knowledge irrespective of narrow bounds of institutions. Bearing the tag of educator and/or teacher does not mean that they are mere instructors, trainers, or preachers, rather, they should move beyond the drab duties for the higher goal stated above. In fact, being steadfast to basic duties and to reach a satisfaction limit is nothing but stagnation of intellectual abilities and skill, which is unethical. It is thus a basic difference in the perception of government teachers who take themselves either as mechanical performers or as those facing growing challenges in a subject.

We may now come to the case of private institutions and teachers in these institutions to consider a number of ethical issues, including private tuitions. Apart from the basic reasons for the growth of private institutions in India, which we have seen before, we now come to other reasons and associated ethical questions. One so-called strong argument is that when mother institution is off colour, the society is in shambles, privatization is the best answer because there is no way to avoid our national responsibility to educate the masses. Private parties are thus best people around us whose benevolence comes at some cost because free benevolence and altruism soon runs out of all wits of which government benevolence is a testimony. The counter view is that in India, the spurt of privatization is a late phenomenon, earlier it was a low-key affair. The spurt was mainly owing to some basic factors involved in business with effect from the late eighties because India witnessed a relatively dry run for the major corporate sector when profit potential was not very high. Naturally, diversions in interests of the profit-oriented business took up private educational institutions because they attract funds; there is low organizational fuss and unrests. The returns are good enough for the houses. The failure of government schools, colleges and universities to give quality education to a large number of students drew private institutions to earn some profit by way of educating those who can afford. The distinction of class-based education at some cost resulted into the leftovers as due to the state governments to educate. If this be the basic reason for the spurt of privatization in education, it is out and out profit-oriented, classism at best and service-based ideal to impart education relegated to a secondary matter. This amounts to the unethicality of the business because India is not a fertile ground to exploit the well-off people; it needs help for the extremely poor and ordinary people. Further, the unethical consumer psychology percolates deep in the minds of ordinary consumers of private educational facilities. Students are offered awful courses, costly books and stationeries, which have to be purchased at arbitrarily fixed prices by booksellers in connivance with school authorities in particular. Costly extra-curricular programmes are provided so that there is all round flourishing of character but allegedly, truncated human values prepare a group of students who are egoists, power-trackers, over ambitious and jealous. Though these institutions are affiliated to central councils and other central bodies, they are far above strict monitoring for supervision and checks. The tuition fees are taxing, capitation fee exorbitant, malpractices rampant and exploitation at its worst. However, all these adjectives are true if someone cannot afford such education though wants to be educated. Private schools and colleges are not benevolent institutions who lose their pocket to educate and remain beggars themselves. Is it not natural that private people have right to thrive decently and for that generating sufficient funds is necessary? In fact, these institutions have not forced us to join them. In reality, even most ordinary people run for admission in these institutions knowing well that they may be financially taxed. Hence, to harp the agony of exploitation is needless; it is all fair in business that guarantees quality and work climate that people do not get at subsidy in government institutions. Hence, pretending to be benevolent is worse than unpretending business to educate that in turn does some good to some people of a nation. In fact, good things do not come free; they should not come free because free-education is a big public hoax. Only able people do welfare, poor cannot be welfarist. Aristotle famously remarked in the *Nicomechian Ethics* that beggars should not be altruists and welfarists because that is unethical. Take this from the former director of Education in Himachal Pradesh, Mr. Atma Ram, who happens to be a good advocate of privatization: "Education in the country is highly subsidised. But for whom? Who gets the benefit? Mostly those who manage the system.... 97 per cent budget of our university is spent on salaries. That is very true of most universities and State Departments of Education. Little is left for students and their development."[16] However, Professor Malay Choudhury, IIM, Bangalore, in an interview to *The Times of India* (2004) said, "There are few ethical private institutions. This is because private entrepreneurs and industrialists in India do not follow ethical norms. There is no regulation set up by the government. Honesty does not fall from heaven. There is need to step up a regulatory authority in the field of education."[17] Hence, there is a hidden appeal for privatization but with moral policing because the idea is that there is no business ethics in private institutions, the only touted ethics is stockholders' benefits, which is gross enough to keep stakeholders in abeyance. Is there any logic and ethic in policing in private institutions?

In a remarkable judgement the apex court ruled in 2005 headed by the chief justice Mr. R.C. Lahoti stated that "Unaided institutions as they are not deriving aid from state funds, can have their own admissions, *if fair, transparent, non-exploitative and based on merit*" (italics mine). This was in view of the "larger interest and welfare of the student community". However, the *capitation fees and profiteering by colleges* was strict no-no because "it could be regulated in the interest of preventing profiteering and capitation fees."[18] It appears that students' welfare and their interests are basic to moral policing because more often than not they are exploited by private institutions in the name of capitation fee and unlimited profiteering. However, in the same newspaper an editorial advocated that the Bill to regulate private institutions regarding fee etc. is to unethically curb them because "thousands of Indian students pay millions of dollars to third rate British or Australian institutes for degrees in management and business administration. The government does not have the money to invest. Private capital is the answer and there is no dearth of it. But why would anyone invest in a sector hemmed in by so many restrictions? Why shouldn't the service provider also be allowed to make a profit? Restricting the freedom of those who are willing to invest and willing to pay for education is self-defeating. This is not to suggest that there should be no regulation. But regulation is distinct from control."[19] There are interesting points that make a good ethical debate here but two things are important to notice: first, thousands of willing and economically able students in India make an infinitesimally small population needing educational justice and second, crores who are willing but economically handicapped need the same. Can private institutions be so broad to cover them? Or, is it time again to revisit the past when public institutions basked in glory?

Returning finally to the case of private tuitions in the backdrop of private institutions, and the moral questions, it appears that the problem is almost non-existent because moral curse is on the government teachers. Are private teachers not covenanted? Do they not have institutional statute to follow? No one really argues that private teachers do not have serious responsibilities. Many of them fall in the categories of either the "committed" or "serious" or "satellite" teachers who do not have any intention to give tuitions, but nothing should be unethical if they do so because the argument goes, many students in an institution are deprived of knowing things from good teachers and the teachers do not enjoy the same benefit and security as government teachers do. Hence, in a business atmosphere the contributors must be well-off. Yet, the moral question is, do they have any supererogatory role as professionals? Do they have internal and external checks on themselves when it comes to profit maximization in educating? With this, we need to stop our survey of value questions popping up from the controversy of private education. It is time now that we come to ground reality to go for an ethical dialogue climaxing in a moral consensus. This was considered by me on 28-01-1999 under the topic "What is Moral in Privatizing Education in India?" with the following people:

1. Dr. Mithilesh Kanti, Former Principal, Netarhat Government School, Netarhat and Director, "Dipshikha", School for the Challenged Children, Ranchi.

2. Dr. N. Datkeoliyar, Former Principal, Government Teacher's Training College, Ranchi and Lawyer.
3. Fr. C. De Brouwer, Former Head of Physics Department, St. Xavier's College, Ranchi and actively engaged in educational management.
4. Dr. J. Ashraf, Professor of Management in the Xavier Institute of Social Sciences, Ranchi.
5. Dr. S.N. Prasad, Professor and Chairperson, Academic Affairs, NIFFT, Ranchi.
6. Dr. Ramesh Sharan, Professor of Economics, Ranchi University, Ranchi.
7. Mr. S.K. Chatterjee, Businessman and Parent of Children in Private Schools, Ranchi.
8. A number of teachers and students.

Let me analyse the "construction of the panel" because this is an important part of what I call intersubjective corroboration. This may be a guide to the way in which a panel for ethical discussion should be constructed. From the foregoing discussion, we came to know that to avoid structuralism on the part of the ethicists in constructing a panel for discussion and framing a questionnaire, ethicists need to have some knowledge of the problem in consideration and public interpretation and evaluation of the problem. For both, apart from reading important books, it is important to have the clear idea of context in which the problem appears. In this case, the Indian educational context, which is distinct in many ways from other such contexts should be known clearly. Hence, books concentrating more on Indian educational issues than general academic treatment of education and private education (we have no dearth of them), should be given importance. Another important literature is newspaper where we get number of news items, editorial, debates, interviews and so on that gives us clear idea of public view on a problem including ethical views. Finally, we need to talk to common men who find interest and know something about the problem. Armed by this a non-co-opted ethicist just takes lead in initiating a dialogue by selecting parties and framing questionnaire. Books, newspapers and people help us in knowing who are most suited or most concerned persons in our society who face such educational ethical dilemma and strives for resolution. Privatization in education is a value-laden issue that certainly asks for teachers, students and administrators of education to participate. The parents are important contributors in this regard and so are lawyers. These are the people directly related to the problem and its resolution. It is important to keep in mind that among students we should include students of private and public schools and colleges. The same is true of parents, teachers and administrators. Among lawyers, those with service law specialization are preferred in these cases, other experts are welcome. Principals and administrators of public and private schools and colleges form important parties. Someone having knowledge of educational planning and management is needed and equally important is to have someone with economics background. The selected panel is a testimony to what I thought was most appropriate to do not by any whim but by having some experience gathered among the public. Questions as I said before must be straightforward, simple and ethically oriented. The dialogue should be so conducted that at no stage it becomes theory-laden, jargoned, factual, data-based and having little or no moral arguments at play. It will take the desired course if questions really take out the moral views of participants. This should be backed up by reading a passage or two while switching from one question to another that are ethically stimulating as well as provocative for the people having pro or con attitudes regarding the moral problem. Keeping these things in mind, the questions put were as follows:

QUESTIONNAIRE

1. What according to you should be aim of education and why?
2. What is the desirable relationship among students, parents, teachers and managers of education? How do you evaluate professionalism in education?
3. Does privatizing education encourage classism in education, which is good as well? Does government impart pseudo-education in the name of class-less and non-profiteering education?
4. Do you think that renewed efforts in quality and quantum of public education are desirable in India? Or, is it more desirable that the private institutions find out ways for qualitative as well as extensive education?
5. Do you think that morally the most desirable way in India is public-private joint ventures? If that be the case, should

government impose imperatives and checks in admission, fee, private tuitions and on other things to maximize profits?

6. How do you evaluate the role of NGOs in Indian education? Is it imperative on them to be morally restricted in fund raising and profit making in education?

It is important to notice that the first question tries to bring out what is the desirable goal of education. Whereas the second question unravels the implicit ethical opinion of people regarding essential relationship among the important parties involved in education and educating and clarifies the conception of teachers as professionals. The third and the fourth questions are about the ethic of class *versus* mass-based education which takes us to profiteering *versus* welfaristic ideals in education. The question of "quality" along with "extent" makes the moral evaluation more intensive. The next question tries to clarify the moral opinion of the participants with regard to collaborative efforts in mass education and the role of the government in practical decision-making and profiteering. The last question evaluates the role of the NGOs and the ethic of moral policing on their activities.

My experience is that with seven panellists and a number of teachers and students such discussion might extend up to three hours or more. It is important to record the views for a later analysis. The ethical corroborator should be extremely patient, remain neutral in moral debates but stimulate the discussion with intermittent messages and comments until the house reaches a consensus. Most of the time the points of corroboration are placed systematically by a participant or by the corroborator after a consensus has been reached. Let me now produce the details of the moral arguments of the esteemed panellists with regard to the questions put to them. Let us proceed from one question to another. To start with, we have inaugural remarks by Dr. C.R. Laha who inaugurated the discourse. Professor Laha said that education is the fundamental right of the citizens in India. But it is different from gathering information, which was the motto of the so-called education since a long time, that is, since the British era because passing and gathering information for them meant to means of material well-being. Hence, education as information became valuable in terms of market, money, benefits and as such a commodity. The teachers were linked to the commodity, market and money as workers in education. There is a need now to rethink what education should be like, what values should be brought in it so that it remains education as it should be. The private sector, thinks Professor Laha, looks at education as a commodity and aims at the maximization of benefits. These private houses impart education that fits well with market and profit values. Such education is, therefore, money oriented education, which, however, should not be the case when it comes to the moral desirability.

Mr. Dattkeoliyar started answering the first question by saying that the aim of education should be all-round development of human personality. This is an ethical aim but in the modern times, there is a crisis in education in terms of corrosion of its moral aim because it has moved far away from character building or holistic development of human personality. We are thus concerned more about human values in education in recent times because we lack in moral character. This was emphasised by both Dr. Radhakrishnan and Mr. Kothari in the Report of Education Commission. The aim of value-based education or character building education starts from classrooms, which has deviated a lot from its older vogue to become more utilitarian, that is, more material value oriented but not moral value oriented. This does not refute the ideals of professional and material training in our times but warns that these need not be at the cost of value degradation.

Dr. Kanti thinks that education has a broader significance. It covers the entire realm of human life in terms of knowing. Hence, the aim of education is not one but there are many aims of education. It takes us to learn the ways of living a meaningful life in its totality. One aspect of holistic learning or knowing is to learn about the value of good health, the way one should live in family and society in a healthy condition, including the learning of basics of personal hygiene because unhealthy people make others unhealthy. Such people cannot balance their body and mind. Next, we have self-dependence that education inculcates in us because it makes us aware of freedom in society. Further aim of education is to learn to cooperate with social beings without any sense of bossing, rather to become an able leader who is also a good follower. Next is to remain ever attentive to the constant flow of information around us and to try to catch them because this is needed for self-study, thinking and meditating. Finally, the aim of education is to inculcate values for man, so that they are accultured, sympathetic, empathetic and involved in social good. Character making should be included in this aim of acculturation. All these aims of education are possible to attain or that they should be made possible to the utmost at the school level. Hence, basic school education is most important in our life because it gives us a number of good or valuable things in life. Dr. Prasad thinks that the purpose of education is to create a society, which is non-violent. It is also to build moral character of the population. Education should give us proper work ethics and human values. Discipline is also an important aspect of education. Dr. Ramesh Sharan looks at education from three angles; it should develop human capability to earn his or her livelihood honestly. Education should develop self-esteem in all humans. Finally, education should give us freedom from dogmas, orthodoxy, bigotry, superstitions, ill values, and to think rationally as humans should. To develop certain human values like living in unity in community, sharing, compassion, equality and dignity are also important in education. Mr. Chatterjee proposes that education should be a constant effort towards broadening of human perception and values that frees us from narrow attitudes and to rationally analyse and intellectually evaluate human life. Without these, we have in our societies three types of people: well-educated, uneducated and the mal-educated. An education system devoid of human values churn out in our society a sizeable population of mal-educated people, they are most injurious. An educated person without perception of self, national and global good is mal-educated; they are devoid of human values. Hence, education is the one that gives us universal perspectives of living a life as humans. Since, the days of Macaulay we have been under the huge debris of information which dumped human values and a life of values resulting into people who are mal-educated, corrupt and not resisting to corruption.

In reply to the second question, Mr. Dattkeoliyar said, he does not hold the view that education is a mechanical process where students are seen as stakeholders, and managers and educators as stockholders and that there is a relation of give and take among them. It is not a commercial relation rather, a cooperation among the students, teachers, managers and guardians coming together by virtue of noble ideals and not merely for needs and their fulfilment, which is good for education. A feeling of disharmony will prevail once students and teachers are seen related externally in terms of users of facilities and providing same at some price. The whole system of education goes by the feeling of harmony between the teacher and the taught. If education is declared a fundamental right, it should be a huge responsibility of all sections of people to see that education beyond the limits of the artificial market relation is seen as essential aspect of social welfare. Mr. Dattkeoliyar holds that education should not be conceived of having a market value because it is not a commodity. If proper education is needed, the sense of education as a commodity should be eradicated from people's mind. Mr. Kanti thinks that education is not a baseless activity. If professionalism in education means achieving a target in education ably, it is desirable. Hence, professionalism in education speaks of a sound method to obtain desirable objectives of education and is, therefore, good. But this is not business or commercialization because such professionalism in education need not be profit oriented. In fact, education truly speaking is an intimate (*ātmika*) relation between the teacher and the taught wherein both are related as if the former is devoted for the good of the latter, that is, without which the latter cannot flourish in life. Hence, education is not an activity of providing information or inputs of certain topics by teachers by taking some fee. Rather, education is the best way of empowering the assimilation of desirable knowledge to the knower. The best way to do so by following immaculate methods is professionalism in education. It is without a profit motive that professionalism in education is desirable. Mr. Prasad agrees that professionalism is not profitability. But Mr. Ramesh Sharan disagrees to the extent that when we speak of education as a good for man, it is a commodity. Education is in fact a "mixed good". It is a "social good", which has no demand and no supply with respect to individuals in society. Hence, education is not a commodity having a market and market value when it is a "social good". However, when we speak of "private good", which unlike the 'social good' is demanded by a person, supplied by another person or a group of persons, both linked in some monetary transaction, gain, loss, benefits etc. and which may be denied to a person or a group of persons because they do not have adequate purchasing capacity to fulfil their needs, certainly education is a commodity. Nevertheless, when we speak of basic education in schools it is a social good because it is the basis of making a social being, a citizen with input of values and humane elements. Hence, almost universally, school education is taken as social or public good in which distinctions, profits, private benefits are ruled out. It is thus a matter of public production, which should be taken over by governments at no profit orientation. It is however, not in an ideal level in India and elsewhere largely due to social structures, the gaps in these structures owing to income distributions. There are huge gaps among the very poor, the poor, the middle class, the upper middle class and the affluent. The private needs of those who can afford privately beneficial education to a class or a strata, have created islands of a flow of demand and supply and thus a market within the welfare state which otherwise ideally does not like to commodity school education. Truth is that even school education has become a private good and the government is pleased to share the responsibility at the cost of class-based monetary exploitation. Going to the higher and technical educational institutions, India tended to accept initially that professional courses like engineering, medicine, management are all within public education scheme for the good of the society at large. It was due to this that at no profit motive IITs, IIMs, AIIMS was started. Yet, market for profit were created by planners and professionals trained in these institutions, who turned out to be thoroughly profit oriented individuals having least care for the government objective of social good or welfare. Now it is here that the ethical question of public spending on students comes in higher and technical education. What can be the ethic of huge public spending on educating such people who do not strive for public good? People educated in public institutions who later on look at private benefits are unethical. Should we not stop subsidised education here and open up for private institutions if private good is so important for the educated? Truly if all educational benefits end up in private good, those benefiting from it should make financial arrangements whether less costly or very costly. Certainly, there is a rationale of private, profiteering institutions in such cases. However, the withdrawal of (even partial) public spending on education hits the poor and the non-affluent most. In such cases, we should have safeguards like freeships, scholarships, subsidies to help them, but with an assurance of imperative social service. If that is not the case, we fail again. Dr. Sharan agrees with Dr. Kanti and others who said that in education professionalism need not be confused with profiteering because non-profit making teaching may be equally professionally oriented. There is a need for commitment, dedication and feeling on the part of the educators to not only gather information and supply them in the name of imparting education. Rather, try to work for social good and prepare people having the objective of social good. Teaching has to be a mission with highly-dedicated professionalism that prepares students for social good. Mr. Chatterjee holds that so far as the question of 'relationship' among the teachers, students, managers and guardians are concerned, it ought to be one of mutual trust and confidence because education is a collective interest. In case of such collective interest if trust and confidence lacks, there is widespread corruption and exploitation in education. In the lack of these, there is no professional and professionalism in education because then we confuse professionalism (and a professional) with a rampant profiteering person, which in any case is undesirable. Education is thus least profiteering with the great missionary zeal of professionalism that leads to the good of the society.

Mr. Prasad in reply to the third question agrees that privatization is no solution to quality education unless there is accountability on their part of the private institutions as fixed by the state agencies. In fact, if private institutions are left to their freedom, it is bound to class-based quality education, though at times the so-called 'quality' education might be pseudo-education. In fact, in private education, there is a lot of high-talk of quality education but they are low at what they do. If there is no parity and check and balance in thought and practice at this level, private education is pseudo-education. Mr. Dattkeoliyar argues that knowledge, skill and education of values being three important aims of education together they build our character. If education fails to do this, it is pseudo-education. Without completely agreeing to Dr. Sharan that education, as a private good is a commodity, education is for him a character-making without much concern for profiteering or earthy benefits. When education is based on profit making as in private education, it will naturally create classes within a society—the classes of haves and have-nots. There are tensions among the classes, physical, spiritual and psychological, and in this atmosphere, there is no character making rather destruction of characters. Mr. Dattkeoliyar argues that in a democracy there should not be class-based education system because that weakens our society and polity. Hence, there should be a proper balance in private education, a lot of government checks on such education so that they do not turn to rampant class-based education. Mr. Kanti agrees that there should be no class distinctions in our education system; it should be truly "classless" whether or not such education has been guaranteed by the Constitution. Such education without distinguishing the classes is perfectly in accordance with our social ethics, which does not speak of encouraging classism. In fact, all this is true particularly of basic school education. Tragedy is that we like it or not, we have fallen in the trap of class-based planning and strategy in basic education in India, which gave impetus to big houses for class-based education in these schools, about which Mr. Kothari himself felt very sorry. There is really a gap in what we think we should do and what has been done. In any case, higher education is not essential for all people but we have somehow made it necessary most unwisely at the cost of preparing people without basic skills to earn a living. However, in case of higher and technical education, we need more resources and it is not necessary for government or the public to afford such education in a heavily subsidised manner. It is here that checked and quality controlled private education is a necessity. Dr. Sharan said that it is very difficult to imagine today a classless society and classless education in the given socio-economic and political scenario in India because since a long time, we have built a society divided along classes—haves and the have-nots. We have deprived people systematically from basic education as well. Yet, what is still left as a moral goal for us is to provide basic and universal education to the people even at the lowest strata—to the most unprivileged people. It is here that despite all arguments, education for all should be an imperative because a society with regard to education has to grow both horizontally and vertically. Horizontally it should extend basic education despite the class chauvinism prevalent in society and vertically grow up to a qualitative higher education with a mission of public good, which should be backed up by private agencies. Dr. Sharan said that starting from Adam Smith, the political economy is ruled by the concept of self-benefit and not benevolence, though there has been a turn in the Marxian ethic of classless society, which turned out to be difficult ideology to assimilate. We are thus till date as good as Adam Smith's 'self-interested people'. However, we cannot completely neglect Harsyani's conception that we are rational beings as well, self-motivated towards critique of self-interests. Yet, this concern for a critique of unlimited self-interest in the ideal structure given by the capitalists turns out to be a needed critique of self-interest today. It is due to the needs of political stability and to check social unrests and rebellions that the ethic of benevolence of capitalists in modern societies have crystallised in the field of education in the form of educating the unprivileged classes to some extent at least at the school level and more or less so at the higher level. Whereas school education in India should have been a completely government affair, reaching to the last person as a matter of social guarantee though at the higher education level, there may be some liberty of private participation. However, we may consider the method of issuing 'vouchers' to highly educated people to guarantee a pay-back when they meet their expenses of education in the public institutions at huge subsidy. Given the directive principles of state policy and the fundamental rights, it would be a little premature on our part to start this project of issuing "vouchers" with great force in India. More ethical is larger horizontal and vertical justice done by the states with judicious encouragement to the private parties. Mr. Chatterjee argues that drawing from above arguments it is important to add that the government's non-participation or lackadaisical participation in basic education is unethical. It is neither possible nor desirable for our government to do such things keeping in mind the welfare of the public. However, it should be noted that private participation in basic education is neither undesirable nor impossible if it keeps checks on rampant profiteering. In India, we have instances of private institutions contributing to the public welfare at minimum profit-making. We have seen active participation of some missionaries and the NGOs in this regard. Therefore, to find out faults in any private institution will be unethical. If some such institutions' character is like a private limited company, their ethic is clear and we should not encourage them in basic education. However, these companies are flourishing these days. Yet, if there are private institutions whose character is of the missionaries, it does contribute to basic educational welfare. As India is a nation migrating along the path of Nehru's socialism to globalization of economy and open market, we should have serious thinking about whether everything in education should be left for the government. However, when we give freedom to private education, the individuals and institutions participates in a huge market, and whether the said market has any ethic or should have an ethic becomes the moot issue. It is a matter of concern that there can be no ethic or should be no ethic in an educational market. The market values and educational market values needs to be redefined so that we can find out the ethical value of private participation for the public good because the idea that market has no ethic, is a morally repugnant idea, it exploits ordinary people.

In reply to the fourth question, Mr. Sharan first of all disagrees that the best known missionaries as backed up by government aids have true missionary zeal which we thought is most important in education. Most of them in reality are profit-making institutions, thoroughly exploiting their students and teachers without any social good in mind. Further, educational renaissance is extremely important at the basic stages in particular. However, the moot issue is which ethical values should govern the renaissance? It cannot be the one advocated by Adam Smith, neither can it be that of Marshall. A renaissance backed by Marxist ethics is unsuitable now. In the midst of such dilemma, we find that education today is encircled by market forces and its mechanisms, the profit ethics, the effects of globalization, the social and value changes and the growth of castism, social conflicts and corruption. Nevertheless, we should be concerned in such complex situation about our social objectives and entitlement despite communalism and other vices challenging us. One way to face such adversities is to have public dialogues. This should be the basis of neo-renaissance in education. However, we must also keep in mind that markets in the global era has a simple ethics, that is, he who buys is able to survive in and with the market. The question is, who buys what in the market of education and who should buy in what ways? Given the ethics of income and survival, our ethical concern calls for a judgement of ways to control the weeding out of the non-entitled people, the needy, and the poor, who has no income and cannot buy good things in the open market at good price. We need to face the problem of entitling these people. Hence, the ethic is to empower common people in education market, which empowerment does not come from the market itself or from those who govern the market, but from the power of the public and thus from the government. Public renaissance in education is thus most important in basic education than a private renaissance. We should thus have broader participation of the civil institutions the broadening of the public participation at least in basic education, which is the backbone of nation's education. It is not that private institutions have no role in higher education or at the basic level of education, but participation of public institution is a prerogative. Better said, there should be a judicious balance between the two in this regard. This includes participation of enlightened people that is, those not guided only by egoistic welfare, rather, who have altruistic motives. Even good NGOs of other regarding motives are important. In such renaissance in education, there should also be a strong element of protest among the public towards all unethical decision-making. The protest should be joined by the teachers and the lawyers who should be at the front to protest so that any disparity between the so-called educated and their immoral deeds may be resolved.

With regard to the fifth question, Mr. Dattkeoliyar holds that collaborative venture of the private and the public bodies in education is difficult to conceive, though government cannot impart education at all levels all by itself. On the other hand, if certain things are left to the private houses, there must be government checks and controls. Therefore, we cannot disregard the basic infrastructural facilities available to the private institutions, which are however, a part of the duty of the government. Nevertheless, these houses need to be checked for ruthless extortion of money in the name of quality education and infrastructural facilities provided to the students. Dr. Kanti believes that the government, given its near helpless governance and facilities, cannot impart an extremely broad based public education in India. It should thus collaborate with the private institutions with some degree of control in its hand. The greatest problem is the way such balanced collaboration is made possible. The basic factor in this regard is the growth of consciousness of the people in private houses that education is a great social responsibility where profiteering is not most important. The greatest problem among the educated today is that people of good will and well thinking have been outwitted by the so-called educated but evil people. If private-public collaboration is needed, it should ultimately boil down to the people finally, who needs to be ethically charged. The lack of power of human goodness prevents any educational collaboration to be successful. Owing to the lack of social consciousness and urge for peoples' welfare has risen the problem of private tuitions in such rampant way, which is unethical for its anti-people attitude and for its adversity to the noble aims to education stated before. Even if some schools arrange for tuitions for weaker students in the schools, the common public are crazy about private tuitions for they feel insecure for many reasons, like competition, admissions and so on. One reason is that the less intelligent people feel insecure about the future of their wards, which many teachers cash. Dr. Sharan thinks that the main problem in this regard is the lack of dedication and sense of duty among the government teachers, which invites private participation. In the modern times, the governments have politicised education in a way so that the private houses flourish and a large chunk of the common mass remains uneducated. This is worst seen in higher education, which has been systematically rented to private houses. Another way is to increase participation of the teachers empathetic to the people and culture of a region, one who is empathetic to the masses as own brethren. It is here that grassroots education in local language becomes so important at least at the basic level of education. Another point is the systematic neglect of the participation of the teachers, students and guardians in educational decision-making and programme implementation because in lack of it, everything is left to some power assuming non-empathetic people, who ruin education. The sense of educational right and the right to proper education are the basis of educational renaissance, which can replace the unethicality in education mentioned by us. Mr. Chatterjee urges that though capitation fee cannot be freely charged by any institution, at times private institutions do need it for extending benefits. Even the private tuitions are not so evil if guardians are to be believed but the great human values and aims of education need not suffer for that. Private institutions have every right to free their teachers for private tuitions which government teachers do not enjoy.

Fr. Brouwer took the questions together to argue that in school education most important is to read, write and speak correctly. At college level, we should be able to think deeply and judge correctly. The most important party to enable pupils for having such education are the parents who extend education to them by means of some investment. State is responsible in overlooking broad base of pupil's basic education at the cost of some investment of the public, though the public here means the parents. So the parents should be morally and practically free to choose the type of education for their ward's benefits. This responsibility of the state is, therefore, to ensure liberal education, which is morally based. Private institutions have a great role to play, particularly, if they are preferred for liberal education. It would be unethical to stop that liberty on the part of any state. There is no doubt that there is an ethic beyond the mere wish of the parents for best education and the state and the private institutions wishing to participate in the process of imparting best education. The private and the public institutions should go hand in hand in quality education that contributes to the personal and the social life. This is basic to assure that there is minimum ethical concern of both the private and the public institutions in education. Father cites several instances to justify that private institutions and even private tuitions by any government teachers is not a necessary evil lest the teachers do not in any case neglect their duties. The experts are so highly qualified and skilled that maximum benefit should reach to many sections of the public who have the liberty to get best education. Ethically speaking, we should have no objection whatever be their financial status, if their parents choose to go for quality education at some cost for betterment; there is no harm because what matters is sound education leading to high expertise. It is not that several government institutions in higher education are not very stringent about admission. The best always demands certain things from teachers as well and if the best private institutions demand so, at a reasonable limit and great professionalism there is nothing ethically wrong in it. Mr. Dattkeoliyar in a response to a query of Dr. S. Mishra said that the fundamental right to education is to be educated. This is morally based because it extends the base of general well-being of a nation. The ethic that should govern privatization in education on the other hand is restraint on maximization of profits or material gains and the maximization of welfare. Institutions should not be industrialised at any cost, whether it is public and private. Mr. Chatterjee in response to the question of a student regarding role of NGOs said that it is interesting to notice that barring Gujarat, there is no education act and as such there is no legal checks on the public and the private institutions in education to ensure good education with minimum service guarantee to teachers. It is very important, therefore, that the teachers and the public should be legally safeguarded against any malpractices and exploitation in the face of either private or public institutional education. Dr. Sharan replies to a question that many known NGOs in education are also voluntary organizations, and we have to be careful about confusing the role and status of both. Voluntary organizations need not be understood responsible in mass education or even substantially contributing to it as does private schools or colleges. As we stand now, there is no denying that whatever degree of freedom and liberty we have, we should not overlook the ethical value of mass education as undertaken by the state at basic level irrespective of class, caste and sex. There should be a renaissance in our mode of thinking about class, caste, sex and affordability based education at all levels in the society.

The house reached the *consensus* that the ethically desirable goals of education are *empowerment of all sections of people* and the *flourishing of human character*. Education aiming at such moral goals conceives of a *relationship of love and empathy among students, teachers, parents and others* important parties in education. Teaching as a profession should thus *refrain from the motives of maximization of benefits for oneself and making optimum profit out of professional expertise*. Nevertheless, *professional teachers need sufficient financial encouragement as students of all sections need justice in educational distribution;* when it comes to school level education, it needs to be *largely a government affair*. The house concluded that though private institutions imparting school and college education do not necessarily be branded as imparting unethical education because they are providing class-based education and profiteering, whereas the government institutions are branded as imparting pseudo-education in the name of mass education. Rather, it is ethical on the part of both the government and the private houses to reach the goals of education which ultimately does a lot of good to the people and the nation. Hence, educational policy-making at all levels in India should be fine-tuned for a *perfect balance among the government spending in education and encouragement of private parties including the NGOs* with some humane rules that does not harass the private contributors but deters them from unethical practices. This is also true of control over unethical practices in government management and government institutions. The quality and quantum of education in India should be assured by the public and the private bodies because education is mainstay of *welfare of the people*. The consensus revealed that keeping aims of education in mind well-paid teachers in any institution should *not be allowed for rampant private tuitions*. This is all the *more important in case of teachers of public institutions*.

Keeping the moral dialogue in view and the moral consensus that emerged (which got clearer as we proceeded along the debate), it is now the task of ethicists to analyse the moral views of the participants carefully to find out which theory or theories found in academic ethics were active in the debate and the consensus that emerged thereof. This is *post-corroboration* theoretical task *exclusive* to persons knowing academic ethics, having its unique *academic value*. Hence, this has not to be confused with chauvinism of ethics experts because any interested person can take up this analytic task as well but with the condition that the person must have participated in real life moral debates as corroborators and has some knowledge of academic ethics. Analysis of the moral views of the participants reveals that though the participation of governments (Central and State) is found to be almost an imperative in school education, particularly, at the level of basic education, the same force of "imperative" lost ground gradually as they proceeded to answer the questions regarding quality and quantum of education and the role of public-private cooperation in this regard. This is a testimony to the truth that the overriding moral principle of *human welfare* that was visibly the basis of accommodating privatization at the cost of minimizing public participation and public spending was not fairly clear to us because well-being or welfare is a complex notion. When we consider it as a *non-economic* thesis, that is, a thesis in morality, it consists of *holistic good* for man. Hence, "non-economic welfarism" is an ethical principle that recognises well-being of people of a nation by considering several good things, some are good as means, some are good as ends and for that matter, some are material good, and some others are non-material good such as ethico-spiritual and metaphysical good. This was evident from what most of the panellists said. However, Dr. Sharan's arguments which was later on accepted nearly uncontested except for mild objection by Mr. Dattkeoliyar, focused the shift from non-economic thesis of welfare to welfarism more widely advocated in economics because education was seen as an economic activity, having definite economic goals, such as empowering people to work, earn, spend, be party to teeming market activities and so on. Hence, bereft of the economic conception of "welfare", it is trite to say that "welfarism" is the moral theory that governs the idea that after all public-private cooperation ultimately helps in any level in education both in terms of quantum and quality. Thus, the gradual shift in almost every speaker, including Mr. Sharan was noticed due to inherent clumsiness in the moral thesis called "welfarism", which however, no doubt ruled supreme in resolving the issue of the necessity of the participation of private houses in education in India. We have to understand why the shift was natural to economists like Mr. Sharan because his initial stronghold in the conception of education as means to a higher good, that is, economic well-being ultimately gave way to a broader conception of "welfare" once the issue of education *beyond* basic education and the assurances of quality with quantum came into the limelight. Evidently welfarism as an ethical thesis could not relegate the value of economic welfare as part of 'holistic' welfare of masses when it comes to educate them. Let us, therefore, settle the issue that the welfarism as an assimilation of economic and holistic good is key to or basic to the acceptance that in India, governments should be surely but only partly responsible in imparting extensive quality education. It should thus allow free access to private players at all levels of education (formal and non-formal) with full conception of profits going to the private houses, but under social vigilance and humane rules. Profits cannot be ethically ruled out, as it is unpragmatic to imagine education without generating enough funds whether it is imparted by the private parties or the public. It would be grossly unethical to imagine that an economic activity, as is education, should be wholly free even at the school level becausc that amounts to encouragement of immobility on the part of the public and the government to run an efficient economic activity depending largely on availability of funds not only for salaries but infrastructure and other things. However, the government is not a profiteering institution. Hence, ethicality demands that it assures *efficient fund generation* through tax collection and effective budgetary allocation and implementation of programme. In addition to this, it should encourage private players to harness profits but to contribute in educating the masses. In fact, a non-callous government that imagines holistic well-being should realise the basic truth that the public has to be brought into active participation in educational programme, and for that matter, it cannot behave as a hermit who lives on begging. This ensures government activism in fund generation though not with a profit motive, which is, however, not the same with the private players because their economic activism is different. And nothing is ethically repugnant if somebody makes profit lest people's welfare is assured and exploitation minimized. In reality, complete government role in education in India would only demand a ruthless government financial activism that catches the well-off to do justice in distribution for the worst-off as if that way worst-off would be at par with the well-off and justice will be done. Where we stand now in India, is that we are left with either the options to do this unimaginable distributive justice which is most unethical in terms of welfare of the whole of population because such utopianism should better give way to a complete social revolution, or we have to do justice to the whole of society in accommodating the private players under rule of the land which is humane, not ruthless. The choice is ours. One message came from Dr. Sharan and others that public institutions cannot be at the begging end and educate the poor people to push them to a high status. If somebody is pushed up, he or she should be bound to pay, which is one way in which government can earn for sustained educational programmes. Hence, it is hopeless to imagine that government education can run only at the cost of widening the tax net and increasing budgetary provisions because that is the *mantra* for success in almost essential sectors in India. Equal to education, industrialization, agriculture, housing, sanitation, water management all require the same *mantra*. All vie for priority. Yet, funds are hard to find. Then the need and aspiration for holistic welfare being unchallenged and unmoved, the message of the people is clear in the dialogue we have just read: "Go judiciously for privatization in India at all levels in education".

NOTES

1. Mr. Adrian M. Dupuis quoted in Bantock, G.H., *Education and Values*, Faber and Faber, London, 1965, p. 124.
2. *Ibid*, p. 124.
3. Ray, Suprakash, "Volatile Mixture" in *The Statesman*, Kolkata edition, 20.05.2001, p. 8.
4. Rajput, J.S., "Equity in Education" in *The Times of India*, New Delhi edition, 02.10.2002, p. 8.
5. Joshi, Kireet, "Value Judgement" in *The Times of India*, New Delhi edition, 18.01.2002, p. 14.
6. Mitra, Tirthankar, "Students opt for English-medium Schools: SCGRT Study in three sub-divisions" in *The Statesman*, Kolkata edition, 11.05.1998, p. 5.
7. Dasgupta, R.K., "Perfect Language II", *The Statesman*, Kolkata edition.
8. Sanyal, Sunanda, "English Classes III", *The Statesman*, Kolkata edition.
9. *Ibid.*
10. Srivastava, Radhika D., "Teachers may no longer spank school students", *Sunday Times of India*, Patna/Ranchi edition, 23.04.2006, p. 4.
11. *Ibid*, p. 4.
12. Pervez, Shahid Md. "M.P. Parents say yes to sex education", *The Statesman*, Kolkata edition, 01.03.1999.
13. Mohan Lal Seal as quoted in *The Statesman: Voices*, "Is Sex Education necessary?" 1999.
14. K.P. Roy quoted in *The Statesman: Voices*, *Ibid.*
15. Pervez, Shahid Md., "M.P. Parents say yes to sex education", op. cit.
16. Ram, Atma, "Education Today: Privatization Only Answer", in *the Statesman*, Kolkata edition.
17. Choudhury, Malay, "Business of Learning", *Times of India*, Patna/Ranchi edition, 24.02.2004, p. 12.
18. Report on "SC bars Pvt. College quotas: Institutes have unfettered Right to choose students" in *The Times of India*, Patna/Ranchi edition, 13.08.2005, p. 1.
19. Editorial column "Learning Curb", *The Times of India, Ibid*, p. 6.

5

Is Educational Ethics all Good to Read but not Good to Make us Good?

In the four chapters of the book, I was trying to deconstruct the nature of educational ethics in terms of its tasks because I felt that the best way to know what educational ethics is or means, we need to state its different tasks in an unambiguous way. We have seen that educational ethics as an independent field of study that undertakes the metaethical, normative and practical tasks, are related and in some sense similar to the same tasks undertaken by ethics or moral philosophy. However, the basic difference between moral philosophy or ethics and educational ethics is that the latter as a branch of the former takes on ethical inquiry in another field called 'education' because there are ample grounds to show that the field of education opens for ethics an interdisciplinary venture, that is, it invites ethical scrutiny or *ethically relevant study* of some important aspects in the field of education. For instance, it invites ethics for metaethical study of what is the meaning of "education", "ethics" and "educational ethics", and the justifications of "educational ethics". It invites ethics for "metaethical" study of bearings if any of theories of truth and meaning of ethical language such as emotivism, prescriptivism and so on to analyse the significance of language of moral and/or value education. Education invites ethics for a *normatively relevant study*. For instance, to study the bearings if any of the normative theories such as Kantianism, utilitarianism and so on in the moral evaluation of some tasks of education and decisions taken in the field of education, as we find in cases of the task of value education or character formation education or virtue inculcation or religious education and so on. Finally, education opens *practical or applied ethical study* as in cases of *resolution* of several ethical or value-laden practical problems like privatization in education or sex education and so on, which belongs to the professional life of the educationists. Hence, as we have said before, educational ethics stands out as a branch of ethics and not education because none of the above ethically relevant tasks belongs to education proper rather; they belong to ethics proper, which *approaches* education for an interdisciplinary study. By virtue of taking on only some aspects of the field of 'education' and not the whole of it, educational ethics as an independent field have unique features different from both, education and ethics. But the independence and uniqueness of educational ethics does not prevent the field from borrowing insights from both education and ethics as all interdisciplinary study does. Nevertheless, not merely for all practical purposes rather for the reason that basic theories and principles of ethics becomes the major tools for the interdisciplinary study as is with biomedical ethics or environmental ethics, educational ethics needs to be seen within the broad field of ethics and not education. Given these points after deconstructing the tasks of educational ethics, we now come to construct what it really amounts to. Educational ethics amounts to a branch of ethics which empowered by basic tasks of ethics applies them to issues in education which are first order or normative, second order or metaethical and practical. Educational ethics thus assures us (those taking interest in an interdisciplinary study as this one), of three ethically relevant ways in which some educational enterprises needs to be studied.

Many misgivings about the nature of education, ethics and educational ethics are due to the lack of understanding of what has been first deconstructed and then reconstructed by us. Proper understanding of educational ethics further enable us to answer whether it is all good to study but not good to make us good. However, we will not jump to give an answer to the problem mentioned above because we should start seeing what confusions are about educational ethics in the popular parlance. Educational ethics in fact, is as ill-fated as its precursor, moral philosophy or ethics because many among us believe that much like ethics it aims at making us people of moral character or morally good character. Similarly, educational ethics is as ill-fated as value-studies, particularly study of moral and human values to imagine that like such studies it is sure to make us persons of value-studded character or thoroughly value-oriented as well as virtuous. Most important expression in the above assertions is "us", that is, persons who deal with ethics and educational ethics. This is important to note because all persons on earth are not conceived of as having great moral character by virtue of educational ethics because not all on earth are said to have come across educational ethics. Only those persons (*some* among 'us') who are serious about education or who are serious about educational ethics are conceived as great moral persons. Naturally, the conception (or misconception?) about educational ethics is that it aims at inculcating moral virtues, values and human virtues to build high character individuals in civil societies. In fact, people do not contest much that education aims at inculcating several values and virtues and most of the time comes out to be successful, but it is highly debated that the same may be true of ethics and educational ethics. The debate is interesting when we consider an important argument that being parts of academics, both ethics and educational ethics are indubitably under the broad enterprise of education, therefore, like education, ethics and educational ethics aims at charging us with values and virtues and shape us as good people, though failure in such cases does not prove that education with ethics and educational ethics are all bogus. Yet, the counter-view is that though education in its narrower sense have many aims or objectives, such as value-charging us or making us people of good character, what it does or aims to do is not what it 'should' do because everything we have traditionally expected of formal education or education as academics are not *desirable*. Hence, it is a matter of debate whether education, and ethical and educational ethical education though conceived of making us good, should nevertheless, do so because *per se* these enterprises having nothing in their nature or tasks that confirms the said glorious aim of making us good. It is due to this that despite all traditional pressures, we hesitate to accept that through education, virtues and values can be inculcated in us to make us good people. The point is, ethics and educational ethics cannot and should not teach us to be morally good people. If education or any enterprise therein such as above, fails to make us morally good, they remain good themselves. However, more intense argument is that as educational enterprise in general and any part of it more often than not *practically fails* to make us morally good, therefore, ethics and educational ethics as parts of education have to fail practically when it assumes to be so noble to make us good. It is bad to be pretending than being honest to our basic subject matter. If we come to accept the truth of the extreme version, we need to face the challenge whether ethics and educational ethics should be given up as practically hopeless things and thus undesirable in life because these are merely academically worthy in *theoretical terms*. They are good to read but turn out to be a fuss when it comes to value in our life. Where does the problem lie in such dilemmatic questions? It must be in the understanding of the nature and tasks of ethics and educational ethics (also education) rather than anything else.

I should not indulge too much in the discussion of the value of teaching moral philosophy or ethics because we have seen it in *The Primer* (Vol. 1) in details. In *The Primer* I have also discussed briefly the different approaches or methods in teaching ethics, and in this book, I have discussed the ways in which value-based education may imparted and what is proper in this regard, though not much has been said whether value-basing is at all practically and ethically desirable in educational ethics. Similarly, I have not discussed in *The Primer* whether educational ethics should take up inculcating moral values and virtues. Here, it is sufficient to say that ethics or moral philosophy as I understand it, is not merely good to read but to do something good by way of resolving questions of value in society in association of the public. However, reading, thinking, analysing, criticising, assimilating, writing on ethical issues along with solving value-laden issues does not imply that the participating moral agent has assumed a moral character, virtues and values by virtue of all the above activities because a number of non-ethicists who do not partake in any such activity, possesses high moral characters, virtues and values. Ethical enterprises are thus *not necessary and sufficient* in the evolution of moral persons. Yet, morally charged or morally conscious persons evolve when they partake in moral activities, who may be both philosophers and non-philosophers, or ethicists and non-ethicists because being morally conscious, having moral intentions, deciding to act morally, able to evaluate moral acts and decisions are beyond academics, that is, they become our habitual states when we simply care to be reflective about what is going in and around us in this vigorous life of participation in the vast ecological community. Hence, *to partake in ethical matters and being ethical are different things*, the former is exclusively academic, needing specific *education* (ethics education, for instance), whereas the latter is 'beyond-academics', needing participation in community life. Naturally, without being educated in ethics or moral philosophy, and having less formal education is not a hindrance in moral evolution of man, and therefore, not a hindrance to the evolution of moral intentions and character. Perhaps ethical wisdom of some ethicists enabled them to suggest, therefore, that teaching ethics and education in ethics does not have any logical implication that by virtue of these we become morally good. In fact, unsocial, anti-social and a-social persons fail to be ethically oriented though they may be educated in ethics or educate ethics. Naturally, more often than not the teachers of ethics fails to be ethical despite teaching academic ethics or by participating in academic ethical enterprises if they have anti-social or unsocial intentions; so does those educated in wholesome ethics fail because they remain anti-social or unsocial in their attitude. However, those who teach ethics or are educated in ethics might show encouraging signs of moral evolution because they are by and large social and care for values, which, nevertheless, were not helped by the subject called ethics. Similarly, many among us who neither teach ethics nor get ethics education are ethically good. It is due to these reasons that ethics as a branch of philosophy does not even aim at undertaking overzealous tasks such as making people good or morally good. *Ethics is thus not a means to assure that the world is full of ethical people*. I will stop here because something has to be said with regard to educational ethics now before we come to the moot issue. However, readers need to keep in mind what are the "tasks" of educational ethics.

Three questions need clarification when we come to educational ethics. First, does it assume the role of moral education and thereby include moral values and virtues in people as well as human values and virtues in them so that as final products we have morally good people? Second, does it assume the role of educating people in general values and virtues so that we have people of values and virtues? Third, *should* it assume these roles to boast of production of good people? To consider the first question whether educational ethics imparts moral education, we should first of all see that "moral education" need not be the same as "ethics education", about which we have discussed something just now. The reason is that "moral education" is a sweeping expression that covers the range of common morality, moral traditions, moral beliefs, rules etc. as well as philosophical study of morality, which is moral philosophy or ethics, which, apart from other things, is a critique of common morality, moral traditions etc. Sometimes tradition allows us to take "moral education" as "moral science education" and "ethico-spiritual education", which are, however, not "moral philosophy education". When we are discussing the role of moral education in educational ethics, we need to consider all these cases. It is fairly simple for our readers to follow that educational ethics as a branch of moral philosophy or ethics (as seen before), has nothing to do with moral education taken in the senses of education of common sense morality, moral science and spirituality. Hence, we are left with the option that moral education in this regard should be taken as the education of ethics or moral philosophy, which is clearer to us from an account given in an earlier chapter. If we followed that account, educational ethics does not take up the *education of whole of ethics* rather, the education of a part of ethics that *ex-hypothesi* that is, 'in principle' do not change rules out inclusion of whole of ethics because *a whole cannot be equivalant to the part of the whole*. If this be the case, why do we say that in some sense educational ethics *does* take up moral education? We say so due to bad habit or bad faith because "does" as an assertive is expressive of our traditionalism (as we have seen in the introductory part of the book and in a following chapter). Educational ethics does not aim at "moralization" of people or "moral initiation" of people rather aims to be *critical* of moral faiths, dogmas, principles and so on. In fact, education as a rational enterprise initiates us to be "critical". This may be seen as one step to the ethical orientation of interested people. Hence, "educational ethics does take up moral education" may be seen as an assertive of the truth that it is a *primary initiator* to criticise dogmatic morality and thus a stepping stone to philosophical study of morality and moral education. It is clear that those taking specific education of morality aims primarily to develop basic critical ability as mentioned above and then move on to more academically intensive programmes such as the metaethical, normative and practical enterprise in educational ethics but never to make oneself morally good or a person of good character. Educational ethics as 'primary initiator' of critical thinking of morality is far away from the moral education in which one is taught and trained to behave morally, that is, to act according to fixed set of moral rules as found in society or which is a set of moral faith. We have seen just now that educational ethics develops in us critical powers to evaluate such rules and faiths, and does not teach and train us to adopt them. Hence, we do not or cannot teach (or educate) to be morally good if that is to behave morally as per rules because educational ethics is a critique of such aims and not a contributor to it. Legitimately what it cannot and does not, it should not do so as well. Educational ethics *should not* take up overzealous but pointless things such as making us ethically good. It is but assured that after reading this book none of us may have sound character as I do not have one after reading and writing about this issue because soundness of character does not logically depend on academic ethics or educational ethics. We may be emphatic now in ruling out the possibility of educational ethics as aiming to inculcation of ethical values and virtues and human values and virtues in general public and/or those who participate in the specific academic venture. To add to this, educational ethics as we now understand does not fulfil the needs of general value orientation of general public and/or those who participate in the specific academic venture like practical ethical resolution of value-laden issues.

Keeping this in mind we are now in a position to refute approaches in educational ethics that includes within it efforts to charge people with values and virtues through ethics education. This is a serious point because we are now speaking of "ethics education" and not of the ambiguous "moral education", which we have already discussed. Do educational ethics make us good through ethics education? Before reflecting the important claims that it does, we must be aware of the fallacy that 'a whole is not equivalent to a part of the whole'. Let us proceed with the confusions about educational ethics as inculcator of ethical values and virtues through educating us in ethics (or what is loosely called, "morality"). I will consider in this regard the following models conceived to be of some help in the ethics education of young students in schools.

Ethics education as we understand, it is an extremely difficult proposition when we consider it in public or private schools in multilingual and multicultural countries like India because on the one hand we have to consider the mental maturity of the children who need such education and the level of difficulty that are inherent in ethics, for instance, in metaethics or normative ethics. Nevertheless, we must start somewhere. We cannot overlook the importance of an initial orientation of the young school students towards the *empowerment of critical acumen in* them so that they are able to judge what is desirable, undesirable, right, wrong, good, bad, just, unjust, duty and obligation through the use of *stories*, *anecdotes* and *poems* having the moral messages as well as the use of *role models*, particularly the teachers, great men with the hope of emulation. Using these things in education gradually forms *moral character*, and therefore, known as the model of *character education*. However, the model has its own problems. First, in the name of starting ethics education somehow in the schools, young people are dragged to character formation by peer intervention, that is, direct intervention of teachers, stories and biographies and deeds of great men and women with the hope that these are sufficient to grow in them the 'critical conception' of what is morally worthwhile. But how do students distinguish and teachers let them to critically evaluate what is morally and non-morally worthwhile? How do teachers convey the idea that what the Good Samaritan did was ethically good or desirable for us when we attend a fellow student in case of an accident? In fact, such critical development basic to ethics education is helped not by stories rather, norms, which in turn begs critical inquiry into their nature for comparison. Ethical teaching as different from teaching traditional moral rules is not possible without inviting to see what in reality is ethically good as distinct from non-ethically good. Such basic critical teaching of ethics does not rely on stories, anecdotes, biographical stories and so on, that is, on artificial 'peer intervention'. Hence, the second point is, peer intervention *gives* us what is ethically good and so on, we do not *find* them, and therefore, does not keep us free from dogmatism in the growth of critical thinking. This in turn points towards the failure of forming young pupils' character, because ethics education wrongly understood as telling us stories etc. has no ground to justify that young people have surely formed ethical character. That ethical character is formed, is testified in the long run in the several acts of young people as they grow in the society, which may be different from what stories conveyed to them because their judgement of ethicality is a normative affair that stems from the *pro-community attitudes, decision and acts for holistic good.* In fact, what ethical teaching amounts to is difficult nay impossible at the school level in case of young people, and if it be possible, it does not aim at forming good character rather, enable people to judge what is a good character. In the midst of this, ability to good judgement, good decision etc. may be reflection of a good character, but that is unintended in ethics. Ethics does not aim to form ethical character, and what things are said to form such things is wrongly taken as ethics. In reality, they are not ethics but peer produced common etiquettes, acceptable behaviour patterns, cues to civilized and decent living and ideas about several non-moral duties, obligations, responsibilities and virtues and values.

Many educationists argue that ethics education, as an important aspect of educational ethics is to develop the moral cognition of the young people right from the school days. This is based on the idea of gradual cognitive development of children championed by Jean Piaget and Lawrence Kohlberg. In her book *The Moral Judgement of the Child* (1932), Piaget argued that schools need to put emphasis on decision-making and problem-solving rules gradually, which are morally just or fair. Hence, to arrive at universal principle of morality students should be free to solve moral issues by themselves so that the solutions are fair as based on fair principles. Hence, it is important in formal ethical teaching that teacher should provide all opportunities to the students rather than indoctrinating them with moral aids artificially so that the students discover what is morally good and just. Lawrence Kohlberg modified and elaborated the conception of Piaget in a number of essays found in *Collected Papers on Moral Development and Moral Education* (1973). He argued that the moral education should take note of the six successive stages of moral cognition and moral development grouped broadly into three, the *pre-conventional*, the *conventional* and the *post-conventional* levels according to the age of students. However, at any stage it is pointless to imagine that the traditional conception of moral education in terms of indoctrinating in a basket of virtues with an idea that in doing so great moral characters are formed, which is the goal of ethics education. Rather, agreeing with Piaget he said that we should well programme classroom ethics teaching through active engagement of students and teachers in resolving moral impasse that suit to the age of the students. This is the way in which a student is aware of the inherent contradictions they have with regard to moral issues at the level of their moral awareness and critical abilities so that a shift to higher awareness and reasoning is possible. This way there is successive moral development of children, which at its best prepares students for community participation in moral resolution through consensus, where the moral issues are real-life, not imagined in the classrooms. It appears that Piaget and Kohlberg is my precursor because what I have advocated as a model of ethical resolution of value-laden issues called 'intersubjective corroboration' is possible when the participants are ethics educated in the way Kohlberg advocates for a 'just community'. However, there are a number of problems in this regard and I will write briefly, why 'intersubjective corroboration' does not depend on Kohlberg's model of moral education. This idea is spread throughout the four volumes of the Series of Practical and Professional Ethics. This may be treated as a part of critique of what Piaget and Kohlberg thinks about moral education. Both Piaget and Kohlberg base their educational programme on a process of cognitive development, which is fraught with *a priorism* or rather arbitrary construction of stages or levels of moral cognition among children. Hence, what they conceived of as best suited for moral education at a particular age may be far too imaginary. Moreover, the cognitive developments in children are never uniform or universal. There are several gaps in the conception of the stages because Piaget and Kohlberg do not concentrate on other than psychological factors, the social, economic and political influencing moral cognition of a child. Hence, stage-wise ethical education may be true of a select group of children living in a particular society having more or less patterned forms of life. The avoidance of this other than psychological or rather, the environmental factors of the students is a grave mistake. This was noticed by Elliot Turich later on who advocated a more revised form of moral education. What is more important for me in this regard is that both Piaget and Kohlberg though rightly mention that the model of "character formation" in the way of artificial intervention by teachers armed with the idea of 'basket of virtues' is way off the mark, nevertheless, they wrongly advocate that ethics education is possible only if teachers encourage students to debate freely (but methodically) in classrooms about moral issues and thus become just citizens who later on resolve trifling issues at more ease than others because they have become morally oriented. First, ethics as we know is not simply solution of value-laden issues; it may be an important part of it, nevertheless. Moreover, consensus among students in classroom does not come automatically as the debate does not go smoothly if teachers do not do their bit. Teachers must initiate a moral dialogue, that is fine, then students must be guided along the debate and not end in a cacophony and further the consensus is reached among students if teachers are helpful. The moot issue is, how the students know that there is a resolution of an ethical issue on *moral grounds* and not on non-moral grounds? There are intricate problems in ethical dialogue, consensus and analysis of the grounds of consensus, which needs much maturity, not to be conceived at the school level. (I fear if it is possible at the high school level.) In fact, a confusion about school ethics teaching that amounts to classroom debates should be replaced by either proper ethics teaching or none, the first is rather overdoing by any extension of moral development, whereas the latter may be more prudent up to high school but we do not imagine that in such programme we need only issue based independent dialogues and no theory or only theory and no dialogues. Intersubjective corroboration does not beg theory based dialogue as well as ethics educated people for dialogue, though it needs ethical corroborators and analysts as ethics educated people. Education in ethics is not at all a prerequisite of persons partaking in ethical debates. (See vol. 1 and chapter 4 of this book), and such education is least needed for having a nation full of good people as we need a 'basket of virtues' for good character. Sophistry does not leave us easily as ethics education at some price in schools, even if it is glorious dialogue and not indoctrination. Again, we conclude that in educational ethics, ethics education is a misconception, particularly, if it is what Kohlberg imagines or what we take to be preparatory for good people. It would be unnecessary to imagine that for school ethics education we need to start somehow at a point because doing something at any cost is neither wise nor ethical, ethics education should meet proper justice.

In *A different voice: psychological theory and women's development* (1982), Carol Gilligan argued that what is basic to ethics education in schools is the infusion of a model of care rather than justice and rights because for the children a feminine model that encourages the value of care for those who needs most is morally desirable though care does not overlook rights and justice. In fact, teaching to be empathetic as in care goes long way to be just and right. Another implication of Gilligan's ethics of care model is that the empowerment of children in moral decision-making should take note of *gender specific* differences because different from the male population females are more caring than abiding by principle-based ethical decision-making. Yet, several gaps in this ethics education model leave us for its avoidance. One gap has been identified in the idea that in isolation or in association, children do not show gender specific moral development and moral reasoning. Care may be as basic to males as to females, but both may be deprived of the same. Moreover, fostering the responses of care among children cannot be the whole of ethics education; it may be a part of virtue-based education, which is nevertheless, incomplete. It appears that to start with something in ethics education presses on us certain things that are far from pragmatic. It is strange to believe that though the ethics of care is strange to many officially less educated people, they are oriented in life in care and empathy. Stranger is to believe that bereft of ethics of care, one is not a good male or female.

There is stiff controversy about the models of ethics education for older children and in higher education, particularly found in

European and American countries. The lines are drawn between the *conservatives* and the *liberals* in these countries, the former speaking more like the indoctrinators or interventionists who are *authoritative* in teaching what are ethically good and bad for children with an idea that in due course the older children will mature as responsible citizens who are worth of ethical decision-making by virtue of basket of values and virtues. It is needless to repeat the defects the model suffers from. The *liberals* on the other hand advocate *freedom* in moral thinking and problem solving because authorities such as the teachers are said to refrain from the misconception that growing boys and girls necessarily depends on them for critical moral thinking and decision-making. Rather, society may be averse to such ideas. However, liberal conception of ethics teaching is much like Kohlberg's artificial independence in classrooms, which have the same problems as mentioned before. It is needless to repeat them either.

Taking a cue from cultural relativism and Gilligan's idea of gender specificity, A. Cortese in *Ethic Ethics: The restructuring of Moral Theory* (1990) argues that *multiculturalism* is key to ethics education. To corroborate Cortese draws from cultural relativists and gender relativism to argue that the ethical principle of justice, for instance, need not be taken as absolutely valid ethical principle in the universal perspective and thus taught to make people good because such principles are in the main given to us absolute sacrosanct morality by the western culture, which may not be universally acceptable. In different cultures as in genders, the very conception of justice as overreaching principle may be completely repugnant or unethical in different moral views about what is right and just. Hence, it would be rather difficult to teach overreaching principles of morality in the name of teaching ethics. In its place it is desirable that we teach the relative values of principles of morality as they appear in different cultures so that moral perception of learners broaden and they become more caring about the culture specific values and virtues. Nevertheless, in high school ethics education we need to be careful about teaching the value of what is objectively valuable. For instance, irrespective of cultural differences we need to teach people that being right and just are objectively valid in the ethical perspective because within cultures and beyond them, at any point of time, at any socio-economic and political condition, people on earth should care to be just and right towards other beings and even things, though what means to be right and just in those cultures at specific situations are not objectively valid. There must be, therefore, some role for universalizability of principles in ethical parlance, which needs to be taught. Nevertheless, such normative teaching is a part of ethics and not the whole of it. If older children in schools are thought to be suited for normative relativism and arguably universalism (if Cortese allows that), why on earth should their logical justifications be left out as a metaethical discussion is not known to us because without it, perhaps the students do not come to know why normative relativism and/or universalism holds good. Ethics education is an interesting affair, but if we start somewhere hastily, several issues catch up and then it is a matter of prudence to see whether older students need any ethics education at all provided in the high schools, particularly if they have not opted for philosophy as a major subject. For older boys and girls in our schools, therefore, two things become important; first whether they are students of philosophy and thus demand ethics education or, second, whether they are non-philosophy students demanding no ethics education. If the idea is that all students before leaving schools must have ethics education, the idea may be to save the endangered species of value-degraded students in general or to save the endangered species of philosophy teachers. If either alternative is true, the attempt to universalize ethics education as 'basket theory' is unethical. Yet, ethics teaching for non-philosophy students in schools becomes important if some of them takes interest in interdisciplinary study right from schools days or are interested deeply in ethical corroboration for value resolution. Nevertheless, any student who reasonably demands ethics education at the school level must be knowing well that it won't help them evolve high moral character or become great nationalists or the like. Ethics teaching need not be as narrow as Cortese thinks or as broad as many others think because such teaching does not end up either in teaching normativism of some kind or in making us good. In fact, *post-modern* thinkers like Martin Barber on the basis of a *republican outlook* argues that one should dispense with the liberal or the contractarian urge (*cf.* Rawls and Nozick), to provide a sound ethical foundation to those coming to high school education because that gives the learners ample opportunity to be obsessed with normativism and thus produce a ethos of *individualism* rather than committed *collectivism*. The shift from the social self to adore individuality is adoring unethical stance in life through pseudo-ethics education. Naturally, for Barber if ethics education in schools makes some sense, it should take care of the *social-ethos-development* among students of ethics, which is a *social-survival-need* not 'feeling-satisfaction-need' as in case of utilitarianism. Whatever may be the strength of Barber's arguments, we are reminded of the stark truth that teaching ethics needs to be mere means to specific ethos development which in turn makes us great people because without such teaching we may not be perfectly apt at the ethos of social good; however, if ethics does not aim at such things, it still remains good for different academic reasons. If it is meant that teaching wholesome ethics to philosophy students or interested non-philosophy students enable them to be more oriented towards ethical corroboration for public good, it may be true to a great extent but that does not imply that all educated people should do so or that educational ethics has the job cut out for it to orient all students in that desired direction because that does makes us good. The evolution of the spirit of ethical resolution for public goód through ethics education is a more likely phenomenon, not logically necessary phenomenon, nor is it a means to evolution of good men and women or earth because wholesome ethics teaching should never aim at such high sounding, self satisfying things.

Without going to the value of ethics education in schools, let us attend to the question whether wholesome ethics education is a part of educational ethics curriculum because we were concerned with this moot issue in this part of the chapter. The different models or approaches to ethics education (leaving aside their aims), does not do any justice to wholesome ethics education because our foregoing analysis has revealed that far from touching the important aspects of teaching ethics, these models concentrate more on indoctrinating in virtues and values with a complete hodge-podge of ethical and non-ethical virtues and values or, on freedom of learners to debate on moral issues or, on individual and/or social ethos development, all having their own narrowness and problems. However, greater problem or rather defect lies in the complete confusion that teaching ethics in any of these ways or teaching wholesome ethics as done in professional ethics courses forms an essential part of education, as well as educational ethics. Let us concentrate more on the latter. Why should educational ethics, which is a part of ethics, take up the teaching of whole of ethics or any part of it as conceived in the models stated above? The reply is that the nature of educational ethics has revealed that it has three essential tasks, the first order, the second order and the practical which presupposes the normative, metaethical and the practical ethical teachings, but for this it is not educational ethics rather, academic ethics which is needed most. Naturally, it is the task of *ethics proper* to discuss elaborately what are its tasks, what models are proper in taking up those tasks, what are the various application of ethical knowledge in different fields such as education, biology, ecology and so on, and not that it is the task of educational ethics and ecological ethics to elaborate the tasks of ethics and the applications of ethical knowledge in these fields. Hence, it is wrongly, as I believe that in educational ethics, methods of teaching ethics finds a place in great details as if this is needed for clarifying what are the basic tasks of educational ethics. The basic tasks of educational ethics, we have seen are far from ambiguous, it needs to discuss how to teach "educational ethics", but *not* how to teach ethics. To conclude, educational ethics should find out ways to teach ethically relevant issues in education having its own target group and teachers of specific qualifications and requirements for pedagogy and training, which undoubtedly forms a part of ethics teaching curriculum but as ever, special disciplines like these need separate treatment for intensive discussion. In order to contribute something in this regard I have justified that a model of teaching educational ethics as we have discussed here, need to refrain from the ideas that (a) such teaching aims to charge the target group with ethical values and virtues; (b) aims to make people of noble character; (c) aims to prepare people who are apt in the debating about values and (d) aims to prepare social and concerned people. Unambiguously stated, educational ethics should care to teach its three tasks but not to prepare good people for our societies by champion educational ethicists. Can educational ethics teach us to be ethically good? Obvious answer is in the *negative*. This answer is basic to teach interested people (including teachers of educational ethics) what educational ethics amounts to, and the way it should be taught without unnecessarily presumptions. An educational ethics teaching that does not pretend to produce people of great character is thus ethical; the corollary of it is unethical because false pretensions and ideals in teaching programme are averse to human good. I have also justified that the model of teaching educational ethics should be free from the misconception that it needs to teach everything in ethics in depth though basic tasks of ethics are needed to be taught to the teachers who take up the job of educating in educational ethics and to those who take interest in ethical problem in education for their resolution. The above points are vital to the construction of both teachers' training curriculum and general educational ethics curriculum. What I have said thus far also justifies that educational ethics need not be a handmaid of theoretical churnings because its practical aspect needs involvement of its learners in active participation to resolve value-laden educational issues. Criticizing Kohlberg we said that teaching about the practical task of educational ethics is not confined to classroom pedagogy where teachers give us issues and we debate freely in an utter imaginary enactment of real life imbroglios and their solution. Intersubjective corroboration as basic to practical ethics lends a cue to understand how participation of concerned parties in educational ethical dilemmas is very important when we educate people how things should go in real life. Educational ethical education is thus a matter of balancing theoretical pedagogy and practical participation where an artificial division of labour giving some task to teachers and others to the students are ruled out. It also abolishes artificial line of demarcation in target groups in education because teachers of ethics and educational ethics learn while they participate in the pedagogical and the practical enterprises. A model of teaching educational ethics should thus keep in view how learners transcend classrooms and formal bindings. I have argued in *The Primer* (vol. 1) that teaching ethics needs to do the same though traditionally in India it is highly artificial and mere clatter and platter. The same may be true of value-based education where pedagogy needs a fresh approach.

We now need to take up for analysis: whether educational ethics by means of teaching values and virtues (both general and ethical) should aim to make us good. We have rough idea about these issues, though more analysis is needed. There are widespread gossips that educational ethics as part of ethics and broadly thought as part of value-study should consider as its *aim* to teach values and virtues to interested learners in schools, colleges and elsewhere so that they become value-charged and build a fitting moral community. However, there is some ambiguity in teaching values because this notion is very broad; it covers ethical and non-ethical values, for instance, dutifulness, obedience, studiousness and so on. Teaching virtues as values are also too wide, they range from human to non-human virtues. The problem is, which values and virtues do we have in mind when it comes to the 'aim' of educational ethics? The simplest reply is that all values and virtues expected of man *qua* man are aimed by educational ethics for inculcation so that we become good people. Humans *qua* humans should have unique values and virtues, which educational ethics should discover, describe and inculcate. These values and virtues as expected, are not only ethical because many of them are non-ethical in nature, those belonging to the physical, mental and spiritual categories, which are called, *non-ethical* values and virtues. For instance, human virtue to maintain good health or the recognition of the value of good health, their virtue to choose rationally among options, or, the values of rational choice, or, the virtue to have steadfast faith on transcendental Reality, or, the value to have faith in metaphysical objects. The moot issue is whether educational ethics needs to discover, describe and inculcate these values and virtues for us because by having them in us, we are called "good"? We need to remember that to call us "good" or "worthwhile" does not always have moral or ethical significance because in many cases we are called "good" in the non-moral sense of good, which *ex-hypothesi* rules out any business on the part of ethics to discover, describe and inculcate. Nevertheless, education may be imagined to have these tasks, that is, to discover, describe and inculcate non-moral good in humans because educating, training, teaching and so on gladly takes up moral and non-moral goods for the learners to pick up so that they build their character. Hence, we educate young to be truthful, diligent, tough, faithful and so on. When we come to educational ethics, it is, a discipline *unlike education and ethics* that considers ethical scrutiny of some educational matters, which do not leave much opportunity for discovery, description and inculcation of human values and virtues. However, an ethically relevant inquiry of education is the *critique of value of discovery, description and inculcation of human values and virtues of ethical and non-ethical kinds*. Educational ethics, which is within ethics, therefore, does not have any practical aim to take up the above tasks that builds our character. In fact, the tasks of discovery and description of human values (ethical and non-ethical) comes broadly under "value studies." Metaethics considers discovery and analysis of nature and meanings of ethical values. Whereas subjects other than ethics backs up with discovery and analysis of non-ethical values. Educational ethics as an anti-climax being within ethics and value-studies does not take up any such study for the simple reason that value studies including ethical, religious, non-ethical, material, ecological value studies completes the job leaving none for educational ethics. We need not be hasty in imagining that in educational ethics we discover and analyse educational values but it is wrong to do so because the task should be taken under the field of education and not educational ethics. We are thus left with only one option, that is, educational ethics takes up the task of *inculcating* human values and virtues (ethical and non-ethical). I will make a passing remark now in this matter because at this place we have to be clearer about what exactly serious people think about the ways in which values and virtues are to be inculcated. In any case by way of a passing remark, 'ethicists do not take up the task of inculcating good things to make people good but *moralists* do so. Did we get the difference right?'

One popular conception among educationists is that educational ethics being responsible in carrying ethically relevant jobs in the field of education, should *transmit values* and to do so, the teachers and other responsible people in the institutional management should well plan about the set of values and virtues the institution believes are most important. These values and virtues become prime motto of the institutions reflected well in the institutions' codebook, diaries for students and even in the emblem used by the institution. Given these set of values and virtues which are thought to be vital as persons, all responsible parties are careful to *transmit* them to those coming for education. These reflect in the pedagogical procedures in the classes, in the co-curricular activities, off the classroom interactions among students, teachers and responsible persons. Transmission of values is taken up habitually by these concerned and committed educationists. Some institutions bind teachers and students with sets of ethico-spiritual values, others with non-spiritual and even anti-spiritual values, and many others with democratic, socialist, communist values and so on. What is common to them is that transmission or rather systematic and constant intoxication in sets of values and virtues prepare people of great character in the long run and thus people of a great nation. The methods of intervention, which are authoritative in nature, are on the part of the educators taken to be natural. If necessary, enforcement of these things as backed up by soft and hard punishments basic to the discipline of picking up good things. This is perhaps the most ancient and popular conception of value based education carried with vengeance to this age in almost every institution. Nothing is bad with schools and colleges relying on sets of values and virtues because they are intrinsically good and not bad for learners but the design may be evil if a set of these intrinsically good things are taken to be *absolutely* good over others and thus artificially fine tuned to transmit or intoxicate pupils in the imaginative hoax of making people good and making good people. Another point of concern is that set of absolute values for intoxication is sure to hit the mark because the intoxicators are either obsessed or paid people to do the job, very apt at service ("committed" is a good title delivered for them), whereas those intoxicated are most of the time simple, innocent and voiceless children in schools as well as students who are timid, rule-governed and threatened by disciplinary actions in higher institutions. Most of the time so-called good colleges take these advantages to transmit values at will though little or no commitment on the part of the students, rather, most of the time are disliked by them causing inner urge to throw them in the garbage bin of memory as soon as they are out of the campus. The reasons are simple for not liking absolute values and their intoxication. Students as they grow up realise the agenda that they are not free to find their values and virtues, not free to challenge sets of values and virtues thought to be absolute and thus institutional formal education that demands high degree of rational acumen, critical understanding and appreciation of whatever is worth knowing is curbed and axed. This is grossly unethical, as we have seen before. Most dangerous is that the simple school students are exploited most by the value transmission agenda because catch-them-young tactics for any propaganda has to succeed. Yet, parents and guardians need to be either ignorant of the agenda or have to be neutralised for any criticism. In any case, transmission of values in schools succeeds when there is a "hidden agenda" that carefully avoids grown-up people to raise questions. One way to do so is to have methods of deterrence for guardians as well as in-house teachers and the other way is to camouflage the intended agenda with several other agendas that remain largely unsuspected. All these things are again grossly unethical. The most repugnant ideas in value transmission are having fixity of values by not letting contesting values calling for value-criticism and threat perceptions in not succumbing to any open or hidden agenda that is almost an imperative in institutions. However, I have argued before that there is no way to shut the doors on the flow of values and virtues in educational institution and one nice way to do so is to free the classrooms from value-chauvinism on the part of the teachers though not forgetting the basics that while you teach a subject do not skip the elements of value in it for a good discussion involving perception of students at freedom. Secular institutions do not transmit values, they teach subjects of different kinds inviting students to see for themselves what lies beyond these subjects, what are the questions of values and how they might be resolved. In any case, such a method of teaching subjects do not *aim* the least that doing so we make people good or make good people because opening questions of values in subjects is to open socially related aspects of subjects which otherwise remain implicit in them, these help to develop our critical ability further. No doubt, when we do these things, they might socialize us, and make us good on the basis of evaluation of people around us, but that should not be an *intended* agenda in our institutions. Value-added education aims at a more comprehensive study of subjects, it should not aim at making us good people. We will hopefully become good if education has the power in it to do so and if it enables us to be relatively free among several bindings. A point of concern is before us while we move to discuss the model of value clarification. In the modern times, some educationists think that though value-related issues are unavoidable in classroom education, the role of the teacher is to completely keep off value-related debates and subsequent resolutions when students are at work. Such *value-neutrality* on the part of the teachers is undesirable because the teacher, even if he or she is careful not to intoxicate in values, they do have a positive role to corroborate the value-related debates. M. Taylor and M. Warnock argues that in value-based education all is not good when teachers shut up because it is the teacher who helps students to discover, analyse and corroborate about values. The brilliance of a teacher is always needed in value-based education. In any case, we come to conclude that educational ethics as such has no role in the transmission of values but education has great role to play in finding out ways to secular, scientific value-based education though not with a guarantee to make us great people.

Banking on the recent upheavals against value-chauvinism in schools and colleges that aim at moralising and giving values to students many thinkers such as L. Raths, M. Harmin and S. Simon and many others have advocated *value-clarification* as a method of teaching values and virtues. The model aims at bringing out the best in pupils so that they get in touch with their own values, make them explicit and have critical acumen to appreciate them for evaluation. In this way, a person concerned about questions of value clarifies the moot value issue freely, that is, evaluate or clarify them without pedagogy and intervention to dispel confusion regarding the matter. However, the inherent idea to clarify value conceptions is to be a worthwhile person. Nevertheless, one doubts whether the same needs to be done in an institutional setting or in isolation and what if any is the role of the teachers. If the students have to clarify value perceptions all alone, it is hardly of any use. Moreover, value questions do not emerge in isolation. Hence, such clarification makes any sense in association in institutional set-ups. About the role of teachers, it has been said that they incite students in classrooms to play roles in a game situation to ponder about what they think about the value or worth of certain things they have in possession. They are incited to *see* for themselves what if any is the "worth" of things they "possess" and evaluate whether the assumed worth is really of some worth. This way students are able to clarify values by themselves and in doing so, they are value-oriented. Hence, the institutions make people free to see the worth of things to make them good. Borrowing insights from relativism in values, critics of this method J.P. Shaver, W. Strong and J.P. Fraenkel argues that value clarification is insufficient and in some sense way off the mark to make people good because what the students find to be worthwhile in one community will be different from those in other communities, thus all of them will be good enough. Another point is that if values are clarified by the critical insights of students, in the final run all values turn out to be same, none are better than the other. Hence, value clarification fails in evaluating values. As such, it fails in the evaluation of some values as objectives than relative. Failure such as these amounts to the shortcoming of the method itself, which does not make persons good either.

Another way to make us good is to be *considerate* towards others in life, which is possible by means of role-play, drama, play-writing and several activities at the initial stages moving gradually towards involvement in real life problem solution. However, the model advocated by P. McPhail and others have been criticised on the simple ground that evolution of the worth of considerations in us cannot be the chief in making us good because the ideal is fulfilled by several worth. In any case, we have some answers to the questions whether educational ethics should include the discussion of value education for making us good. I believe strongly as ever that educational ethics has great role to play in raising the issue of *aim of value education* because a proper critical analysis of the issue is extremely important as ethically relevant discussions about certain types and methods of education. It is due to this perhaps that in a number of books including this one an educational ethics relies on the critical study of what needs to be done in value education. However, educational ethics does not leave for us any role in making people good, though serious ventures in educational ethics might make many of us able to do good actions, but aiming to make people good and people turning out to be good are different propositions, the former is a specific intended course of action that becomes basic to an educational enterprise, whereas in the latter case, the enterprise itself is basic to human life. In some sense, rather than the conception of a particular end in mind, educational ethics for its intrinsic value *should* be carried on which, in many cases hopefully gives us some good or worth for us, even if that does not happen in some cases, that is, despite all efforts people turn out to be evil minded, the end result does not justify the fruitlessness or valuelessness of the basic enterprise in question. It is due to this that even if the basic programmes of educational ethics are carried out perfectly well, some among us, the teachers, the students and others who are directly related to the programmes, need not necessarily expect to be good or morally good in life though there is every chance that they will be called good for their creditable academic efforts. Educational ethics on the whole have every chance to credit us for doing well in *what are expected of us* in that field, but do not confuse that by virtue of that we will be great moral people or a nation will be full of great people. It is important to remember that to do "what are expected of us to do" is ethically vital than doing what were not expected of us to do. It is not expected at all that in educational ethics we find out ways to make others virtuous, therefore, it is unethical to justify that this was important and thus we are good people. When ethicists assume the role of "moralists", the same unethicality is exposed.

If ethicists do not forget the basics, they must not confuse between tasks cut out for them as ethicists. As philosophical critiques, they need to be fairly clear in their minds that unlike moralists they are not moral incarnations on earth carrying a heavy burden to correct evil people and to prevent people becoming evil rather, empower them to be good. Since time immemorial saints, prophets, *gurus* and preachers acted moralists. They based their mission on different thesis of morality and values, in most cases fixing a set of such thesis as against contesting ones because they fixed for the definitions of 'morality' and 'values', and standards which they would never give up as illogical or unwanted. The moralists as absolutists imagined sets of *universal* values as well, which however, were most important for them as sacred potions to feed humanity because in that way we become morally good. The enterprise of the moralists unlike educationists and ethicists is, therefore, non-critical indoctrination which is the foundation of their entire humane enterprise, though people turned in big numbers to be extremely evil after solid *guru-jñāna*. When this happened, the moralists rubbished criticism with a snob smile that people becoming bad does not disprove worth of *guru-jñāna* rather it is they and the external pressures in which they live are to be blamed for the failure. Truly, moralists knew that their sacred efforts could not be failed at human follies because in itself it stood worthwhile. But that could not be justified because they have an obsession that absolute end or aim of moralism is that it makes us good and nothing else, whereas the same could not be seen in many cases, even when followers of staunch moralism religiously followed a set of virtuous actions and not another and yet turned out to be anti-human and anti-social. The reasons are many because religious following of *guru-jñāna* remained vulnerable to the evaluation of their worth on several relativistic standards. Hence, humanity never stopped quarrelling about the *jñāna* for moral sanctity. People remained iconoclasts, belligerent, unorthodox, non-absolutists among various toxicity of the magic potions for becoming good. The frantic cries of humanity to let them free of the indoctrinating bondages of the moralists whether it be spiritual or official, never died.

Ethicists never attempt at what should not be done if it can be done, nevertheless, because they are aware that *no one has given them a moral authority to do what they can but they need not and should not do*. Ethicists are not moralists; they do not aim at making us good through indoctrination of absolute thesis about worthwhileness because even if they can, they know that being philosophical critiques, they should not lose the good habit to refrain from acting moralists. It is due to this that we are still freely scrutinising the logic of moralism but not falling in the act of moralists. Gilbert Ryle reminds us of Socrates who said: "Subjects like arithmetic, geometry, astronomy, rhetoric, wrestling, medicine and so on can be taught, and there exists professional teachers of them. For a person to become good at engineering, swimming or shooting he needs to be and he can be instructed by experts; and they will make him good, if he has the aptitude and the industry. But for a person to become good man… we do not seem to provide or require expert coaches. There are no technical colleges where honourableness is taught; there are no periods set aside on the school timetable for classes in unselfishness…. If virtues were teachable, we should expect there to exist experts to teach it and examiners to test progress in it. But such teachers and examiners do not exist. So it begins to look as if virtues cannot be taught."[1]

Gilbert Ryle argued that though as a matter of fact it is difficult to buy Socrates' words that virtues cannot be taught because in formal conditions of schools and colleges and at homes we do learn *derivatively* about several values and virtues while we learn about something. Ryle says: "A person learns to be honest or learns not to be a cheat; only derivatively do we need to bother to say, he then knows that honesty is a good thing, or realizes that cheating is wrog."[2] If this be the case then our institutions are able to teach us the value of being honest or that honesty as a virtue is good. Hence, if we rephrase Socrates, in our institutions we do not learn to be virtuous rather we learn to be so-and-so, which only *derivatively enable us to teach* about virtues. Institutions should not be in the misconception that through sophism (at some cost) their task is to teach pupils to be moral or ethical or virtuous. Educational ethics, has nothing to do with imparting the techniques of becoming virtuous or making others virtuous though through ethics and formal education in many subjects, we learn about so many things that enable us to *derive certain things as worthwhile*, and truly, *some of us do well in life to behave well* out of such derived teachings. Ethicists in educational ethics thus need not and should not nourish the idea that they need to make people good by any means. Educational ethics is not 'all good to learn or read, if it is mostly coming to us through hackneyed formal pedagogy and if it completely avoids the practical aspects of the same. But to be involved in practical educational ethical enterprise is not a surity to make people good.

NOTES

1. Ryle, Gilbert, "Can virtues be taught?" in R.F. Dearden, P.H. Hirst and R.S. Peters (eds.), *Education and the development of reason*, Routledge & Kegan Paul, London, 1972, p. 434.
2. *Ibid*, p. 445.

Bibliography

Austin, J.L. *Philosophical Papers,* O.U.P., Oxford, 1961.

Austin, J.L. *How To Do Things With Words,* O.U.P., Oxford, 1962.

Ayer, A.J. *Language, Truth and Logic,* Gollancz, London, 1936.

Bantock, G.H. *Education and Values*, Faber and Faber, London, 1975.

Barrow, Robin, *Moral Philosophy for Education*, Allen & Unwin, London, 1975.

Beck, C.M., Crittendum, B.S. & Sellivan, E.V. (Eds.), *Moral Education: Interdisciplinary Approaches,* Newman Press, 1972.

Beck, L.W. "Kant On Education" in *Essays on Kant and Hume*, Yale University Press, New Haven, 1978.

Bhagia, N.M. "New Values and Education" in S.P. Ruhela (Ed.), *Human Values in Education*, Sterling Publishers Pvt. Ltd., New Delhi, 1986.

Bhagia, Sushma, "Approaches to Value-Oriented Education" in S.P. Ruhela (Ed.), *Human Values in Education*, Sterling Publishers Pvt. Ltd., New Delhi, 1986.

Blum, V.C. *Freedom of Choice in Education,* The Macmillan Co., NY, 1958.

Brandt, R. *Ethical Theory: The Problems of Normative and Critical Ethics,* Prentice-Hall, Englewood Cliffs, NJ, 1959.

Brown, S.C. *Philosophers Discuss Education,* Macmillan, London, 1975.

Cahn, Steven M. *Morality, Responsibility and the University: Studies in Academic Ethics,* Temple University Press, Philadelphia, 1990.

Carter, R.E. *Dimensions of Moral Education,* University of Toronto Press, Toronto, 1984.

Chadwick, Ruth, (Ed.), *Encyclopaedia of Applied Ethics,* Academic Press, San Diego, 1998.

Chaudhury, Malay, "Business of Learning", *The Times of India,* Patna/ Ranchi Edition, 24.02.2004.

Chazan, B.I. & Sollis J.F. (Eds.), *Moral Education,* Teachers College Press, Columbia, 1975.

Cortese, A. *Ethic Ethics: The Restructuring of Moral Theory,* The State University of New York, Albany, 1990.

Crittendum, B. *Forms and Content in Moral Education,* Ontario Institute for Studies in Education, Toronto, 1972.

Dasgupta, R.K. "Perfect Language II", *The Statesman,* Kolkata Edition.

Dearden, R.F. Hirst P.H. & Peters R.S. (Eds.), *Education and the Development of Reason,* Routledge and Kegan Paul, London, 1972.

Dobson, James, *Dare to Discipline,* Tyndale House Publishers, Illinois, 1978.

Downie, R.S. Loudfoot, E.M. & Telfer, E. *Education and Personal Relationships,* Methuen & Co. Ltd., London, 1974.

Drinkwater, F.H. *Educational Essays,* Burns Oates, London, 1951.

Edwards, Paul (Ed.), Encyclopaedia of Philosophy, Vol. V, Macmillan & Free Press, NY, 1972.

Fitzpatrick, E.A. *Philosophy of Education,* The Bruce Publication Co., Milwankee, 1955.

Fraenkel, J.P. *How to Teach about Values: An Analytic Approach,* Prentice-Hall, NJ, 1977.

Frankena, W.K. *Towards Philosophy of Moral Education,* Harvard Educational Review, 28, 1958.

Frankena, W.K. *Three Historical Philosophies of Education: Aristotle, Kant and Dewey,* Scott Foresman, Chicago, 1965.

Frankena, W.K. *Ethics,* Prentice-hall, New Delhi, 1989.

Gower, R.R. & Scott, M.B. *Five Essential Dimensions of Curriculum Design,* Mendall/Hunt Pub. Co., Iowa, 1977.

Goyal, B.R. *Documents on Social, Moral and Spiritual Values in Education,* NCERT, New Delhi, 1979.

Guha, Debashis, "Transcending-Transversal Ethicality" in *The Journal of the Indian Council of Philosophical Research,* Vol. XX, No. 4, 2003.

Guthrie, J.W. *et al.* (Eds.) *Encyclopaedia of Education,* Thomson, Gale, 2003.

Hare, R.M. *The Language of Morals*, O.U.P., London, 1952.

Hennessy, T.C.H. (Ed.), *Values and Moral Development,* Paulist Press, NY, 1976.

Herman, Barbara, *The Practice of Moral Judgement,* Harvard University Press, Cambridge, 1993.

Hersh, R.H. Miller, J.P. & Fielding, G.D. (Eds.), *Models of Moral Education,* Longman, 1980.

Hirst, P.H. *Moral Education in a Secular Society,* University of London Press, London, 1974.

Hume, D. *A Treatise on Human Nature,* L.A. Selby-Bigge (Ed.), Clarendon Press, London, 1978.

Jeganathan, W.S. Milton, *Professional Ethics Among Teachers,* ISPCK, Delhi, 1999.

Joshi, Kireet, "An Outline Program of Value-Oriented Education" in S.P. Ruhela (Ed.) *Human Values and Education,* Sterling Publishers Pvt. Ltd., New Delhi, 1980.

Joshi, Kireet, "Value Judgement" in *The Times of India,* New Delhi Edition, 18.01.2002.

Kohlberg, L. *The Psychology of Moral Dèvelopment,* Harper & Row, San Fransisco, 1984.

Langford, G. & O' Connor, D.J. (Eds.), *New Essays in the Philosophy of Education,* Routledge and Kegan Paul, London, 1973.

Lisman, C.D. *Caring: A Feminist Approach to Ethics and Moral Education,* University of California Press, Berkeley, 1984.

Louden, Robert B. *Kant's Impure Ethics: From Rational Beings to Human Beings,* O.U.P., Oxford, 2000.

Luther, M.M. *Values and Ethics in School Education,* Tata McGraw-Hill Publishing Co., New Delhi, 2001.

Mascranhas, M. & Justa, H.R. (Eds.), *Value Education in Schools and Other Essays,* Konark Publishers Pvt. Ltd., New Delhi, 1989.

McPhail, P., Thomas, J.R.U. & Chapman, H. *Moral Education in Secondary Schools,* Longman, London, 1972.

Mitra, Tirthankar, "Students Opt for English Medium Schools, SCGRT Study in the Three Sub-divisions", *The Statesman,* Kolkata Edition, 11.05.1998.

Neill, A.S. Summerhill, Penguin, Harmondsworth, 1968.

Nowell-Smith, P.H. *Ethics,* Penguin, Harmondsworth, 1954.

Pandey, V.C. *Value Education and Education for Human Rights,* Isha Books, Delhi, 2005.

Pervez, Sahid Md. "M.P. Parents Say Yes To Sex Education", *The Statesman,* Kolkata Edition, 01.03.1999.

Peters, R.S. *Practical Problems in Moral Education,* Heinemann, London, 1973.

Peters, R.S. *Ethics and Education,* George Allen & Unwin, London, 1974.

Peters, R.S. *Psychological and Ethical Development,* George Allen & Unwin, London, 1974.

Peters, R.S. *The Concept of Education,* Routledge & Kegan Paul, London, 1979.

Piaget, J. *The Moral Judgement of the Child,* Routledge & Kegan Paul, London, 1932.

Rajput, J.S. "Equity in Education", *The Times of India,* New Delhi Edition, 18.01.2002.

Ram, Atma, "Education Today: Privatization Only Answer", *The Statesman,* Kolkata Edition.

Raths, L., Harmin, M. & Simon, S. *Values and Teaching,* Charles E. Merrill, Ohio, 1966.

Rawls, J. *A Theory of Good*, O.U.P., Oxford, 1980.

Ray, Suprakash, "Volatile Mixture", *The Statesman,* Kolkata Edition, 20.05.2001.

Reddy, V.N.K. *Future Education and Human Resource Management*, Bhartiya Vidya Prakashan, New Delhi, 1988.

Rousseau, J.J. *Emile*, Dent, London, 1961.

Ruhela, S.P. (Ed.) *Human Values and Education,* Sterling Publishers, New Delhi, 1986.

Ruhela, S.P. "Value Orientation of Teacher Education Curricula in India" in S.P. Ruhela (Ed.), *Human Values and Education*, Sterling Publishers Pvt. Ltd., New Delhi, 1986.

Russell, B. *Education and the Social Order,* Unwin Paperbacks, 1977.

Ryle, G. "Can Virtues Be Taught? In R.F. Dearden *et al.* (Eds.) *Education and the Development of Reason,* Routledge and Kegan Paul, London, 1972.

Sanyal, Sunanda, "English Classes III", *The Statesman,* Kolkata Edition,

Scheffler, J. *The Language of Education,* Charles C. Thomas, Springfield, 1960.

Sealey, J. *Religious Education: Philosophical Perspectives,* George Allen & Unwin, London, 1985.

Shaver, J.P. & Strong, W. *Value Decisions,* Teachers College Press, NY, 1982.

Simon, S., Howe, L. & Kirschenbaum, H. *Values Clarification,* A&W Visual Library, NY, 1972.

Singer, Peter, *A Companion to Ethics,* O.U.P., Oxford, 1991.

Sizer, T. & Sizer, N. (Eds.), *Moral Education: Five Lectures,* Harvard University Press, Cambridge, 1970.

Spiecker, B. & Straughan, R. (Eds.), *Philosophical Issues in Moral Education and Development,* Open University Press, Philadelphia, 1988.

Srivastava, Radhika D. "Teachers may no longer spank school students", *Sunday Times of India,* Patna/Ranchi Edition, 23.04.2006.

Stevenson, C.L. *Ethics and Language,* Yale University Press, New Haven, 1944.

Straughan, R. & Wrigley, J. *Values and Evaluation in Education,* Harper & Row, London, 1980.

Straughan, R. *Can we teach children to be good? Basic Issues in Moral, Personal and Social Education,* Open University Press, Philadelphia, 1991.

Strike, Kenneth A. & Egan, Kieran (Eds.), *Ethics and Educational Policy,* Routledge & Kegan Paul, London, 1978.

Taneja, V.R. "Inculcation of Human Values: Educational Approaches and Strategies" in S.P. Ruhela (Ed.), *Human Values and Education,* Sterling Publishers Pvt. Ltd., New Delhi, 1986.

Taylor, C. *The Modern Identity in Communitarian: A New Public Ethics,* Wadsworth, Belmont, 1994.

Titus, H.H. *Ethics For Today,* Eurasia Publishing House, New Delhi, 1965.

Wilson, N. & Sugarman, B., *A Teacher's Guide to Moral Education,* Geoffrey Chapman, London, 1973.

Wilson, N. & Sugarman, B., *Introduction to Moral Education,* Penguin, Harmondsworth, 1967.

Index